全国14家国家特色服务出口基地（语言服务）联合推荐
新文科语言服务学术文库

语言行业多元化
超越翻译的成功

Diversification in the Language Industry
Success beyond Translation

Nicole Y. Adams ● 编

王立非 ● 导读

上海外语教育出版社
外教社 SHANGHAI FOREIGN LANGUAGE EDUCATION PRESS

图书在版编目（CIP）数据

语言行业多元化：超越翻译的成功 / 妮科尔·Y. 亚当斯 (Nicole Y. Adams) 编；王立非导读. —— 上海：上海外语教育出版社，2024. ——（新文科语言服务学术文库 / 王立非总主编）. —— ISBN 978-7-5446-8377-7

Ⅰ. H059

中国国家版本馆CIP数据核字第20245T60H6号

© Nicole Y. Adams, 2013
Published by arrangement with NYA Communications.
Licensed for distribution and sale in the People's Republic of China only.
本书由NYA媒介公司授权上海外语教育出版社有限公司出版。
仅供在中华人民共和国境内（香港、澳门、台湾除外）销售。
图字：09-2024-0058号

出版发行：	上海外语教育出版社
	（上海外国语大学内） 邮编：200083
电　　话：	021-65425300（总机）
电子邮箱：	bookinfo@sflep.com.cn
网　　址：	http://www.sflep.com
责任编辑：	田慧肖
印　　刷：	上海宝山译文印刷厂有限公司
开　　本：	635×965 1/16 印张 22.5 字数 372千字
版　　次：	2024年12月第1版 2024年12月第1次印刷
书　　号：	ISBN 978-7-5446-8377-7
定　　价：	72.00元

本版图书如有印装质量问题，可向本社调换
质量服务热线：4008-213-263

"新文科语言服务学术文库"专家委员会

顾问：
李宇明（北京语言大学）
王继辉（北京大学）

主任：
王立非（北京语言大学）

委员：（姓氏笔画为序）
王传英（南开大学）
王华树（北京外国语大学）
王宗琥（首都师范大学）
王铭玉（天津外国语大学）
文　军（北京航空航天大学）
艾　斌（上海财经大学）
冯光武（广东外语外贸大学）
司显柱（北京第二外国语学院）
吕世生（北京语言大学）
任虎林（北京科技大学）
刘　宏（大连外国语大学）
刘和平（北京语言大学）
孙　玉（上海外语教育出版社）
李　梅（同济大学）
杨明星（郑州大学）
张　政（北京师范大学）

张天伟（北京外国语大学）
张法连（中国政法大学）
张慧玉（浙江大学）
罗慧芳（当代中国与世界研究院）
屈哨兵（广州大学）
赵蓉晖（上海外国语大学）
胡开宝（上海外国语大学）
俞敬松（北京大学）
祝朝伟（四川外国语大学）
贺永中（美国蒙特雷高等国际研究院）
高明乐（北京语言大学）
高　霄（华北电力大学）
郭英剑（中国人民大学）
黄立波（西安外国语大学）
曹　进（西北师范大学）
崔启亮（对外经济贸易大学）
蒙永业（北京悦尔信息技术有限公司）
蔡基刚（复旦大学）
穆　雷（广东外语外贸大学）
Arle Lommel（美国CSA咨询公司）

前　言

语言服务兴起于 20 世纪 90 年代的欧美。2010 年，中国翻译协会首次正式在我国提出"语言服务"的概念。语言服务指以语言能力为核心，以促进跨语言、跨文化交流为目标，提供语际信息转化服务和产品，以及相关研究咨询、技术研发、工具应用、资产管理、教育培训等专业化服务的现代服务业。

根据统计，尽管全球经济不断受到挑战，但语言服务行业依然保持增长，2022 年，全球语言服务产值突破 600 亿美元。我国对外开放、中外人文交流和"一带一路"建设不断促进我国的语言服务市场增长。2022 年，我国的翻译公司和各类型的语言服务企业总计超过 42 万家，总产值突破 554 亿元人民币。语言服务发展的同时也带来巨大的人才需求。

语言服务教育在我国是一个新生事物，目标是培养行业需要的口笔译、语言技术和项目管理人才。2007 年，我国开办翻译硕士专业学位教育，为语言服务行业培养翻译人才。近年来，部分高校通过开设研究方向或独立设置二级学科点等方式，招收本地化管理、技术传播、翻译项目管理、医学语言服务、国际语言服务研究生，培养"语言+技术""语言+专业"和"语言+管理"的复合型和应用型人才。部分高校成立了语言服务研究院所、应急语言服务基地（中心），举办语言服务论坛，编写语言服务研究报告等。2020 年，中国英汉语比较研究会批准成立语言服务研究专业委员会，出版《语言服务研究》集刊。2022 年，商务部、教育部、中国外文局等部委批准成立特色语言服务出口基地，国家发改委和商务部批准语言服务进入鼓励外商投资产业目录。以上举措有力地促进了语言服务的发展。

为了帮助广大师生了解国外语言服务领域学术研究和行业发展动态，满足高校语言服务学科建设、人才培养、教学科研的需要，上海外语教育出版社组织专家精心策划了"新文科语言服务学术文库"，从国外原版引进多种语言服务学术著作。本文库涵盖翻译及语言服务的职业技能和企业管理两个方面，包括翻译教学、技术文档写作、本地化技术、质量管理、服务管理、众包翻译管理等，体系完整，内容丰富，值得推荐。同时，为了方便读者理解重点，文库各书还专门配有中文导读和推荐阅读书目。

本文库可用作研究生教材，也适合语言服务行业人士和对语言服务感兴趣的广大社会读者作为参考书使用。希望文库的出版能为我国的语言服务发展贡献一份力量。

专家委员会主任

王立非

2023 年 12 月

导　读

一、本领域概述

语言服务指个人或企业依托多语言能力和信息技术能力，以信息转化、知识转移、文化传播等为目标，为各行各业提供人工/机器翻译、本地化、外语培训、多语种数据处理、多媒体加工、语言咨询等服务，以及与语言相关的营销、贸易和投/融资等衍生服务或系统解决方案。

语言服务行业（language services industry）是一个包括所有提供语言转换和语言管理服务的企业和个人的全球产业。它为不同语言和文化背景的人群的沟通、交流和全球化经济活动提供支持，主要包括以下几类服务：笔译、口译、本地化、语言技术开发和应用、字幕和配音、多语种内容管理和制作、语言教学与培训、行业咨询等。

多元化发展战略是指企业通过扩展业务领域、增加产品或服务种类、进入新的市场或行业，以实现业务多元化的战略。多元化发展战略的目标是通过拓展不同领域或市场的业务，降低风险，提高盈利能力，增加企业的竞争优势和市场份额。多元化发展战略使企业将注意力和资源投入多个业务领域或市场，以降低对单一领域或市场的依赖，更好地应对市场风险和变化。通过开展多元化业务，企业可以扩大客户基础，提高市场占有率，并在不同的市场中寻找新的增长机会。多元化发展战略的实施需要企业进行充分的市场研究和竞争分析，了解新领域或新市场的需求和特点，并制定相应的市场进入策略和业务拓展计划。同时，企业还需要具备足够的资源和能力来支持多元化发展，包括人力资源、财务资源和技术资源等。

语言服务行业多元化发展战略是指语言服务提供商通过扩大业务

领域、增加服务种类、拓展市场范围等方式，实现业务多元化发展的战略。它能使语言服务行业更好地适应市场变化和客户需求，提供更全面、专业的语言服务，提升市场竞争力。

　　常见的语言服务行业多元化发展领域包括：（1）跨行业服务领域。除了传统的文学和商务翻译外，跨行业服务涵盖了科技、医疗、法律、金融、媒体等多个行业，这些行业需要高质量的翻译和语言服务，确保信息传播及时和准确。（2）多语种服务领域。企业跨国经营越来越需要翻译与语言服务公司提供多语种的服务，涵盖世界各地的主要语言，如汉语、英语、西班牙语、法语、德语、俄语、阿拉伯语等。（3）语言技术支持领域。语言服务行业不断应用新技术提高服务效率和质量，机器翻译、语音识别、自然语言处理等技术的引入促使翻译与语言服务更加自动化和智能化。同时，云平台和在线协作工具也为翻译人员提供了更好的工作环境和合作方式。（4）本地化服务领域。跨国企业的发展要求其产品和服务在不同国家和文化背景中具有适应性，需要语言服务行业提供具有文化适应性的翻译和本地化服务，确保产品和服务在目标市场中具有良好的接受度和可用性。（5）教育培训领域。国内外的语言服务机构积极开展翻译、语言及相关领域的培训和教育活动，提高人员的翻译技能、语言水平和专业能力。

　　常见的语言服务行业多元化发展战略包括：（1）拓展业务领域，如语言服务提供商可以在原有的口笔译服务基础上，把业务拓展至本地化、技术写作、语言行业咨询等多个领域，以满足不同客户的多样化需求。（2）增加服务种类，如提供语音识别与合成、机器翻译、文字与图像合成等增值服务。（3）开拓服务市场，如进入不同地区的市场，开拓国际业务，拓宽市场范围，扩大客户群体和市场份额。（4）建立合作伙伴关系，如与科技企业、教育机构、旅游公司等共同研发和创新语言产品或服务，实现资源共享和优势互补。（5）培养人才和技术创新，如员工语言技能和业务知识培训，引入先进的翻译技术和工具等。

语言服务行业多元化发展战略具有以下五个特点：

1. 多样性：强调业务多样性，即通过扩展业务领域和增加服务种类，满足客户的多样化需求。服务领域不再仅局限于传统的口笔译核心业务，而是涵盖更广泛的服务范围。

2. 客户导向：强调满足客户需求的重要性。语言服务提供商需要深入了解客户的需求和行业特点，根据客户的需求提供定制化的服务，以提高客户满意度和忠诚度。

3. 创新性：鼓励创新，包括技术创新和服务创新。语言服务提供商需要引入先进的技术和工具，提高翻译质量和效率，同时积极探索新的服务模式和商业模式，以适应市场变化和客户需求的不断演变。

4. 合作性：强调建立合作伙伴关系。语言服务提供商可以与其他相关领域的企业建立合作伙伴关系，共同开发创新的产品或服务，实现资源共享和优势互补，提高综合竞争力。

5. 国际化：追求国际化发展。语言服务提供商通过开辟新市场、开拓国际业务来实现全球化布局和更大的市场份额。

国内外有许多语言服务企业成功实施多元化战略的案例。如我国的新东方和科大讯飞，总部在英国的 SDL 和总部在美国的 Transperfect，它们原都只提供语言培训、语音识别、翻译等单项服务，后实施多元化战略，将业务和产品扩展至相关领域而最终成为语言服务行业的翘楚。

二、编者简介

本书编者 Nicole Y. Adams 毕业于英国雷丁大学的现代英语语言和语言学专业，获硕士学位，是澳大利亚认证商务德英翻译和编辑，澳大利亚翻译协会（Australian Institute of Interpreters and Translators, AUSIT）的资深会员，获得 2012 年澳大利亚商业质量奖和 2013 年澳大利亚卓越奖，2014 年获翻译领域的语言专家认证资格。她深耕翻译行业 20 多年，专注于语言服务市场营销、企业传播和公共关系研究。

三、内容概要

（一）本书概况

本书是一本语言服务行业的实务手册，分八章论述了语言服务行业多元化的发展之道。第一章为序言，介绍了本书写作与出版的背景。第二章对多元化概念进行定义，探讨多元化对语言服务行业及译员的影响。第三章聚焦语言服务行业的多元化业务类型，包括机器翻译译后编辑、非母语文本编辑、配音、字幕、转录、术语服务、创意翻译、文案撰写、跨文化咨询、语言验证（linguistic validation）、在线语言教学等。第四章探讨语言服务行业的非语言业务多元化，涉及翻译项目管理、战略联盟、博客和社交网络、社交媒体和在线营销、垂直领域多元化、客户群多元化等。第五章介绍语言服务行业的被动多元化，即通过语言产品化，如提供出版物、持续职业发展（continuing professional development, CPD）、在线培训课程等创收。第六章讨论语言服务行业的跨行业多元化，如为语言服务公司和翻译同行提供专门服务，包括辅导培训、机辅翻译（Computer-Aided Translation, CAT）工具咨询、网站及与网络相关的服务、多语种桌面排版（desktop publishing）等。第七章分析了夹缝中求生存的独特多元化策略，列举了 Mox 漫画博客（Mox's Blog）、翻译国际支付平台"译员支付"（Translator Pay）、"翻译无国界"（Translators without Borders）组织、雨都伦敦品牌塑造（Rainy London Branding）等四个行业创新的典型案例。第八章为结论，作者基于从业者的经验分享，总结了多元化发展战略，梳理了自由译员所面临的现状，并对未来发展提出了建议。

（二）各章概要

第一章　书中隐藏的故事：开篇

当今社会，多元化已成为备受关注的议题。作者凭借丰富的经验和敏锐的市场洞察力，深入探讨了多元化在自由译员中所蕴含的巨大潜力。本书不仅为翻译行业的自由职业者提供了提升自身价值的独特视角，还为有意进入该行业的人提供了宝贵的指导与启示，帮助他们更好地理解语言服务行业和市场，从而在竞争激烈的环境中取得成功。

第二章　多元化的概念：是否需要多元化？

本章首先详细定义了几类不同的多元化策略：语言业务多元化（linguistic diversification）、非语言业务多元化（extra-linguistic diversification）、被动多元化（passive diversification）和跨行业多元化（external diversification）。

语言业务多元化是指在语言服务领域中，语言服务提供商通过提供多种语言的口笔译和本地化等服务实现业务的多元化，包括拓展不同语种的语对、涉足专业领域的多语种翻译等，以满足客户对多种语言服务的需求。

非语言业务多元化是指在语言服务业务之外，语言服务提供商通过提供与语言无关的其他服务或产品实现业务的多元化，包括市场研究、内容创作、咨询服务等，以扩大业务范围和增加收入来源。

被动多元化是指企业或个人面临外部压力或机会时，通过接受或适应环境变化来实现多元化。这种多元化通常是被动的，是为了应对市场变化、竞争压力或其他外部因素而采取的措施。

跨行业多元化是指企业或个人跨越当前所处的行业边界，进入其他行业或领域来实现多元化。这意味着将业务活动扩展到与当前行业无关的领域，以寻求新的增长机会并降低风险。

通过访谈不同语言服务从业者形成案例，本章深入探讨了四类多元化策略对自由译员的影响。

Inkrea.se Consulting 公司的首席执行官 Anne-Marie Colliander Lind 指出，随着全球化和信息化的发展，翻译需求呈现爆炸式增长，技术进步也给自由译员带来了更多挑战。译员需要不断学习新技术，提高生产力和翻译质量。同时，去中介化的趋势为自由译员提供了更多机会，但也带来了市场价格压力和质量控制方面的挑战。

GxP 语言服务公司的英德法语翻译 Anne Diamantidis 认为，多元化是一种选择，而非必需。她提出业务多元化和个人多元化两种类型，强调翻译核心业务仍然前景广阔，多元化应该建立在利益和需求的基础上，而不仅仅是为了赶时髦。

《互联网自由职业：译员实用指南》(*Internet Freelancing: Practical Guide for Translators*)的作者 Oleg Rudavin 总结了翻译行业的几大趋势，包括业务不断增长但质量参差不齐，翻译内容日益复杂，技术进步日新月异，机器翻译蓬勃发展，产业集聚增加导致大公司主导市场，自由译员的地位下降、收入不断减少。他建议自由译员寻求新机会以拓展业务范围、提升专业知识技能、开辟全新业务等。

全球最大的语言服务公司经营部门员工 Jane Freeman 认为，信息爆炸和客户需求的变化使得翻译行业存在大量机会。关键在于译员要成为行家里手，通过学习机器翻译译后编辑、文案撰写、新技术等方式拓展技能，主动适应技术发展，以提高自身的生产力和产品质量水平。

Wordsmith Communication 的创始人兼首席执行官 Pritam Bhattacharyya 强调，译员多元化发展不仅是一种选择，而且是一种大势所趋。他介绍自己多元化的经历：从一名在线文化杂志编辑，拓展到为 ProZ.com 网站的网友讲授业务开拓课程，再到后来创建一所自由职业者商学院。他指出，个人一旦走出职业的舒适区，就能获得丰厚的回报。

第三章　语言业务多元化：翻译核心服务的拓展

本章邀请了多位语言服务行业从业者分享各自的经历和对行业的看法，介绍除翻译外的其他多元化语言业务，例如机器翻译译后编辑、非母语文本编辑、配音、字幕、转录、术语服务、创意翻译、文案撰写、跨文化咨询、语言验证、在线语言培训等。

LexWorks 机器翻译公司的创始人 Lori Thicke 首先介绍了规则引擎、统计引擎和混合引擎的优劣，提出要根据翻译内容和质量要求选择最佳方案，同时要持续投入机器学习，使得译后编辑不仅能提高译文质量，还能不断改进机器翻译系统，真正发挥机器翻译的价值。

艾奥瓦州口笔译员协会主管 Jeana M. Clark 认为，信息就是力量，在信息数据创造与传播价值链中，译员肩负着巨大的责任，需要成长为人机结合的"人机混合译员"，充分利用技术完成高质量的翻译。多元化发展方式包括与专业同行合作开拓新领域、增加语对组合、拓展翻译方向、提供更多服务如翻译培训等，译员在多元化的同时可以扩大收入渠道，扩大客户群和知识面，激发创造力。

德国自由译员和配音专家 Martina Heine-Kilic 介绍了翻译配音的技能需求和设备要求。她指出，随着行业的快速发展，适当的多元化可以让译员利用专业知识获得更好的项目和客户，从而防范经济危机带来的风险。

Felicity Mueller 是一名自由译员、会议口译员、教师和兼职字幕员。她认为，不同的职业身份可以相互补充和相互促进，这种多元化的尝试无论就个人专业能力提升还是就职业发展而言，都是宝贵的经历。她认为，翻译和口译入行需要长期学习和实践，字幕工作需要快速准确地将对话转化为文字，跨学科背景可以为这个领域带来新的视角和价值。

Karolina Kastenhuber 是一名转录员、编辑、校对和多语种翻译。她认为多元化最大的好处之一，就是可以为新晋自由职业的语言专业从业者提供更多机会。通过拓宽行业视野，探索翻译之外的其他语言服务相关工作，新人可以瞄准更多的潜在客户，更快建立业务网络。

dbterm 术语服务公司的创始人 Diana Brändle 指出，每个公司都有自己的术语，"多语言知识管理"对于公司对内和对外清晰、统一地使用术语来说十分必要。译员可以通过参加培训、阅读书籍、参加研讨会、学习行业工具等方式，专攻某个专门领域，建立独有的专业术语库，超越竞争对手。

"创意翻译"常用于营销和广告行业，要求翻译内容必须能引起当地市场的共鸣，以产生与原创内容相当的影响力。具有多重身份的自由译员 Percy Balemans 介绍了创意翻译的工作内容和能力要求。她认为，创意翻译领域不太容易被机器翻译取代。

自由译员和文案撰写者 Alessandra Martelli 指出，为应对市场竞争，专业译员可以与企业建立长期关系，通过专业化或多元化战略实现个人职业发展。文案撰写将翻译和创作两者有效结合，译员可以专攻几个专门领域，结合实践经验和职业发展机会，拓展和完善翻译技能和商业技能。因此，这不失为一种新的多元化发展思路。

2M 语言服务公司的首席执行官 Tea C. Dietterich 指出，推销语言服务不容易。语言服务从业者应自我定义为跨文化咨询师，不断了解目标受众、翻译项目、目标语言和源语言的相关知识，从跨文化的维度思考语言的含义，帮助客户解决实际问题。

Nora Torres 是获得认证的生命科学语言专家。她介绍了参与语言验证工作的经历。语言验证主要应用于药物临床试验领域，内容是翻译和改编外语版本的"临床结果评估"（clinical outcome assessment, COA）工具，目的是确保临床评估在各国和各种文化中都能被接受且数据真实。每个调查对象国至少需要 8 名语言专家，专家要技能成熟、知识面广，这项工作劳动强度非常大。

澳大利亚阿德莱德大学教授 Vanda Nissen 表示，在线语言培训具有效率高、成本低和技术新等优势，越来越受欢迎。在线语言培训技能包括信息与通信技术（information and communications technology, ICT）技能、软件应用技能、媒介选用技能、在线沟通技能等。

Polaron 语言服务公司首席执行官 Eva Hussain 分享了她本人的职业经历，呼吁译员必须保持敏锐的眼光，在机会出现时迅速抓住，将技术和知识转化为可以提供给他人的服务。

第四章 非语言业务多元化：拓展商业战略新领域

本章重点探讨语言服务行业中的非语言业务多元化策略，涉及翻译项目管理、战略联盟、博客和社交网络、社交媒体和在线营销、垂直领域多元化、客户群多元化等。这些内容由多位从业者的经验分享组成。

自由译员 Meike Lange 身兼作家和项目管理者两重身份。她首先介绍了翻译项目管理的工作流程和能力要求，并鼓励更多译员投身该领域。项目管理经验能为译员带来诸多积极影响，如扩大翻译客户网络、拓展知识面、提升翻译技能、获得物质和精神满足等。

Sam Berner 同样拥有多重身份，如作家、出版商、教师、商人、导师、译者、励志演说家。她分享了自己如何组建团队并推动"战略联盟"不断成长的故事，呼吁译员不仅要在职场上保持联系，更要在心理上息息相通。

Lingua Greca Translations 公司的共同创始人之一 Catherine Christaki 认为，自由译员还应成长为优秀的营销人员、社交媒体用户、博客作者、簿记员、社交达人等。她通过分享自己的线上经历，梳理了博客和社交媒体为译员带来的优势，并提出了升级在线形象、突出技能专长、研究潜在客户并创造商机等发展建议。

Sharp End Training Russia 公司负责人 Olga Arakelyan 介绍了自己如何通过社交媒体和在线营销促进职业发展。她认为，多元化对个人成长和企业发展都大有裨益，能让译员保持警觉，获得更多财务稳定性和自由，同时提高企业在潜在客户中的知名度。

俄罗斯 Tomarenko 翻译公司负责人 Valerij Tomarenko 指出，专业化很大程度上取决于客户的产品和服务需求。随着翻译服务日益面临被模仿和商品化的风险，译员将越来越难以保持个人特色和竞争优势。因此，只有持续加强创新意识，寻找独特的营销思路，译员才能增强自身独特性，在产品和服务多元化竞争的时代脱颖而出。

Arancho Doc 公司的高级业务开发经理 Inge Boonen 指出另一个多元化视角，即谋求客户群的多元化。她建议译员在实践中向翻译公司和客户更多展示个人专长，因为只有专业水准高，翻译出众，才能为公司带来更多忠实客户，获得高薪，得到长期聘用。

第五章 被动多元化：通过产品多元化创收

主动多元化是通过积极主动地寻求新的机会和领域来实现多元化，

而被动多元化则是通过接受或适应外部环境的变化来实现多元化。被动多元化通常是企业或个人在面临外部压力或挑战时采取的一种策略，外部压力或挑战可能包括市场需求的变化、竞争的加剧、政策的调整等。企业或个人可能会通过扩大产品线、进入新的市场或领域等方式来实现多元化。

自由译员面临的风险之一是，一旦停止工作，收入也随之停止，因此需要被动多元化来稳定收入来源。本章中，几位从业者通过经验分享探讨如何通过语言产品化，如提供出版物、持续职业发展在线培训课程等途径实现被动创收。

《告别盛宴与饥荒》(Say Goodbye to Feast or Famine)的作者 Joy Mo 是一名自由译员和认证法庭口译员。她以自己著书的经历说明，现代技术的快速变化和翻译软件的发展给译员带来巨大的压力，译员需要寻求更多途径施展才华，获得收入。出版电子书或纸质图书是一个不错的选择。她为想要进入该领域的译员提供建议，例如，关注大众的真正需求、建立个人信誉、选择有趣话题、像和朋友聊天一样写作、聚焦一个主题、制定营销策略等。

Lucy Brooks 在 2010 年创立了 eCPD 网络研讨会，为口笔译员提供持续职业发展在线服务。目前，eCPD 几乎涵盖了翻译人员的所有培训需求，已经成为语言服务行业从业人员高质量职业发展的代名词。通过分享自己的创业故事和四则案例，Lucy 呼吁更多译员加入促进持续职业发展的行列。因为分享和帮助他人不仅会带来强烈的满足感，还可以帮助参与者了解其他行业，拓展行业知识，并增加曝光率，获得更多翻译客户，带来更多收入。

Désirée Staude 分享了自己从雇员到自由译员与在线培训师的角色转变的故事。她表示，自己非常享受作为培训师带来的愉悦，鼓励更多译员加入培训师队伍。她建议译员阅读大量材料，多与人交流，努力在新领域进入前 20 名。知名度越高，翻译业务就越受认可。

第六章　跨行业多元化：为语言服务公司和翻译同行提供专门服务

随着技术的发展和翻译工具的不断涌现，一种新型的多元化开始出现。越来越多的自由译员开始将"同事"作为服务对象，为他们提供翻译工具使用咨询、技术培训等服务。在本章中，商业培训教练、公共演说家、CAT 工具咨询专家、网页设计师和多语种桌面排版专家分享了各自的经验。

Marta Stelmaszak 经营着一个"翻译商学院"（Business School for Translators）博客，为口笔译员提供业务案例分享与技能升级培训。她指出，多元化发展是译员的必然发展方向，译员需要建立多元化的收入来源。同时，看到其他同行的不同业务相互驱动、内在与外在的和谐共生，让她对整个职业的未来感到非常乐观。

作为一名培训师、演讲者、商业教练和自由译员，Konstantin Kisin 基于自己成功经营自由职业的实践经验，为译员实现多元化发展提供了实用的解决方案。他强调，任何人都可以为他人提供有价值的培训，了解自己已有的优秀技能，能够理解受众，就可以开启培训之旅。只要确保参加培训的人觉得物有所值，自然而然就会有收入。

海德堡大学翻译学院的讲师 Nicole Keller 通过提供 CAT 工具使用咨询服务创收。她知道如何及时了解 CAT 工具和术语管理的最新技术理论，也掌握将理论应用于翻译技术实践的方法。她坚信，未来的译员必须用技术武装自己才能保持竞争力。

Magdalena Dziatkiewicz 和团队一起创办了"译者网站"（Websites for Translators），为译员提供网页设计、营销和管理服务，帮助译员在全球范围内开拓业务。她鼓励译员探索多元化发展道路，建议资深译员可以考虑为从事翻译职业的年轻毕业生提供咨询服务，成为私人职业教练；可以教授自我推销艺术和工具使用方法；可以成为语言程序员或语言培训师；可以进行艺术设计或创意文案撰写等。

Jaber Maycid 分享了对语言行业多元化的看法，以及他从事多语种桌面排版和光学字符识别（optical character recognition, OCR）服务的经历。他呼吁译员在如今经济不佳的形势下，多元化自我发展，保持现金流。一旦译员在专业化需求和多元化需求之间找到平衡，目标市场就会增长，带来更多的收入和客户群。

第七章　夹缝中求生存的独特多元化策略

"独特而多元化的个体"（distinctive diversifier）指在业内提供独一无二的创新内容的人才，他们所提供的产品或服务在以前的语言服务行业中并不存在，如今却家喻户晓。本章分享四个案例，介绍独特而多元化的个体最终如何开辟发展新途径。

案例一

Alejandro Moreno-Ramos 是一名爱好绘画的全职译员。2009 年，他创建了讽刺翻译行业的 Mox 漫画博客，这不仅满足了个人兴趣爱好，也带来了额外的收入。一开始，博客吸引了大批读者，但并未带来多少翻译业务。直到 2011 年，Alejandro 出版发行了实体漫画书，奠定了稳定的商业模式基础。目前，Mox 系列漫画书占到他收入的 18%。Alejandro 说，自由译员非常适合创业，他们掌握多种语言，熟悉不同文化，善于网上运营，时间和空间都比较自由，可以灵活安排多元化业务，这是传统职业所不具备的优势。他指出，译员在做自己喜欢的事时，也要考虑清楚投入产出比，找准用户群体，才可确保商业可持续性。例如，Mox 漫画深受同行欢迎，原因在于 Alejandro 成功培育和锁定了目标用户群。他建议，自由译员可以思考自己的个人兴趣能否为同人带来共鸣或价值，将他们转化为潜在客户；译员也需要保持开放和灵活的心态，随时调整商业方向，才能成功。Mox 漫画博客的成功为自由译员的多元化发展带来启发。

案例二

澳大拉西亚最大的专业文件翻译提供商新西兰翻译中心有限公司（New Zealand Translation Centre Ltd.）创始人 Paul Sulzberger 在公司运营中发现，自由译员在国际业务中经常会遇到各种跨境支付的问题。为解决跨境支付昂贵、低效的问题，2011 年，Paul 找到了国际支付专业会计师 Neil Hamlin，两人合作开发了"译员支付"免费国际支付服务平台。该平台通过批量交易获得较优惠的汇率，并让利给译员、翻译公司和客户。该服务提供免费且简便的集中支付方案，解决了翻译公司支付管理的诸多麻烦，吸引了较多翻译公司使用，由此构建了译员、翻译公司、支付平台三赢局面，所有参与方都从中受益。这个成功案例也为自由译员提供了全新思路，即敏锐察觉并专注解决行业痛点，构建互利共赢的商业模式。这也是可持续发展的秘诀。

案例三

Lori Thicke 是 LexWorks 机器翻译公司的创始人。他创新翻译技术，引领机器翻译，创立了世界上最大的非营利性翻译社区"翻译无国界"。该组织总部位于美国。"翻译无国界"组织每年通过捐赠数百万字的专业翻译服务支持全球救援组织，还在肯尼亚内罗毕成立翻译培训中心，致力于消除全球最弱势群体的语言知识障碍。Lori 认为，翻译既是一种艺术形式，又是一门实用工具；翻译行业本身不只是翻译服务，译员需要在更广阔的背景下审视翻译行业，为消除人类语言障碍贡献力量。

案例四

Valeria Aliperta 是一名意大利自由口译员。她成立了一家专门服务自由译员的品牌咨询公司——雨都伦敦品牌塑造，并开始推广个人品牌，期望以此激励其他同人。她通过总结自身的多元化创业经历，为译员提出个人职业发展建议。她的品牌咨询业务源于她本人对品牌塑造和品牌营销的兴趣，她也见证和经历了很多品牌塑造的成功案例。她希望分享本人的经验，帮助更多译员塑造个人品牌和提升知名度。品牌咨询新业务为 Valeria 带来额外的收入和工作机会，也丰富了她的核心语言业务，让工作更加丰富多彩和具有挑战性。因此，她更加坚信，多元化和差异化是自由译员取得成功的关键，译员应要么围绕兴趣，要么结合工作，及时调整核心业务与规划，把握不同阶段的工作机会。Valeria 预计，五年内，自由译员的多元化发展会因技术发展而前景广阔。她呼吁译员努力成长为企业家，而不仅仅是做一个语言转换的工具，因为只有多元化业务才可以保持工作稳定；译员要与时俱进、拥抱变化。

第八章　结论

本章基于众多从业者的经验，总结了语言服务行业多元化发展的策略，梳理了自由译员所面临的处境，并对未来发展提出建议。尽管分享者们的业务侧重点有所不同，对语言服务、产品和商业策略的观点也存在差异，但他们都有一个共同点，那就是拥抱多元化。自由译员选择多元化策略的原因是多方面的，主要包括响应客户或市场需求、渴望从事多种工作、利用现有技能拓展业务等。然而，成功的关键都是基于现有专长。因此，核心永远是夯实现有专长，而不是盲目涉足不熟悉的领域。译员要弄清楚自身的优势，再以此为基础开拓其他业务。

编者建议，自由译员应该从内向外、自下而上地拓宽多元化业务领域，即先巩固现有翻译业务，再拓展其他业务，不要过分分散精力，而是应该注重发掘和利用自身的专业领域和专业优势。过去十年，翻译行业发生了巨大变化。目前，许多自由译员已不同程度地实现了业务多元化，对行业前景比较乐观。拥抱多元化和变革往往能够让翻译从业者取得更大的成功。当然，编者也强调，多元化并不是必须为之，而是一种风险管理策略。自由译员需要保持开放的心态，因为客户也可能会提出各种与翻译无关的服务需求。因此，译员需要主动寻找机会，以合理和专业的多元化来应对翻译行业的变化。随着全球化和数字化技术的不断发展，翻译行业将继续保持快速增长的态势。未来，翻译行业将更加注重技术创新和人才培养，以满足不断变化的市场需求。同时，翻译行业也将更加注重质量和效率，以提高客户满意度。

王立非

推荐阅读

Angelone, E., Ehrensberger-Dow, M., and Massey, G. *The Bloomsbury Companion to Language Industry Studies*. Bloomsbury, 2020.

雷纳托·贝尼纳托、塔克·约翰逊. 翻译公司基本原理. 知识产权出版社，2021.

王华树. 翻译技术研究. 外语教学与研究出版社，2023.

王立非. 京津冀、长三角、粤港澳大湾区语言服务竞争力报告. 对外经济贸易大学出版社，2023.

王立非. 语言服务产业论. 外语教学与研究出版社，2019.

王立非、李昭. 中国语言服务出口现状分析与建议. 李小牧、李嘉珊等. 中国国际服务贸易发展报告（2023）. 社会科学文献出版社，2023.

王立非、任杰. 中国语言服务行业国际竞争力评价与分析. 李小牧、李嘉珊等. 中国国际服务贸易发展报告（2022）. 社会科学文献出版社，2022.

文秋芳、张天伟. 国家语言能力理论体系构建研究. 北京大学出版社，2018.

Praise for *Diversification in the Language Industry*

'Changes in technologies, procedures, requirements and roles affect us all, and the translator is certainly no exception. Typical professionals are likely to be kept up-to-date by their employers, but translators are often working on their own and must struggle to adapt. This collection of interviews and essays provides excellent advice from a "who's who" list of language professionals. It is a valuable resource for translators, from novices to mid-career professionals. With information from this book, translators can not only adapt but excel in these changing times.'

—*Donna Parrish, Editor-in-Chief of Multilingual*

'Nicole Y. Adams has assembled an impressive array of translation-industry experts in this investigation into the implications of the very rapid pace of development that the industry is experiencing, and the opportunities that this presents for freelance translators. Contributions from authorities on topics such as machine translation, post-editing, subtitling, CPD, business skills, social media and public speaking are interspersed with interviews with practitioners that provide an insight into what the theory means in the real world. In addition, a series of case studies takes an in-depth look at how some of the most distinctive examples of diversification succeeded in carving out their unique niche. Whether you think that diversification is a sign of the translation industry growing up, or you view it with fear and trepidation – as an indication that the standards and status you are aiming for in your work are going to be severely diluted – this book should help reshape your understanding of the term.'

—*Iwan Davies MITI,*
Freelance Translator and Chairman
of the Institute of Translation & Interpreting (ITI)

'Today, starting any kind of business has become easier than ever, but this also makes it harder for clients to choose their prospective service provider. What I love about this book is that it actually describes my own path to successful entrepreneurship. I learned along the way that my customers need more than just translation. [...] Nicole has felt the heartbeat of our industry in 2013. [...] Diversification is certainly a major issue in our industry!'

—*Tanya Quintieri,*
President of the German Association of
Freelance Translators and Interpreters (DVÜD)

'Freelance and translation have long been content bedtime partners. It was inevitable that a publication discussing diversification in the language industry would eventually appear. Particularly pleasing is the collective authors' positive spin on how technological changes and new mediums of communication are broadening and lengthening the translator's field of opportunities.'

—*Daniel Mueller,*
Executive Officer of the Australian Institute of
Interpreters and Translators (AUSIT)

'Like electricity, water and the Internet, translation is becoming one of the basic needs of human civilization. In its current state the translation industry lacks the capacity, the skills and the vision to fulfil such a strategic role in the globalization of business and governance. Billions of new co-citizens and consumers on new continents speaking a thousand or more new languages are waiting to be "served". Zettabytes of information (including more multimedia and speech) are waiting to be translated, faster and cheaper than ever before. Technically it's possible. But it requires a paradigm shift, an open mind and an innovative spirit. Nicole Adams has done a great job showing the way to new opportunities and diversification in the language industry.'

—*Jaap van der Meer,*
Director of the Translation Automation User Society (TAUS)

Diversification in the Language Industry

Success beyond translation

Nicole Y. Adams

'When you come to a fork in the road, take it.'
—*Yogi Berra*

Contents

Foreword	*Annamaria Arnall*	xi
Chapter 1	**The story behind this book: An introduction**	13
Chapter 2	**Defining diversification: What is it, and do we need it?**	17

    Industry trends and consequences for translators

        Anne-Marie Colliander Lind   22

        Interview with *Nataly Kelly*   26

    Diversification – choice or necessity? *Anne Diamantidis*   31

        Interview with *Felicity Mueller*   37

    A freelancer speaks out on trends in the

        translation industry *Oleg Rudavin*   40

    A language service provider's take on diversification

        Jane Freeman   53

    Diversification – not optional, but imperative

        Pritam Bhattacharyya   60

Chapter 3   **Linguistic diversification: Expanding your portfolio around your core service of translation**   66

Post-editing of machine translation   *Lori Thicke*   68

Interview with *Tineke Van Beukering*   73

Editing of non-native texts   *Jeana M. Clark*   78

Interview with *Sheila Wilson*   85

Voice-over   *Martina Heine-Kilic*   90

Subtitling   *Felicity Mueller*   96

Interview with *Melissa McMahon*   103

Transcription   *Karolina Kastenhuber*   105

Terminology services   *Diana Brändle*   110

Transcreation   *Percy Balemans*   118

Copywriting   *Alessandra Martelli*   125

Cross-cultural consulting   *Tea C. Dietterich*   132

Interview with *Clare Gallagher*   136

Linguistic validation   *Nora Torres*   139

Online language teaching   *Vanda Nissen*   148

Interview with *Laura Ball*   153

An interpreter's story   *Eva Hussain*   159

Chapter 4   **Extra-linguistic diversification: Developing new business strategies**   165

Project management   *Meike Lange*   168

Interview with *Alberto Ferreira*   172

Strategic alliances   *Sam Berner*   175

Interview with *Attila Piróth*   180

	Blogging and social networking *Catherine Christaki*	187
	Interview with *Corinne McKay*	196
	Social media and online marketing *Olga Arakelyan*	198
	Diversification through specialization *Valerij Tomarenko*	203
	Interview with *Fernando D. Walker*	211
	Diversifying your client base *Inge Boonen*	215
	Interview with *Judy Jenner*	220
Chapter 5	**Passive diversification: Income through productization**	223
	Publications *Joy Mo*	226
	Interview with *Luke Spear*	233
	Continuing professional development *Lucy Brooks*	238
	Online training courses *Désirée Staude*	251
Chapter 6	**External diversification: Specialized services for language service providers and fellow translation professionals**	256
	Coaching and business training *Marta Stelmaszak*	257
	Teaching and public speaking *Konstantin Kisin*	263
	CAT tool consulting *Nicole Keller*	270
	Websites and web-related services *Magdalena Dziatkiewicz*	277
	Multilingual desktop publishing and optical character recognition services *Jaber Maycid*	283
Chapter 7	**Distinctive diversification: Creating a unique niche**	290
	Case study 1: Mox's Blog *Alejandro Moreno-Ramos*	291
	Case study 2: Translator Pay *Paul Sulzberger*	298
	Case study 3: Translators without Borders	303

Interview with *Lori Thicke*	303
Case study 4: Rainy London Branding	307
Interview with *Valeria Aliperta*	307
Chapter 8 Conclusion: Freelance translator – quo vadis?	311
Interview with *Lisa Carter*	314
List of contributors	320
Index	321
About the author	331

Foreword

DIVERSIFICATION IS AN economic necessity we hear increasingly these days. I would like to go further and propose that diversification can be a *life-management necessity*. Diversification in work is a wonderful approach to achieving a healthy balance between all those activities that we do trying to lead a successful and fulfilling life. Adding variety to what we do to earn a living can have a hugely beneficial impact on the entirety of that living.

It is often said that translation is an art and a craft; an intellectual pursuit equated to dancing on a tightrope whilst your arms and legs are hobbled. Good translation is celebrated for the feat it amounts to of transferring complete meanings within strict boundaries. Your mind and heart are engaged in this pursuit, but is your creativity able to operate at its most fundamental level? No. When you are translating, you are expressing other people's thoughts. You choose the words and you erect the structure, but you cannot have any input into the meaning. It is someone else's meaning, someone else's message. When you translate, you must not have a message of your own. This self-denial aspect of the job is rarely pondered, yet also significant. Diversification is a way to free your ego from the constant repression. When you are engaged in your other-than-translating job, you can generate new ideas, you can let your inventiveness soar where it would, and you reap economic and self-affirmatory rewards.

Translation is solitary work. Isolation might suit some of us just fine for some of the time, but when we are asked about the negative aspects of our occupation we tend to complain that there are limited opportunities for us to interact with peers and the outside world. This is one of the reasons that we join professional associations. AUSIT, the Australian Institute of Interpreters and Translators Inc., has conducted member satisfaction surveys twice during the past few years. Results revealed on both occasions that the most highly praised service AUSIT offers to its members is the connection to a community. Electronic correspondence lists, face-to-face meetings and various networking events facilitate the spread of thoughts and ideas. These confirm our worth and contribute in innumerable practical ways to our personal, professional and economic growth. Participation in the life of a community enables us to help others and also to ask and receive assistance when we need a hand. For most of us, AUSIT is a circle of friends who are also colleagues.

Nicole Adams, the author of this timely and inspirational book, is an AUSIT member; so is the editor, Adele Anderson. Several contributors – in fact, almost everyone from Australia – also belong to our organization, which warms my heart and gives me enormous pride. AUSIT seems to be fulfilling its role as a community where the avant-garde of the profession comes together and cheerfully unites to influence the future.

Professional development is at the core of AUSIT's existence; we help our members to help themselves by bringing the most relevant information to their attention and making the best resources available to them. This book is a fantastic resource. It brims with useful information and exhilarating examples for us all to learn from and encourages us to contemplate our own approach to diversification. Enjoy.

Annamaria Arnall,
National President AUSIT

The story behind this book
AN INTRODUCTION

WHEN I SET OUT TO write this book in 2012, diversification seemed to be omnipresent, yet nobody was talking about it. Today, it has become a buzz word and is being discussed everywhere. First let me outline the reasons for this book. Last year, I noticed that more and more colleagues – including and especially experienced colleagues who have been in the industry for quite some time – started to publicly complain about 'the translation industry' in forums, on blogs and on social media. Some of them even announced that, because this industry is continually becoming more 'unstable' and 'volatile', they would retire from freelance translation altogether this year. What struck me was how different their experience seemed to be compared to my own and that of other successful freelancers I know.

I started my freelance translation business on a part-time basis in 2003. By 2007, I was earning more from translating part-time than I did in my in-house role as a quality manager, so I decided to freelance full-time. Shortly after that, my two children were born and my husband chose to take an extended career break to look after them so I could continue running my translation business full-time. As a result, I became the sole income earner and supported a household of four for a period of four years. During that time, I did not do any other work apart from freelance translation and editing. I, therefore, consider freelance translation a very viable business model.

Having said that, it is undeniable that we all work in different markets, depending on our language combination, client base, specialization, the technology we use (or don't use) and the types of services we offer. For a variety of reasons, some freelancers struggle to make ends meet with translation services alone. Others have been translating for 20 years and are starting to feel claustrophobic in their home offices, experience a lack of job satisfaction or simply crave a change of scenery.

Leaving the industry and changing careers altogether often appears to be the only option left to those freelancers, be it to earn more money or to broaden their horizons and do something different for a change. What seems to be overlooked more often than not is the huge range of possibilities freelance translators have to diversify without leaving their existing freelance translation business behind.

A survey I carried out among 250 freelance translators in July 2013 showed that 80.4% offer proofreading and 65.2% editing services in addition to translation (see Figure 1.1). So far, no surprise. What strikes me is the huge gap to the next services in the list: only between 4% and 21.2% offer another related service such as copywriting, transcription or terminology management. So I believe there is huge untapped potential for language professionals to exploit.

In this book, I have compiled the stories of successful language professionals who have capitalized on their different skills, both language-related and beyond. In their contributions, they share their view on diversification, explain their area of specialization and discuss how offering this additional service has affected their existing core translation business. You may note that I did not include interpreting in the list of potential services or lines of business to investigate. This was a conscious decision, because I consider interpreting a different profession altogether, with qualifications and skill sets not necessarily related to translation. I am, however, sharing an interpreter's story and experience with diversification as an example of how relevant this theme is to the entire language industry, even beyond the translation profession.

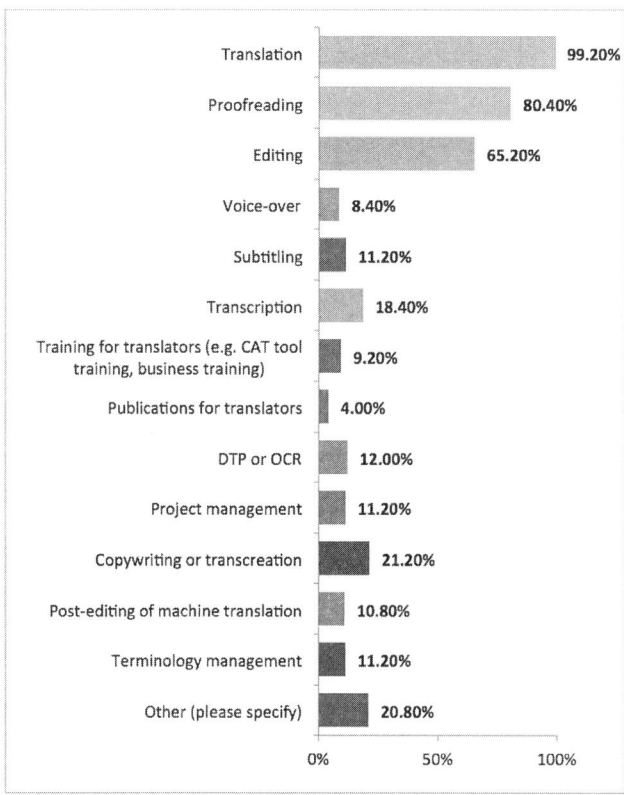

Figure 1.1: What services (or products) do you currently offer?

I would like to express my gratitude to the many kind and generous contributors who have helped me create this book and shared their valuable insights into the industry and their area of expertise. Each and every one of them is an example of successful diversification in the language industry, whether this was a planned process or an accidental journey. I am thrilled to share their journeys with you in *Diversification in the Language Industry.* I have also received a large number of additional suggestions of services, including ghost writing, alignment, translation exam grading, teaching translation, localization, sight translation, CV coaching for foreign markets and subcontracting. Unfortunately, it was not possible to include them all in this edition – but it may be enough to start putting together Volume 2!

2

Defining diversification
WHAT IS IT, AND DO WE NEED IT?

As I MENTIONED IN THE introduction, diversification is a much-discussed topic at the moment and it is certainly not without its critics. Interestingly, just under half of the freelance translators I surveyed consider themselves as having diversified, and the other half do not (see Figure 1.2).

By the same token, almost half of those surveyed (48.8%) believe that freelance translators of today offer more services than they did five

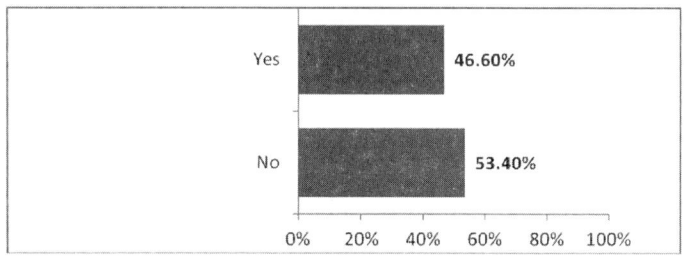

Figure 1.2: Do you think of yourself as having 'diversified' in the language industry?

years ago, and only a small minority (3.6%) think this is not the case (see Figure 1.3). So there seems to be clear agreement that in 2013 freelance translators are offering more than 'just' translation services.

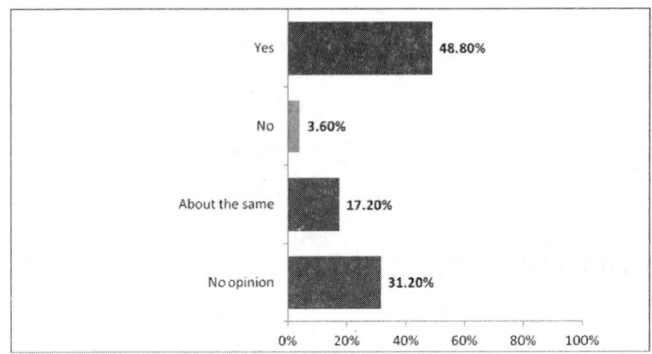

Figure 1.3: In your opinion, do freelance translators today offer more services in addition to translation than they did five years ago?

The question that arose from my survey was how it is possible that most freelance translators offer services beyond 'mere' translation and the majority of respondents agree that, in general, freelance translators today offer a wider range of services than they did just five years ago, yet more than half do not consider themselves as having diversified. My theory is that many freelancers are in fact diversifying but simply aren't aware that they are already doing this.

We therefore need to redefine diversification. The traditional dictionary definition of diversification is 'to give variety to' and 'to extend (business activities) into disparate fields'.[1]

In my view, this is too narrow a definition, and diversification is much better defined by the Entrepreneur Small Business Encyclopedia, according to which diversification is 'a risk-reduction strategy that involves adding product, services, location, customers and markets to your company's portfolio' [sic] based on the observation that:

> Many small companies are one-trick ponies, betting their entire futures on

---

[1] diversification. *The American Heritage ® Dictionary of the English Language*. Fifth edition. Houghton Mifflin Harcourt, 2011.

a single product, a single service, a single location or even a single customer. And there's nothing wrong with that in the beginning: A narrow focus lets a startup concentrate energy on doing one thing extremely well.

But as you grow larger, you'll find opportunities to add products, services, locations, customers and markets. Diversifying in this way can help your business weather tough times by providing alternate sources of revenue in the event that your original market dries up, stops growing or is hit by new competition. Most companies that survive for long periods of time find that they have to develop new sources of revenue as tastes change and opportunities evolve. Growth through diversification can help your company have options in place when they are needed.[1]

This is especially true of freelance translation professionals, whose diversification efforts can take the form of adding another source language (product), offering an additional service (service), marketing to a new target audience (customers), or adding a new area of specialization (market). All these options can be classified into one of the five categories of diversification for freelance translators I have devised.

Types of diversification

1. *Linguistic diversification*: expanding your portfolio around your core service of translation (Chapter 3)
2. *Extra-linguistic diversification*: developing new business strategies or areas of entrepreneurship (Chapter 4)
3. *Passive diversification*: income through productization (Chapter 5)
4. *External diversification*: specialized services beyond translation which you can offer to language service providers and fellow translation professionals (Chapter 6)
5. *Distinctive diversification*: creating a very unique niche for yourself in the language industry with a one-of-a-kind product or service (Chapter 7).

---

1 http://www.entrepreneur.com/encyclopedia/diversification

Criticism

As my survey has shown, a large number of freelance translators are already offering services closely related to translation (proofreading and editing), but the survey has also revealed that many of them do not consider these diversification precisely because they are connected to their core service of translation. I would classify these services as *linguistic diversification*. When we talk about diversification, many freelancers automatically think of *extra-linguistic, passive* or *external* diversification. Most discussions about diversification therefore tend to revolve around the following arguments:

- Diversification is only for bad translators. I'm successful and make a lot of money from translation alone, so I don't need to diversify.
- I'm not an outgoing person; I'm not comfortable selling or putting myself out there.
- I have no time to diversify because I don't want my core activity (translation) to suffer.
- I trained to be a translator; why would I want to do anything else?
- I'd rather improve my existing translation business and become a better translator.

My redefinition of diversification in the language industry seeks to counter these arguments by changing the categories in which freelance translation professionals have traditionally thought of diversification. As we've already established, I absolutely consider freelance translation in itself a viable business model, and 84.8% of those freelancers surveyed for this book agree (see Figure 1.4).

Having said that, careers evolve, new personal interests develop, markets change, new technologies emerge all the time and, most of all, why would you want to put all your eggs in one basket? It is prudent to have a risk management strategy in place, and diversification certainly lends itself to this purpose. Many of the experts who contributed to this book ended up diversifying almost by accident. The common theme in all their stories is that their diversification was not a planned strategy but rather an opportunity that presented itself, and which often led to another opportunity, and another, and so on. So it pays to keep our eyes open and at least be aware of what's out there and what options we have, whether we need to do anything about them right now or not.

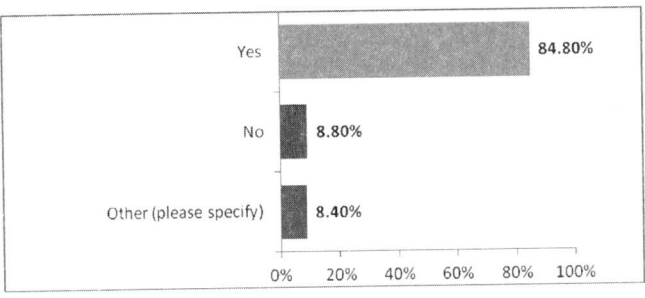

Figure 1.4: Do you consider freelance translation a viable business model?

Different perspectives

To offer as broad an angle on the issue as possible, let's look at five different perspectives on diversification in today's market: those of an industry expert, a reluctant diversifier, a freelancer, a language service provider and an enthusiastic diversifier.

INDUSTRY TRENDS AND CONSEQUENCES FOR TRANSLATORS

Anne-Marie Colliander Lind *is a recognized force in the language industry landscape. She has spent more than 20 years helping multinational organizations solve their language issues, serving in executive sales and management positions at leading service, technology and market research companies. Currently, Anne-Marie is the CEO of Inkrea.se Consulting AB, a management consulting company based in Sweden that assists companies in their growth and development strategies. She is appointed Director of Fundraising for Translators without Borders and organizes localization and technology events in the Nordic countries. Anne-Marie is a sought-after speaker at international industry conferences.*

ARE YOU AFRAID THE WORLD is ending? That your existence as a freelancer is at risk? Don't worry. This chapter covers three trends in the language industry that will ensure a lifetime of joy and employment for you as a freelance translator. The three trends that I see shaping the language industry today and in the near future are volume increase, technology as a productivity enhancer and disintermediation.

For as long as I have been in the language industry, there has been an ongoing debate about freelance translators becoming obsolete. There has always been a fear, for a variety of reasons, that individual translators will be outdone; that they will be overtaken by cheaper resources in emerging markets or by technology, or that single sourcing will decrease volumes – or even, that English will be sufficient in these times of globalization and internationalization, diminishing the need for local languages! I disagree; on the contrary, the market for individual translators has never been more promising.

Volume increase

More content has been created in the last decade than in the entire history of mankind – and access to information has never been easier. I believe that the more global we become, the more important will be the role of local languages. Information in your native language drives your buying behaviour and influences your capabilities. I would even like to take it one step further and say that access to information in your native language could, and should, be a fundamental human right.

Language has become a differentiator. From a commercial perspective, language will give you competitive advantages, because it acts as an enabler. Multilingual communication opens up access to new markets, and the companies using it as the powerful weapon it can become will always be a few steps ahead of their competitors. After all, the cheapest and easiest part of successful globalization is translation!

The good news is that volume is increasing – and at a very fast pace. But translation resources are scarce! There aren't enough linguists in the world to fulfil all the requirements for translation, which in turn drives the need for technology and automation. Freelance translators often mistakenly fear that technology takes work away from them. Technology takes away the boring, repetitive, transactional, low-value jobs, which no one enjoys anyway. There are millions of words stored in knowledge databases with support and user-generated content which no company can afford to translate; at least not with traditional processes. As weird as it might seem, technologies like machine translation drive the need for human translation. As the aphorism says, 'the rising tide lifts all boats.' If volumes increase for translation companies, then volumes for individual translators will increase too.

Technology

The fundamental characteristics of the translation profession have changed in the last decades, as have those of most other professional services. In the past, translation was simple, as you only had to convert content from one language to another with the help of a dictionary. Today content has exploded, not only in volume but also in formats and delivery mechanisms. It's not enough anymore to have access to a typewriter or a computer. The keywords for a professional freelance translator today are productivity and multimedia. These two words are viscerally tied to technology.

When I started in the language industry in 1989, computers were not a given amongst freelancers. There are always the few pioneers who are quick to indulge in new technologies, but sadly, the majority is constantly one or two steps behind. I remember Boris, a fantastic Russian translator whom we used for our most important clients; he refused to abandon his Olivetti typewriter in favour of the brand new Xerox workstation (a €10,000 investment) we offered him to use for his translation projects at our office. As a result of his reluctance to change, we had to abandon him and his excellent translation services for a less experienced professional who could work with the required technology. As far as I know, Boris' inflexibility eventually put him out of business.

If we don't adapt to change, we risk being left behind. We can't stop the evolution of technology, but we can learn how to use it to our advantage. Boris wasn't ready for the change. He produced his 2,000 words per day on his beloved Olivetti, whilst modern individual translators, with the help of technology, can generate outputs of 5,000 to 10,000 words per day. Translators need to see technology as a productivity enhancer, as an enabler, not as a threat. Embrace technology!

Disintermediation

Technology and automation lead us on to the third trend – disintermediation. The language industry is a long chain of production steps, where work flows from the end client through multi-language vendors (MLVs) to single-language vendors (SLVs) and finally to the freelance translators. There are steps in this process that add little or no value to the end product. They only increase costs.

MLVs – who traditionally own the relationship with the end client – are under pressure to produce more with less. One solution is to transfer responsibility for keeping costs down throughout the supply chain by demanding discounts from their vendors. But they can also achieve cost reductions by removing one or two steps in the production chain. This is called disintermediation and means that freelance translators do not carry the entire burden of the price pressure on the market at the client level. Remember that the core service or end product of the language industry is still translation, which is done by translators. Therefore, it is likely that those who perform intermediary tasks (those who don't own the relationship with the client or produce the end product) will be removed from the process rather than the translator.

Disintermediation should also have a positive effect on quality. By removing human steps from the production process, opportunities for the introduction of errors are eliminated. In a streamlined production environment, the professional translator is put back in control of linguistic quality. Disintermediation also puts the linguist in closer communication with the end user, and that means better quality sooner.

Recommendations

Given the trends of volume increase, technology as a productivity enhancer and disintermediation, is it vital for an individual translator to diversify? For any successful business, differentiation is important to be competitive. I see diversification as only one way to differentiate. My advice would be not to diversify too much, but there are a few things that you can do:

- **Add a new language pair.** If you can add a language combination to your portfolio you immediately expand your service offering.
- **Add another domain of specialization.** Become the expert amongst the experts, and choose topics that are close to your heart. Translate what you love – passion is contagious and it gives you energy. Passion is the key to any successful professional career.
- **Become the expert.** Whatever you decide to do, make sure you become the best and make sure that your clients and colleagues see you as such.
- **Embrace technology.** Learn how to use the available tools. Freelance translators should develop their own machine translation engines within their niche of expertise. Start building repositories from translation memories and bilingual files and become your own post-editor. To increase output and become more productive, you need technology to do the bulk of the repetitive work. Reduced price per unit (per character, word, line or page) is not a threat if you can increase your productivity.

- **Build a community.** If you give, you gain. By sharing your knowledge and experience in interest groups, social media and professional development events, you become more relevant and assignments will flow in your direction.
- **Collaborate.** If you are a committed, professional translator, you probably already have a network of translating colleagues. They are not your competitors; they are potential co-workers. Before turning a project down (because of time constraints or other reasons), check if there is help at hand in your community.
- **Make yourself equal before you differentiate.** Make sure you can do what everybody else is doing and then supplement your skills and resources with value-added services.

Always keep in mind that what really matters in the language industry are good customer service, responsiveness and a level of linguistic quality that meets the customer's expectations. Availability and capability!

Diversify, differentiate, disintermediate

Whatever strategy you choose to get more business as an individual translator, don't forget that the free market economy will reward those who are extremely good at what they do and those who know how to sell themselves. Focus on becoming the best and most productive in your area of expertise. Then focus on learning how to use all the tools at your disposal to make yourself known to those who need, and are willing to buy, your services.

Conquer your fear by adapting to change.

Interview with Nataly Kelly

Nataly Kelly is the VP of Market Development at Smartling, the cloud-based enterprise translation management company. Her latest book, Found in Translation: How Language Shapes Our Lives and Transforms the World, *was published by Perigee/Penguin (USA) in October 2012. A former Fulbright scholar in sociolinguistics, Nataly has published articles on various aspects of Ecuadorian Spanish in academic journals from Colombia and Mexico. She also writes about community interpreting and its impact on the integration of linguistic minorities in highly diverse societies, with a special focus on the role of emerging technologies. Nataly is a certified court interpreter (Spanish), has worked as a freelance translator and editor, and is a familiar face on the language industry conference circuit. She has served as an elected member of the board of directors of the National Council on Interpreting in Health Care and currently serves on the American Translators Association interpreter certification committee as well as the advocacy committee for the National Association of Judiciary Interpreters and Translators.*

1) Nataly, you are a trained interpreter and translator, but you have worked as a researcher, author and consultant in the language industry, and now work as VP of Market Development at Smartling, a translation technology company. What motivated you to shift to these roles rather than sticking to pure translation and interpreting?

I think diversification is extremely important in one's career, especially if, like me, you happen to be interested in many things. Diversification in my case stems from two major factors – first, a healthy sense of curiosity with a willingness to learn, and second, a desire to jump in and help where help is needed, even if I previously did not have experience in the area. As an interpreter, I received many types of assignments, ranging from medical to court. When telephone interpreting, I interpreted everything from 911 calls to someone paying their electricity bill.

Early on in my interpreting career, when I worked with AT&T, I was sent to management training, and shortly afterwards I began managing an array of activities, including writing for a newsletter for Spanish interpreters (and eventually becoming the editor), leading various projects (including a certification endeavour) and developing and managing a hire orientation programme for new interpreters. I'd say that leading teams and managing people has been a part of my work life for most of the time I've been in the translation and interpreting fields. I've always kept an open mind to things that come my way, and when I didn't have expertise in a given area (test development, for example), I did extensive research to come up to speed.

Also, I have often seen the need to bridge the gap between the translator-interpreter community and the worlds of business and technology. Many times, I have jumped in primarily due to a desire to bridge these gaps. I've often thought that what I have been doing for much of my career relates to bridging gaps between the professional community and others – the lay public, the media, the technology sector and the business world. In that figurative sense, I'll always be an interpreter and a translator, and more importantly, an advocate for overcoming language barriers.

2) What impact have these activities had on your translation business, and do you enjoy this diversification from the translation career you originally embarked on?

I don't derive any income from translation today, but I still volunteer as a translator. In particular, I enjoy translating Ecuadorian poetry, because Ecuador is a place with many beautiful indigenous voices that are not yet known to the world. One poem at a time, I try to help those voices become known.

With regard to whether the diversification is enjoyable, I'd say if your work is led by passion, you'll always find it enjoyable. Personally, I only take a job if I see a prospect of contributing to a broader change in the world, so whatever job I am in, I tend to love it, and when I no longer love it, I move on to something that I can be passionate about instead. I definitely enjoy working with other people – especially being part of a team. I'm a firm believer that we can accomplish more collectively than as individuals, which is why I've always gravitated toward positions that enable me to work with others. I've always enjoyed that, but when you're an individual translator or interpreter, teamwork is a skill that does not get used as frequently.

For me, it's definitely enjoyable to see an impact from my work, and the way I tend to see this most is through my writing. People often tell me they have enjoyed my books or articles, and that they changed their mind or discovered something new thanks to me, and that is extremely important to me. I've always felt that if I can leave any legacy behind in this world, it would likely be through my writing.

That said, I'm also proud of many things I've developed while working at different companies over the years, especially if they give back to the field in some important way. In one job, I helped develop a cultural competence training programme that was certainly something I could be proud of – extending beyond just language barriers and into one of cultures, too. I also feel proud of the research I conducted and led for nearly five years while at a research firm. I'll always be happy with my work if it's something that I feel made a difference and that I can proudly stand behind.

3) When we talk about diversification, most of us tend to consider it as something only translators can branch out into. Do you feel interpreters can also benefit from diversifying, and in what ways?
Absolutely. Many interpreters have not even scratched the surface of the opportunities that exist. When I was working as a telephone interpreter, I didn't need to become court certified, but I studied and pushed myself to obtain additional knowledge and skills, leading to additional credentials. Many community interpreters do not use simultaneous interpreting skills, but these can be extremely useful. Other interpreters have never tried video or telephone interpreting. Again, these are skills that are very useful, and important. Interpreters can also diversify through the types of specialization and knowledge they obtain.

In addition, I always advise interpreters to set goals for themselves, even with regard to language learning. That could entail deepening their knowledge of a specialty terminology area, local dialect or other area. One goal I set for myself recently was to enrol in an Irish Gaelic course. I studied in advance so that I could opt out of the first level, and I enrolled directly in the second level course, because I wanted to set a goal for myself that wasn't overly easy to achieve. Surprisingly, I enhanced my knowledge of my other languages by studying Irish. Even if it's something as simple as studying another language, it's absolutely worth the time and commitment it takes. It's fun to go back to school, to have homework and to be tested – at least it is if you're addicted to learning, as I am. It also pushes us outside of our comfort zone, which is always a good thing. Our brains grow, our minds expand and we benefit tremendously when we respond to such challenges.

4) What would you say to freelance translators who are sceptical about the developments in the language industry and the increasing level of diversification we are experiencing?
Diversification is a good sign, and a natural progression for a field that is evolving. I've written and talked about how translators are the new blacksmiths, because that field diversified and led to many other professions – welders, mechanics, engineers and so on. Of course blacksmiths still exist too, but just look at the many professions that were born out of theirs. Translation represents the same possibilities.

One of the things I was careful to highlight in the most recent book I co-authored, *Found in Translation*, was the tremendous diversity of the language professions. What does an interpreter for NASA really have in common with a translator of Harlequin romance novels? What does a baseball interpreter have in common with someone who translates and summarizes government intelligence data all day long? And what do the people who 'transcreate' cards at Hallmark have in common with the translator who is working on a technical manual, or a video game translator, or an interpreter who accompanies a journalist into a war zone? It would appear that they have very little in common, but they're all part of a field that is already extremely diverse. I would not say that diversification is part of the future, but rather, that it's already happening before our very eyes. It's a trend in the here and now, one that all translators and interpreters need to be aware of.

DIVERSIFICATION – CHOICE OR NECESSITY?

A French medical translator for English and German, **Anne Diamantidis** *works at GxP Language Services, a medical and pharma translation company based in Germany. A member of the BDÜ (German association of translators and interpreters) and active Translator without Borders, she also works as an Internet marketing and online reputation speaker and trainer within the translation profession and for various industries. Her services were hired by a party in the French 2012 elections to manage the online campaign and image of one of their candidates. An experienced trainer and conference speaker, LinkedIn consultant, certified social media manager and regular author* (Social Media Today, LinkedIn & Business Magazine, BDÜ's MDÜ...), *she has already helped hundreds of translators boost their online visibility and image.*

WHEN NICOLE ASKED ME TO write this contribution, my first reaction was 'What is diversification and why is she asking me?' I had no idea that I was actually 'diversifying' myself. Now everybody talks about diversification in the industry and it seems to be the hot topic of the moment. It took me a while to get my thoughts straight. I had no real opinion on diversification, as I was not aware of the growing trend it represented and had never taken a closer look. In addition, I was not really concerned about what other people were doing, as long as it did not impact negatively on what I did. I am by no means an expert in 'diversification' matters and all I can do here is share my experience (which I hope will give you some food for thought).

What is diversification?

Let's get to the point. What is diversification? I don't know the official definition, if there is one. The way I see it, it could be anything. Adding a specialty field to your freelance translator offering is a way of diversifying. Doing pro bono translation work for charities is a way of diversifying. So is adding a new language to your source languages, or offering additional services to your clients such as desktop publishing, copywriting, transcreation, maintaining their multilingual website or any other 'plus' your translation business can do for them. These could all be considered diversification. An interpreter who offers software localization is also diversifying. The core activity is interpreting, and localization is an additional service this person can offer.

Two types of diversification

Browsing through online discussions and translators' groups, one could be under the impression that diversification means doing something else, as in having a second activity or income stream. I don't know about you, but in this case I hear teaching, training, consulting, authoring, etc., in other words, having some kind of second job complementary to freelance language services. So there are two types of diversification:

- Type 1: **diversifying your business**, i.e. offering additional related services to your clients (new language, new field, new skills, desktop publishing, etc.) to make extra income from your business.
- Type 2: **diversifying yourself**, i.e. starting another activity, a second job, in addition to your translation business, to make extra income.

In both cases the core activity remains – providing language services. If you stop offering them and start teaching full-time, then you're not diversifying anymore. You're a teacher.

Diversification: what for?

There's nothing wrong with trying to make extra money. There are bills to pay, fridges to fill, loans to pay back and kids to raise, so it seems normal to diversify with the purpose of making additional income. That includes pro bono work, though indirectly. Doing pro bono work is also a way to do well while serving one's image. If you highlight the fact that you help NGOs, you never know how this may impact your image positively among your clients. This might lead indirectly to more jobs.

So diversifying = earning more – I think we agree on that.

Is diversification necessary?

I can't help wondering if we really all need type 2 diversification in our industry. Everybody talks about this form of diversification and how necessary it is. I've heard it said that we should all write books or give webinars, or even that translating full-time is not a viable business model. I know some freelance translators who earn more in a month from their translation work than they can spend. I also know a large number of freelance translators who make a decent living of translating full-time and who are happy with their income and their life as it is.

The decision is yours. You are in control of your business, your career and your life. Just that some say we should diversify does not mean we all have to. We are free to do so or not. There are many reasons why one would choose to diversify. It could be for fun because it makes you happy, it could be for the challenge, it could be to broaden your horizons, or it could be to try out something else while making extra money (which never hurts). You may feel you need to, or you may really need to. Whatever your reasons, you are in control. You should not feel obliged to diversify because it's trendy and others are doing it. Their needs are not your needs; what works for you won't automatically work for someone else and vice versa.

No, diversification is not necessary

In my opinion, our industry is not insecure, nor is it 'not viable anymore' despite many claims. Our industry does have a bright future, and it would realize that if it would stop burying its head in the sand and start accepting and adapting to changes that are happening anyway. Instead of fighting changes and being defeated without any idea of what's coming next, why not try to adapt to these changes, which would give us a chance to have better control over the direction of events?

If a translator feels they do not earn enough, then they could consider increasing their rates and/or diversifying their existing offering, before immediately taking on a second job or writing books. Diversifying in our industry does not automatically mean having a parallel career or a new business branch. It can be as simple as adding a 'plus' to your offer. It is up to you, depending on your needs, goals and expectations.

Type 1 vs. type 2 diversification

Type 1 diversification seems easier and more stable than going for the full package of a new career, second job and even crazier hours. In type 1, you already have a client base. You know each other, they (hopefully) know the worth of your work and respect you, and they may be happy that you provide additional services they won't need to do themselves or outsource to a second provider anymore. You enable them to centralize as much as possible by outsourcing more to you. Everything is in place. The risk of wasting time, energy and money is more limited and manageable. The reputational risk is real, but manageable too as long as you don't overdo it. Are translators who claim they can translate in any specialty field and that they can do absolutely everything really that credible?

In May 2013 Kevin Hendzel published an excellent article about this on his blog, entitled 'Everybody lies'. The article is a gem; I couldn't have said it better. To make my point, here is the beginning of the blog article:

> A handyman knocks on your front door. 'I can fix anything,' he announces when you answer.
>
> 'Well, my roof leaks,' you reply, 'and I was thinking of getting some estimates—'
>
> '—I am the best at roofs!' he says, interrupting you. 'Better than those roofing companies that rip you off.'
>
> 'OK, but sorry, I can't talk right now,' you say, trying to be polite. 'I need to take my daughter's computer in to have it looked at and—'
>
> 'Computers! Yes! I can do that! I built a desktop from scratch once and everybody loves my computer work. Never had a complaint.'
>
> At this point you stop, cross your arms and frown with suspicion.
>
> 'Can you surgically insert a catheter and stent into my carotid artery before noon?' you ask sarcastically.
>
> 'Of course! And at a great price!' he insists.

Food for thought, don't you think?

In type 2 diversification I feel the financial risk can be much higher (time is money) – not to mention the 'burn-out' and reputational risks: burning yourself out, but also burning other people out and hurting your credibility (the two go together).

Just as in type 1, just as in the handyman example from Kevin Hendzel, diversifying too much in type 2 may lead to people growing dizzy, annoyed and bored with you. Worse, you can seriously damage your credibility: if you do too much and are too loud, people may think you clearly have too much time on your hands and that therefore you're probably a terrible translator because your clients don't give you any jobs. Just like pretty much everything in life, it's all about balance.

Finding the balance between too much and not enough is a tremendous (probably lifelong) challenge, but it is something you will have to deal with if you diversify.

Diversifying also equals specializing

If you decide to diversify – and this applies to both types, 1 and 2 – then *specialize*. I don't see how you can go wrong by focusing on a couple of subjects and working hard to gain full expertise in them, whether as a translator, trainer, consultant or author. You'll be much more credible and respected for that; you'll be seen as 'the expert in...', which will ultimately lead to the sought goal of making more money. Just keep in mind: 'Jack of all trades is master of none'.

My own 'diversification' experience

As explained above, I had not thought about whether what I was doing as an Internet and social media marketing trainer was diversification. I came to do it by accident. The topic of 'online presence' came up very early in my career, during my MA course in translation at university. During the first MA year's internship, one of the goals my supervisor gave me was to create myself an online presence from scratch, which I did. After that he took me to a translation conference and pushed me into making a presentation about this experience. I was terrified and kept wondering what on earth I, a 'baby translator' with zero experience, could possibly have to say to a room full of real and seasoned translators. The presentation was surprisingly well received; some translators even said they learnt something from it. I could not believe my ears.

I finished my last year at university while doing the same presentation at other conferences. The fun grew with it. The Internet is a more 'normal' tool to my generation than to the previous ones and there were (still are...!) a lot of prejudices and fears to respond to.

After graduating I started working as conferences coordinator for Proz.com. Working for a website where translators can market themselves and showcase their services fed my growing obsession with online presence, and this was during the rise of Facebook and Twitter as promotional tools. During my last year at ProZ.com, I used them more intensively to promote the conferences I was coordinating. The huge potential was clear, but I had no time to really go into it in depth – there were events to organize!

The opportunity came when I started working for my current employer, GxP Language Services. The company was young and looking for ways to have a strong online presence. This was my chance to finally discover and learn about the power of these online platforms. After hours of social media training and webinars (many of them just stating 'marketing blabla') and even more hours of doing, trying, experiencing and making mistakes on social platforms, my confidence grew. Around that time, a friend of mine in France who had launched his business (singing classes) a few months before asked me what he could do to boost his Google ranking – he was ranking desperately low (page 7 on Google.fr) when searching 'singing teacher in Lyon'.

That was a real challenge. I now knew my way around social platforms, but I had no idea about search engine optimization. After a second round of training, webinars and a lot of reading, we decided just to try. I created him online profiles, maintained them and worked on his website. To our surprise, it worked. And it worked really well: within one month, he was at the bottom of page 1 in search results.

After two months, he was in the top three results on page 1. After six months, he had gained 16 new students who all found him via Google, and he finally started making a living out of his passion seven months after we had started the 'experiment'.

That success was a complete surprise and happened by accident. Never had I imagined it would actually work. After that I took a closer look and realized there was an 'online marketing' niche in the translation industry. My university training was still relatively fresh in my mind and there was nothing in there about online presence and online reputation (nothing about marketing your services and looking for prospective clients, as matter of fact). So I simply decided to give it a try and offer training on these questions. I did not take this decision for altruistic reasons. I did this (and still do) to earn extra money.

Along the way, I have lots of fun doing it, meet interesting people, and get to travel to conferences, discover new places and see old friends, which makes the whole thing even better. I do not depend on this activity on the financial level and I can stop doing it whenever I want. I just want to do to it – I don't *need* to do it.

Interview with Felicity Mueller

After completing a BA (Honours) in German and Russian and an MA in Slavonic Languages at the Australian National University, **Felicity Mueller** *lived and worked in Austria. Since moving to Sydney in the mid-1980s she has been a freelance translator, conference and community interpreter and teacher of translation and interpreting. She holds NAATI accreditation as a Senior Conference Interpreter and Translator and is a member of AUSIT and the International Association of Conference Interpreters. Felicity happily diversified into subtitling in 1987 and was a permanent part-time German subtitler/editor with the Special Broadcasting Service (SBS) until 2012. Still a freelance subtitler, she is currently lecturing in Translation Studies at the University of Sydney. Since 2010, Felicity has been teaching intensive interpreting courses at the Centre for Translation Studies at the University of Vienna and working as a contract translator at the Organization for Security and Co-operation in Vienna.*

1) Felicity, you have been a freelance translator, a conference and community interpreter since the mid-1980s and a teacher of translation and interpreting

since the early 1990s. You are also a very experienced subtitler, which we'll read more about later in your chapter on subtitling. One could say you are diversification personified. Have you always considered diversification a must for freelance translators, and how come you've been wearing so many hats since the very start of your translation career – a rather unusual scenario?

I never made a decision to diversify or thought about what freelance translators should or shouldn't do. It was a matter of taking opportunities that came up and continuing with what I enjoyed. I enjoyed freelance translation and interpreting, but welcomed the chance to become a subtitler. For a number of reasons, both personal and professional, subtitling became my main area of work. The university teaching grew out of my professional experience in translation and interpreting and my academic background. It didn't all happen at once, but grew slowly.

2) What impact have these additional activities had on your core translation business? Does most of your income still come from translation or does it come from other services?

Subtitling became my main business when I was offered a permanent part-time position with SBS in 1989. I also continued with interpreting and translation and some teaching. I am still a freelance subtitler with SBS after leaving my part-time position in 2012. Now translation and interpreting, university teaching and subtitling are my sources of income. Since 2010, I have spent part of each year in Vienna teaching simultaneous and consecutive German-English interpreting and translating with an international organization.

3) Some freelance translators are convinced the key to success lies purely in specializing and improving their translation skills rather than diversifying into other areas of business. What would you say to freelance translators who are sceptical about the increasing level of diversification we are experiencing?

Specializing works well in markets where your language combination is in demand and clients are prepared to pay for quality. However, things change rapidly. If a client suddenly has to accept the cheapest quote, or if a new discovery makes your specialized knowledge irrelevant, you could be in trouble. Having extra skills to offer can help.

4) Where do you see freelance translators in five years' time in terms of diversification?
Freelance translators with a specialization should still be in demand, but the ability to diversify and add new skills will be an advantage. Competition and the downward pressure on rates will continue, so most translators will be making more use of translation tools and improved machine translation and may be spending more time post-editing than at present. They will need to quote for jobs quickly, have short turnaround times and be able to put together teams of translators to meet tight deadlines for longer jobs.

A FREELANCER SPEAKS OUT ON TRENDS IN THE TRANSLATION INDUSTRY

Oleg Rudavin graduated from Kharkiv State University in 1985 as an English translator. He started his professional career as a military interpreter in Eritrea; continued as a freelance literary translator (with more than 30 translated books published); and tried working in-house, first at an industrial plant and later at a translation company, only to get back to freelancing. Living in the Russian-speaking part of Ukraine, he is bilingual and translates from English, Spanish and Italian in a variety of technical areas, as well as marketing, ecology, renewable energy, travel and tourism. As a successful freelance translator, he willingly shares his knowledge and experience in conference presentations, in-person training sessions, online webinars and numerous Internet publications focusing on practical aspects of freelancing and trends in the translation industry. He is the author of Internet Freelancing: Practical Guide for Translators, *praised as one of the most comprehensive books available on freelance translation.*

WE LIVE IN A TIME OF CHANGE. Wow! What a revelation! Doesn't everybody know it? We do. Moreover, with changes so global, large-scale, quick and permanent, we've developed a kind of immunity to the world changing around us, instead of monitoring the situation and adapting to it or, even better, anticipating changes and taking proactive steps. The period of active changes in translation started at the end of the 1990s. In order to better understand what's going on in translation now, let's briefly look at how it was not so long ago.

Recent history

Until about 15 or 20 years ago, the only significant change in translators' work had been typewriters replacing pen and paper. Internet and computers changed everything. Dictionaries migrated onto hard disks and CDs, and hard copies gave way to electronic documents, which created the opportunity for tidying up one's work desk (mine is still a mess!) and dramatically reduced the time wasted on picking up bales of printed documents at the client's place and delivering similar cargoes back. Internet and web-based apps destroyed all communication barriers. Outsourcers whose productivity had been limited by the quantity of physically accessible translators started recruiting freelancers from all over the globe. Distance lost relevance; it took a few clicks of the mouse to find a translator with any language combination specializing in any area. Conversely, translators from the most remote places on the planet got a chance to reach clients irrespective of their geographical location.

Formation of the global translation market began where the influence was mutual: cheaper markets affected the rates structure in the high-end markets while the latter helped to improve the situation in the low-end ones. Rates-wise, it lasted till about 2007, and the market sagged during the crisis period, mostly in 2009. The existing global market has basically levelled out now; local variations still remain, but they are not as shocking as they used to be. CAT tools that emerged at the turn of the century proved their efficiency and became an integral part of the translation process. Big translation companies, or multi-language vendors (MLVs), got even bigger, box-shifters came and left, and freelancers grew accustomed to operating in the new environment. Overall, the last 10 or 15 years have been a very dynamic time.

Current trends

It should be noted that the consequences of the same developments may be different or even opposite, not only for the various players in the translation market but also for members of the same group representing different sectors. The 2008 crisis is a good illustration of this point. Many clients stopped buying linguistic services due to the shortage of financial resources. Surprisingly – or, on the contrary, quite logically – some of my colleagues were overloaded with work for months on end. The explanation is simple. The crisis triggered a frenzy of communications between banks and financial institutions, and some translators working in that area had to forget about weekends in order to handle urgent jobs. Also, a number of clients tried to mitigate the situation by going global, and there was an increase in website content translations. A site in many languages is probably the cheapest way of spreading information about one's products or services worldwide.

I've noticed several trends over the last few years and would like to offer my view on both the trends and their potential consequences for the translation market. The order of the list does not reflect their impact on the industry.

Steady growth, demand-supply correlation and quality implications

The translation market is, and will keep on, growing. Globalization says it all: politics, economy, science and culture become more international with every year, and smooth communication is critical for the proper functioning of many spheres of our lives. More documents are generated, they are becoming bigger, and often we see challenges with no feasible solutions at hand. Take Croatia joining the European Union (EU), for example. This means that all EU documentation must be eventually translated into Croatian, in addition to other languages. Will this country with a population of about 4.5 million be able to provide a sufficient number of translators to handle the task? How much will it cost – in total and per capita? Does it make sense? And generally, can the growing demand for linguistic services be satisfied using traditional translation/interpretation/localization approaches and means?

My answer is definitely no! Especially if we consider the available translation resources: professional translators and interpreters are few, expensive and often booked for months in advance. As a result, companies have come up with the unusual term 'acceptable quality'. This could mean anything, from 'approved by the end client' to 'not as good as it should be but passable, because we don't have/want to pay more money to hire a good translator' or 'who cares about the quality of a text that nobody's going to read'.

I once came up with the following definition of translation: a linguistic component of a product or service. A lot of devices wouldn't be used properly or to their full potential without operation manuals, and discussions in the United Nations are impossible without simultaneous interpretation and further translation of the approved decisions. If we accept the definition, poor translation is as ugly as a deep scratch on the paintwork of a newly bought car. On the other hand, with consumerism dominating the minds of many of us, we don't give a damn about the quality of the linguistic component of an item with a service life of a few months or a few years at best. It appears logical then that the quality of translation need only be as good as the quality of the relevant item.

Acceptable quality does help increase the total translation industry throughput without seriously damaging it. Quality matters only for a small proportion of translated documents, specifically documents that, if translated wrongly, can cause damage to life, health, property, financial assets or relations.

Usually the level of the translator's responsibility for the quality of the final document is reflected in a few domains such as finance, medicine, insurance or law. Many other documents are but a formal attempt to waive off liability; still others are for information purposes only and don't actually need to be perfect in terms of style and grammar. In my view, the share of 'acceptable quality' and 'for information purposes only' translations will keep growing at a higher pace. These segments will be increasingly populated by amateur translators, beginners and various arrangements that include machine translation, with fewer opportunities for professional translators.

Content

There is one minor tendency which doesn't affect the translation process much, but which is obvious and deserves to be mentioned. A growing proportion of texts to be translated are intended for use on the Internet as site content. This means certain aspects have to be considered during translation. These texts are usually short in order to fit the web browser window, contain a lot of search engine optimization terms and frequently resemble advertising material (more serious materials are usually offered as downloadable files).

Much more important is the fact that specialized documents, especially those describing new scientific discoveries, innovative technologies, production processes, etc., are becoming more complicated every day. Interdisciplinary research and development, complex design and supermultifunctionality, and integration of essentially different elements into elaborate sophisticated systems require that translators who want to specialize in certain areas have to have a profound field-specific background and keep themselves up-to-date with new developments. I notice that many clients have learned to value specialization more than linguistic excellence and are ready to put up with not-so-perfect style and poor grammar as long as proper terminology is guaranteed and the general logic of the translated documents matches the logic of the relevant specialists.

Technology

What is the purpose of technologies? Presumably they should make things easier. Do they? They surely do. In fact they do it so well that psychiatrists will soon be treating a new type of patient: people who invent problems to add spice to the dull chores they call life.

I was one of the first translators who started regularly using CAT tools (and among the first to buy a licensed CAT tool). Back then, 10 years ago, I voiced my support for CAT tools, unlike a great many of my colleagues who were against them. The software did boost my productivity (and income); I also appreciated the function that allowed me to easily search for earlier translated terms to ensure consistency within separate jobs of a long-term project.

Where am I now? New versions are released at intervals of about two years, and the tool I use is pretty expensive. Consistency has improved – at least when the translation memories (TMs) consist of my translations. When it's a third party TM (sometimes I strongly suspect the 'third party' is a machine translation app), things can be tough, and more often than not I have to spend a lot of time checking and correcting gibberish. A discount grid for 100% matches, reps and fuzzies seems to have been established as the industry standard. Many jobs are assigned only on condition that the files are processed with a particular CAT tool (occasionally the latest version of it) with relevant discounts. Some clients require that I also use a glossary-creating program. Also, a number of clients have crafted together their proprietary web-based translation platforms, and a fraction of the working time should be scheduled for mastering them, too.

Thus, I have to spend more money on purchasing and upgrading my software packages, translate more than I used to in the pre-CAT age and spend time learning how to use the new platforms or latest versions and circumvent the glitches. What this boils down to is, the additional income is counterbalanced by additional expenses and extra time invested, and I can't really say that my earnings have gone up substantially due to the use of a CAT tool.

But technological progress in translation is not limited to CAT tools. The ghost of machine translation lurks in the gloom of the years to come, as do cloud technologies that connect freelancers to a hub to make them into pinions of a single overwhelming system. Irony aside, there's no alternative. The entire bulk of information that will have to be translated daily all over the world can only be translated with the help of all possible means: human translation, machine translation and everything in between. Time pressures, budget limitations and quality-related factors – all of these and many other reasons lead us to a situation where technology will be increasingly employed to process billions of words describing everything, from EU parliament resolutions to adult site content, from user interface to lists of ingredients on packaged snacks, from the operation of computer numerical control (CNC) machine tools to tourist information.

Basically, technical and technological progress brings about results of two types: tools that give us possibilities we don't have naturally (take an axe, mobile phone or aircraft, for example) and technologies that replace human labour – computers and automated production lines belong to this category. The role of humans shrinks to controlling, monitoring, servicing and interfering when something goes wrong. Human-replacing technologies were critical in satisfying the growing demands of the world's population for food, clothing or devices which have colonized our homes. These technologies are perfectly in line with the single use concept of the modern society: they guarantee quick and large-scale supply of mediocre goods and services for mass consumption, whereas when we want something exclusive, solid and long-lasting we go for hand-made things. The modern meaning of 'hand-made' is quite specific though, often implying that an item is manufactured on the most sophisticated hi-tech equipment!

No matter what we think of technological progress in general and its influence on the translation industry – from welcoming it to starting

Luddite whining in forums – the technology is here to stay, and it's up to us to decide what we are going to do with it: submit and let it reign; anticipate, accept and make it work for us; or even create new technologies – why not?

Industry formation

Six or seven years ago, I talked to the director of a translation agency listed among the top 20 language service providers (LSPs) in Europe. The prospects for translation was one of the topics we discussed, and I mentioned industry formation as one of the trends that will change the entire profile of the sector. He waved this away, pointing out that the share of large MLVs amounted to a mere 9% of the market – a nearly negligible figure. I don't know if he was sincere in underestimating the phenomenon or felt too uncomfortable to admit it. Anyway, the proportion of translations gated through MLVs has increased manifold, and caused dramatic changes in the industry. The changes are best illustrated when we compare earlier job-handling structures with the ones existing now.

A decade ago, the translation sector was quite fragmented. (The situation hasn't improved much since then; Renato Beninatto characterized it as 'pulverized' at the May 2013 UTIC conference in Kyiv.) At that time, translators basically belonged to one of the three types of arrangement. One was working on staff; the scheme needs no additional explanation. The other two were 'end client–translator' direct relations and 'end client –translation company–translator' chain.

Both have their pros and cons. From a translator's point of view, working with direct clients is usually more rewarding in terms of earnings; also, translators can easily contact the client with terminology questions and for reference materials. On the other hand, there are the issues of editing and proofreading; the level of responsibility (and liability) in case of errors; lack of feedback or quality assurance (at least for end clients who don't speak the target language); and often, the end client's vague idea of translation as a professional activity. From the end client's standpoint, there's little difference between direct co-operation with freelancers and buying linguistic services via intermediary translation agencies as long as the final result is acceptable. At the same time, the above-mentioned problem of responsibility/liability can be resolved faster and more easily under a business-to-business scheme. Even though most freelancers are essentially one-person businesses, claim settlement with freelancers can be tough, especially when the parties are separated by a few thousand miles and operate in different jurisdictions. Assigning a translation task to an LSP company – preferably located in the same country – seems safer.

If we look at the distance a translation job covers now – and the structure of the chain between the end client and the translator – we'll see what has happened in the past 10 years or so. My assessment is that up to 60% of all translation jobs are currently channelled via MLVs, and frequently the chain looks as follows: 'end client–local MLV office–MLV head office–MLV regional office–local LSP–local translation company–translator'. This appears to be the longest chain possible, though in reality a job passed down from the MLV to an LSP may then be re-outsourced a few times. The opposite is also true: there may be as few as two or three intermediaries between the end client and the translator, and some end clients keep (and value!) direct co-operation with freelancers.

My personal experience of working for MLVs (when I had been contacted by an MLV branch) is not exactly positive. First, the recruitment procedure is long and bureaucratic, involving a test translation (more than one if the translator claims to work in more than one field); signing several agreements, some of them exceeding a dozen pages and containing absolutely unacceptable terms; a long period of test assessment (probably due to the complicated hierarchical structure); and finally, bargaining on rates, sometimes only to learn that they are indecently low. (While we are on the rates issue, I've been using the following trick lately: when a potential client contacts me with an offer of co-operation and invites me to register on their site or otherwise start the registration process, I ask them to confirm that the rates they pay to translators and the payment period match my terms. In most cases, I never hear from them again.)

Back to MLVs. Even after the rates are agreed on, the bureaucracy is not over. There are workflow documents, which might not be the same for different jobs, project-specific glossaries and style guides, quality assurance forms, and, in case a typo creeps into the translation and slips through all the proofreading/editing/review/quality control barriers, the sheer amount of forms to fill in is a punishment severe enough to never, ever let it happen again – or to never work with this client again, as in my case.

There's one more thing to add, and it has to do with the eternal issue of rates. Each time I was contacted by an MLV, or for a job obviously outsourced by an MLV, the highest rate offered was $US0.08 per source word from clients in North America and €0.07 from those in Europe. When my patience was exhausted, I emailed a friend and colleague, who happened to be working at the head office of an MLV I did translations for, with a not-so-ethical request: I asked him about the rates the company charged the end client for the project I participated in (I received €0.07). The answer was an eye-opener: $US0.45.

Please don't get me wrong. Although not exactly a fan of translation companies, whether large or small – especially now that I have had the experience of wearing a small corporate hat for a couple of years or so – I'm fully aware that the market is big enough to accommodate numerous and varied players, from bilinguals who make three typos in every two words to huge translation corporations with lots of staff and offices scattered all over the world. We are allies rather than competitors. Moreover, the relations between freelancers and translation agencies, if fine-tuned, can be beneficial for all parties. It's like a coast where one can see a variety of vessels, from weather-beaten fishers' boats and small but expensive yachts to enormous bulk carriers and showy cruise liners, each doing what they are intended for.

The problem is, some of them (MLVs in particular) demonstrate Darwinistic behaviour, expanding their feeding areas far beyond the rations suitable for their species. Have you ever heard of a translation company refusing to do a job for their client because the job-added value potential was too small? Speaking simply, a straightforward text with no formatting requirements and general vocabulary with no terminology is a job most bilingual people with good linguistic skills could handle – would a translation agency turn down such a job?

In my experience, translation companies remove freelancers from the end client's field of vision (and MLVs step in trying to establish themselves as the first link in the food chain to be as close to the end client as possible). Having secured the client, they email the freelancer offering the same projects but on slightly worse terms. I lost a number of projects in this way. During the years of co-operation, the partnership between me and some of my clients developed into a remote friendship. Every now and then we exchange emails and views on subjects not immediately related to jobs at hand, and I regularly receive 'The bastards from XXX have snatched our customer, so the project you had been involved in for four years is now over'.

Freelancers are reduced from the level of equals to the level of inferiors. In fact, the structure of the translation industry is taking the shape of other industries such as the automotive. Locally sold 'German' cars are usually cars under German brands with obscure ownership and are assembled in Russia from parts manufactured in China.

It's worth mentioning that in the worst case scenario, freelancers will find themselves in a position where their earnings are reduced to those received by in-house translators, but they still have the same responsibilities and liabilities (much higher than those working in-house) while the entire burden of running their own offices, and paying taxes, insurance, etc. will be laid on their own shoulders.

Further developments and potential consequences

Below is my vision of the translation industry in 2018 (plus or minus a year or two).

Quality and process standards have been agreed on, approved and introduced in many local markets; a number of clients and translators alike ignore them as too formal to describe something as intricate and ambiguous as linguistic products. The translation process has been completely impersonalized. Often, jobs are not whole documents but bits and pieces to update the earlier translated ones. Translation continues round the clock like a relay race, with translators from different time zones connected to a remote cloud-based CAT/TM interchanging with each other. Machine translation has improved a lot and is widely used, even after a few major incidents that resulted from wrong translations by machines. It can't compete with human translation yet, but the demand for post-editors of machine translations has never been so high.

Different translation assignments have developed to the stage of almost turning into separate professions; web-conference interpreting, website localization and transcreation all require different sets of professional skills and different availability schedules, as well as the ability to use (and often possess) sophisticated (and often expensive) software. On-site interpreting is on the verge of extinction as too expensive, replaced with remote interpretation via web-based platforms, except for high-end events or clients.

Consolidation has reached 80% of the market, with two dozen MLVs dominating it. The majority of smaller translation companies act as subcontractors to MLVs. Successful freelancers are few. There are two types of successful freelancers: those who have loyal clients they found a decade or more ago, and those with a specialization. The latter group is actually specialists with solid backgrounds in their respective fields who could be good doctors, lawyers or engineers but opted for translation. Translators with a pure linguistic education complain that the demand for their services exists in the cheapest segment only. The large middle group that felt pretty comfortable in the not-so-distant past have two options: either to join the structure of the translation industry, accepting the lower rates and worse conditions, or to search for additional earning possibilities.

International and governmental institutions emphasize the unaffordable cost of translation and interpretation with frightening and increasing frequency, and recently I voiced a suggestion to reform the industry altogether. The reform would provide that all materials that need to be translated be ranked as 'important' (these should be translated with utmost care, in conformity with all applicable standards and quality control), 'specialized' (these can only be assigned to translators and interpreters who have obtained relevant certifications) and 'general' (no requirements specified).

In addition, an authoritative international body would issue a directive stipulating that all translated documents start with the following disclaimer: 'This is a translation of the original document in the XXX language into the YYY language. We assume no responsibility/liability for possible errors or typos in it, nor for losses or damage whatsoever incurred as a result of inaccurate translation. For precise meanings, please refer to the original document...' Five years is a short period, so we won't have to wait too long to learn how close to the reality this picture is.

Conclusions

So what should we do?

Translation is unique in the sense that we never create our products from scratch. Even with a certain degree of liberty in transcreation and localization, we always work with the source words spoken or written by politicians and businesspersons, researchers and advertisers, artists and engineers. As a consequence, our wellbeing completely depends on international political, economic and commercial relations and cooperation. I'm sure the industry will flourish, but I can't say the same about translators, and additional earning opportunities should be investigated – the earlier, the better.

If we categorize the currently existing legal earning possibilities, the choice turns out to be limited to just a few options. These are: investor (one has to have enough money to take this route); owner (of income-generating assets); official (position where influence is sold – often with dubious legitimacy); freelancer (basically, taking any earning opportunity that turns up on his/her way); and staff (highly-paid staff positions exist but are pretty few). Obviously, the two options most suitable for translators are 'freelancer' and 'owner'. At the core, we are often a two-in-one combination, because freelance translation is in fact a small one-person business.

When analyzing potential additional income sources, do consider diversification. For the purposes of this book, diversification may be interpreted in the broadest possible manner. I'd say we can diversify in the following ways:

- expanding our professional portfolio by adding new translation or language-related services, such as proofreading, training or language teaching

- improving our knowledge in areas of specialization – this can be regarded as diversification into a new profession – and combining it with professional linguistic and translation skills to offer a better-quality specialized translation service
- launching an absolutely independent line of business.

A number of translation-related ways of diversification will be discussed later in this book. For my part, I believe and insist that in restricting ourselves to translation and adjacent activities we seriously reduce our options.

The best jobs or occupations meet two criteria: they are enjoyable and they bring income sufficient to satisfy one's needs, with a bias towards one or another depending on one's priorities; the final choice is thus very individual. At the same time, I have found this rule works: every activity, even an innocent hobby, can be monetized if properly tackled. How to do it is a subject for an entirely different book, though.

A LANGUAGE SERVICE PROVIDER'S TAKE ON DIVERSIFICATION

Jane Freeman brings over 10 years of experience spanning the complete localization food chain. Jane qualified as a translator and interpreter in 2002 and has used this academic knowledge to forge a successful career in the localization world. She has covered many disciplines within the localization field including translating, interpreting, project management (customer and vendor), sales, and more recently, strategic account management and sales management. Working for one of the largest global multi-language vendors, Jane has a vested interest in translation, best practice and how the industry will be shaped over the coming years.

BEFORE TACKLING THE SUBJECT of 'translator diversification' from a language service provider's (LSP) point of view, I would like to give some background on why I have been asked to contribute to this book. For over 10 years now I have been involved, in one way or another, with language, translation and localization. I have had the privilege of seeing the industry from a multitude of angles as my career to date has been so varied. As a qualified translator, previously freelancing, now working within the commercial arm of one of the largest global LSPs, I feel I am well placed to put a balanced opinion forward on this subject.

In my career I have seen the translation industry significantly change and I envisage that these changes, developments and process improvements will continue. Translation, like any industry, has to develop and improve to survive; however, it is my experience that these changes bring fear amongst the translation community, when in fact we should be embracing them and evolving with them. I am proud to be a translator and believe that as global business continues to grow, good translation skills will continue to be sought after by LSPs and MLVs (multi-language vendors) alike.

When I say a good translator, I refer to a specialist translator. Translators should be mastering not only the art and skill of translation, but also the subject matter of choice. It is the latter that will ensure a translator always has work. I find there are many people who speak multiple languages and have a high level of proficiency in translating, but who don't really specialize. These people will feel the stresses and strains of the current climate and may be looking to diversify away from the industry.

According to the Common Sense Advisory (CSA), there are 27,668 recognized translation organizations globally, with the vast majority of these relying on the freelance community to service the work. The demand for translation is increasing. The difference today, when compared to five or ten years ago, is that translation or local content is now expected by the end consumer, and has therefore become a commodity in the eyes of global brands, as it cannot be seen as a differentiator anymore. It is this change in attitude and opinion towards translation, combined with the explosion of content available, which is driving the need for advancement.

What is an LSP/MLV looking for in a translator?

LSPs and MLVs will always need translators – in-house and freelance alike. It is the skills of the translation teams that enable their businesses to be successful. I am confident that no amount of technological advances will change this. LSPs are looking for specialization, and proven specialization at that, and it is this high level of knowledge which will see a translator busy now and well into the future.

The localization industry predominantly relies on the freelance community, and one of the key reasons large MLVs and LSPs, even those with in-house models, look to the freelance community is to gain this subject matter expertise.

What do translators need to do to stay in the game and continue to be successful?

This book is looking at diversification. From my point of view, I don't think it is a question of choosing between diversification OR specialization. Diversification and specialization are two very different components, almost polar opposites, yet both are critical to the success of translators and the translation industry as it advances.

As the industry continues to evolve, both these areas are becoming heightened and ever more important. LSPs/MLVs never want to hear about diversification with regard to subject matter; LSPs want and need experts in the subject matter of choice – this is the key differentiator between translator A and translator B and will be a huge factor in deciding which translator is selected. Certain content types and industries require specialist knowledge and skills for an accurate translation. No LSP/MLV or agency can cover all this in-house and they will always look to the freelance community for that support.

I have been approached by translators who say they cannot afford to live with the new rates that are being imposed on them, and I have seen general translators being asked more and more to reduce rates to enable MLVs and LSPs to stay competitive. Larger LSPs and MLVs are developing technology to support this need to do more translation with a smaller budget, and I would advise the freelance translation community to get involved.

This squeeze on the community is unfortunately the fallout from translation becoming a commodity and there being so much content to translate. Whilst this rate squeeze is a conversation I hear day in and day out and is a principal reason for people diversifying out of the industry completely, it is not a common conversation for the more specialized translators. These translators have something which not only the MLVs and LSPs need, but the end customer also – subject matter expertise. There is a place for diversification in today's translation community, but in my experience this lies solely with skill set.

For translators to stay at the top of their game they need to start to embrace these changes, and the only way to do this is by diversifying skill set. I don't mean starting to offer brand new services, such as desktop publishing or file engineering. I believe translation is a highly skilled profession and these skills should not go to waste, as the skills used for translation can be adapted to support these new technologies as well as the industry as it is now.

The ways I would encourage translators to diversify are:

- post-editing
- transcreation
- reviewing
- understanding and embracing new technologies to make the translation process more productive

- language – look to where the emerging languages are and start to train in these areas now, so that when the rest of the world comes online, you are ready to support their local needs.

What I would advise is: do not diversify subject matter. I cannot stress this enough. Translation agencies, large MLVs and LSPs are looking for specialized subject matter expertise, be that specific knowledge within one industry – pharmaceutical, defence, automotive, etc. – or one content type, such as technical writing, marketing, medical or pharmaceutical. Certain industries, simply due to the nature of their business, will never be able to use technologies to translate, and I would advise people to focus on these areas, as well as learning to use the new technologies and processes to their advantage.

Should translators be fearful of new-found technologies?

Many of my translator peers have spoken to me about their concerns with the translation industry and the fact they feel they are being replaced by technology. They feel devalued because their prices are being forced down to compete with these technologies and they cannot keep up with the speed with which these technologies churn out content.

I truly believe that these fears are because they are misinformed about the actual ability of these technologies and the associated risks of relying on them.

Working for one of the largest MLVs in the industry that is responsible for a large part of the technology that we see – translation management, translation memory and machine translation alike – has given me the opportunity to understand where these technologies fit into the translation ecosystem. This insight has enabled me to embrace these technologies and use them to my advantage to improve productivity, as well as appreciate why they are so important.

Let's take a look at a technological advance which we now embrace. When translation memory was introduced into the translation process, the translation community initially, unsurprisingly, feared the solution. Today, over 20 years on, this is seen as an integral part of the process for all concerned – LSPs, the end client and translators alike. Translation memory brings cost savings to the end customer and supports the translation process, adding value to the quality and speed of the output as well as allowing translators to be more productive.

As with the introduction of translation memory, translators need to embrace the new trends of machine translation, post-editing, crowdsourcing, etc. and diversify skill sets to do so, which in turn will open up more possibilities for work.

Is there a future in the translation industry for translators?

If we look at the world of content, I see this as an exciting time for the translation community and language professionals. According to the GeoNames geographical database, only one-third of the world's population has Internet access – two-thirds of the world are left to go. As this access is developed, new areas for translators will open up.

Content and access to content has exploded and is continuing to explode with the constant development of the Internet. The expectations of the end customer are becoming higher, with local language content being classed as a minimum expectation nowadays, whereas in the past it was considered a luxury for global brands to offer local content.

As well as this end customer expectation shift, the amount of content available online has gone off the scale with the huge uptake of social media. Social media data is starting to become critical for global businesses. This data reflects the opinions of their customers and is an uncensored view into their wants, wishes, expectations and buying triggers, allowing businesses to take a truly informed approach to entering new markets, launching new products and generally communicating with their customers.

According to IBM research, 2.5 quintillion bytes of data exist today, most on the web, and 90% of that was generated in the last two years alone. This amount of data is becoming more and more valuable but in all honesty:

- the volume and turnaround make traditional translation processes impossible

- the content is important, but only has a short life span as so much is constantly being created
- this content, whilst important to understand, is only for information purposes, so gist translation will suffice.

Not all content needs to reach premium quality levels – this is very much like using a hammer to crack a nut. Now that the industry has developed, the world understands that varying quality levels are expected and needed to meet the demands of the content explosion.

It is for the translation of the content above (social data, user comments and reviews, etc.) that pure machine translation technology is being employed. This is additional content which traditional translators would never have been involved in in the first place, so no work is being taken away from them.

I mentioned earlier that translator rates are being cut. Translators need to embrace these revolutionary technologies to allow them to come into line with market expectations by increasing productivity whilst having the ability to offer varying quality levels so the reduced rates can still offer a good living.

Summary

Naturally there is a lot of unease within the translation community at the moment, and it is heartbreaking to hear that some translators are diversifying out of the industry altogether, when there is so much opportunity still within the world of global content; it is just opportunity that feels outside of the norm and is therefore scary.

Translators are critical for global business success, having an impact on almost everything we do, buy and read. Research tells us that this will continue well into the future, but as MLVs and SLVs (single-language vendors) have had to do, translators need to stop being fearful of the changes and the demands and embrace them, using them to their advantage and increasing their portfolio of translation-related services to adapt to new pricing and quality levels. Before machine translation, there was no need for post-editing; this is a real window of opportunity. Where one door starts to close, another one starts to open.

Both diversification and specialization are key components to a translator continuing to be successful. LSPs and MLVs are looking for specialized subject matter experts with a range of skills, so to continue to be successful; translators need to invest in their subject matter, whilst diversifying skill set.

DIVERSIFICATION – NOT OPTIONAL, BUT IMPERATIVE

***Pritam Bhattacharyya** is the founder and chief of* Wordsmith Communication *and founder-teacher of* Wordsmith University, *a freelancer business school. He holds an engineering degree in electronics and telecommunication engineering and a master's degree in communication management from Strathclyde Business School, UK, as a British Chevening Scholar. Prior to his freelancing and business ownership career, he worked in managerial positions for several major telecom providers. Pritam's blog on freelance business and business development is* Freelancer's Freelancer. *He can be contacted at wordsmith.bengal@gmail.com. He lives and works in Calcutta – his city by adoption.*

I WILL BEGIN WITH THE argument that diversification is not an option for a freelance translator but an imperative, at least in the long term.

Next, I will discuss what is meant by long term, medium term and short term.

Finally, I will describe a case study from my own attempts at diversification and the experience and learning so far.

Why is diversification an imperative?

If we were living in a static universe, no diversification would be necessary. There are four fundamental processes over which we have no control, and these are driving changes, either alone or in tandem.

1. **Manifestation:** New ideas and new ways of doing things are developed. Technological changes are nothing but the birth of a new way of doing old things. CAT tools are new ways of doing the same ancient thing – translation of meaning using one set of symbols into another.
2. **Un-manifestation:** Whole industries or activities regularly disappear or die. Consider typewriters and, closely following

suit, landline telephones: once very vibrant, active, talked about; now heritage items, museum curiosities.
3. **Wear and tear:** Ideas, things and activities do not remain in their original form under the merciless and incessant beating of time. Just as our clothes undergo the beating of wear, weather and seasons, the same is true for our activities and ideas. As long as a freelancer has a body, this grows old and what was once a project needing just a little sacrifice of sleep for few hours now seems too taxing. We are all growing old under the constant wear and tear of the cosmic eco-system.
4. **Malfunction:** Computer viruses and influenza viruses can both jeopardize the work and life of a freelancer critically and at critical moments. This is not fully preventable. We can take precautions, but there is no 100% protection. Neither computer crashes nor flu or flu-like symptoms can be completely eliminated.

If we admit the above four in principle, the obvious conclusion is that we have to diversify. If we don't, we will be forced to. It is better to at least give this consideration. Government and private institutions down the ages have been devising means to counteract or minimize the effects of these four principles. Pensions, sick leave, insurance, employee training, job rotation, loyalty income, welfare and specific institutional safeguards are examples.

A freelancer has no such institutional safeguard. There are none, and no one has any incentive to think about these issues for the freelancer. For an employee, there is a leader or leader-figure – whether competent or not. Each employee's immediate boss is the default leader.

For a freelancer there is no default leader or guide. Hence, a freelancer has the great fortune and opportunity of choosing his/her leader or guide.

Who can be a freelancer's guide? Here I provide a clue to one of the most obvious diversification paths: an experienced freelancer who has travelled the road.

When shall I think about diversification?

This 'when' is relative as well as subjective. Here are some crude but realistic issues a freelancer might raise:

- I have no pension or savings to take care of myself in old age. What shall I do when I can no longer work as I can now?
- I have an eye problem and working for long periods strains my eyes.
- I am not able to cope (financially and timewise) with these new ideas, new technologies, new concepts and new demands from the client.
- I think the industry is becoming 'nasty, brutish, and short'.[1]
- I think social networking is a fad. But what should I do? Everybody seems to be doing it.
- I shall leave this and start something else – but what?
- I like to do [X].

The above list of examples shows that there is really no 'when'. It depends on one's age, preferences, perspective, experience, association and impression of experiences. A young person may think that in the early days he/she will slog and build up funds and then invest these funds in an altogether different area. Someone else, in an equally logical manner, may decide to invest in skill and experience and become a consultant at a later date.

There is one fact in common among these individual differences: you have to start the activity at some point in time. Thinking about diversification in advance allows you to be prepared and provides you with a sense of mission. This sense of mission can be a great mooring in the wandering freedom of freelancing.

A case study in diversification

I was pushed into becoming a freelancer when I found my corporate job suffocating and soul-destroying. My love of reading and writing helped

---

[1] Hobbes, T. *Leviathan*, XIII. 9.

a lot. Without this propensity, I would not have been able to endure the very difficult initial days. After being a freelancer and business owner for more than five years, I thought that I should also do something else. There was no specific agenda but the urge to do something. I started an online cultural e-zine and then started a small publishing business, Pentasect. The investment in terms of money was minimal, but the involvement was high.

While scanning and cataloguing freelancers' CVs and applications, I also observed that many had excellent linguistic talents but less than ordinary business talents. I started teaching on ProZ.com – mainly about business development. This was very enjoyable and was a channel to communicate my own experience and learning to those who were starting their journey or were interested in hearing a fellow traveller's story. Apart from joy and satisfaction, this provided what ProZ.com calls 'residual income'.

During this period, I wrote three books – mainly on the theme of freelancers' business development and in the form of a personal journey. These were published on lulu.com and a few other online retailers, and more 'residual income' came. Lots of readers were also providing invaluable input, in the form of both praise and critical remarks.

At this stage, my diversification strategy could be summarized as packaging my own experience as a freelancer with the skill acquired from running the e-zine and being a trainer at ProZ.com. My customer segment was clearly visible – aspiring and established freelancers. Then in November 2011 I collaborated with some of my students and other teachers and launched a full-scale learning platform for freelancers, a freelancer business school quite grandiosely called Wordsmith University. The venture so far is proving a nice 'diversification vehicle', both in terms of income and towards building a platform of lasting value.

Challenges and rewards

One of the greatest challenges is to come out of one's comfort zone and work in an unknown area; every unknown area is risky. The next problem is what I call 'transactional fatigue'. A freelancer's income depends on transactions when translated products change hands. This continuous transaction process has the power to inhibit long-term goal setting and the more difficult task of working consistently towards these goals. The last, but hardest, challenge is to remain patient when the goal appears far off and the venture does not seem to be working.

The rewards are endless. I shall be brief and mention only one. When work or projects undergo the occasional downturn due to unknown and unknowable causes in your core transactional business of translation, you will not feel restless.

You will be working with the conviction that you are solving the immediate problem (keeping yourself engaged) and also adding bits and pieces to solve the larger problem of the future. This does not include the satisfaction you experience while building your backyard empire.

Some tips when you start diversifying

Your diversification project should be something that is a naturally pleasurable task for you. This should be the first criterion. I list a few of my own tips that may be of help:

- Choose an area, project or task that does not seem like 'work' however much you are involved.
- Beware of big ideas. A big idea (behind which is ambition) can kill you. Most dotcom failures were pursuing big ideas. There is an ocean of genius between a big idea and great work.
- Choose an area of work which can be completed incrementally if you are building another business while your core revenue comes from full-time freelancing.
- Use your freelancing network to build your new business. This book project is a classic example of building a publishing/content business targeted for the freelance sector.
- Be a disinterested reader. This will allow you to consciously

and unconsciously absorb many useful things for your projects suited to your temperament.
- Use the new business's network to help your freelancing business. I acquired many new clients from the readers of my blog (content business).

Here are a few parting words before you set sail from the familiar shore. As a freelancer, whatever experience you have, you have something that is very rare. You have the authentic and personal experience of being your own guide and master in earning your livelihood. You have given birth to a new person within you. It is a safe bet to presume that you will plant and water the saplings of businesses that will take care of you when you are no longer able to water them.

Linguistic diversification
EXPANDING YOUR PORTFOLIO AROUND YOUR CORE SERVICE OF TRANSLATION

WHEN I SPOKE TO FREELANCE colleagues about what I consider *linguistic diversification*, many were surprised and stated that it had never crossed their mind that offering services such as editing, transcription or terminology management could be considered diversification. Some were even very adamant that this is not diversification at all but simply a standard part of the range of services a translation professional should offer their clients.

In my view, any service offered beyond pure translation is already a type of diversification. Not all translators edit, not all translators transcribe, not all translators proofread third-party texts, but all translators translate. So anything beyond that very core service is by default diversification, and more specifically *linguistic diversification*. Every single service or bonus you can offer your clients serves to set you apart from the competition and can contribute to shaping your unique selling point. In today's market, it is no longer enough to offer only translation services. Many end clients, and even agencies, expect their translation service providers to offer a range of services to suit their needs. The key here is to take a good look at your customer base, talk to individual clients to identify exactly what they need, and then tailor your service portfolio to their requirements, using your existing skill set and preferences. This will make you stand out from your competitors who are 'just translators' and are reluctant to diversify.

Linguistic diversification, however, has another component: embracing technology. Machine translation and post-editing of machine translation (PEMT) are still taboo words in wide circles of the freelance translation community. While I agree that some concerns are legitimate, I firmly believe that freelancers, not just language service providers and large corporations, can benefit from these emerging technologies. The volume of translations required is increasing and this trend will continue. There are not enough human translators in the world today to cover all translation requirements. The availability of machine translation technology will lead to more material being translated than previously, especially material that would otherwise never have been translated due to resource constraints. Rather than machines taking over our work, there is an opportunity here for freelance translation professionals to explore the opportunities that come with machine translation and post-editing. PEMT is becoming more widespread and sought after, so it makes good business sense to at least consider it as a way of expanding one's service portfolio. This possibility is just one of those explored in this chapter.

POST-EDITING OF MACHINE TRANSLATION

Lori Thicke *is the founder of the machine translation services firm LexWorks, an innovator in translation technology and a leader in machine translation. LexWorks is a subsidiary of Lexcelera, which has been providing translation services since it was founded in Paris, France, in 1986. Lexcelera was the first translation company in France to receive ISO 9001:2000 quality certification. Lori is also the founder of Translators without Borders, the world's largest community of humanitarian translators. As a US-based non-profit, Translators without Borders supports global aid organizations by donating millions of words of professional translations each year. With the founding of its translator training centre in Nairobi, Kenya, Translators without Borders is actively taking down language barriers to knowledge for some of the world's most disadvantaged people. Lori, who holds an MFA from the University of British Columbia, is a frequent speaker and blogger.*

THERE'S A REVOLUTION GOING on in the translation industry. Machine translation (MT) technology has revolutionized international communication by making translation available in real time, or near to real time, at radically lower costs. When paired with human linguists who post-edit the raw output, MT can even improve quality and consistency. I've seen MT ably do the job even when fully human quality is needed thanks to this pairing with a human linguist.

So what's the catch? The catch is that there is a shortage of human post-editors who want to accept the sometimes thankless work of taking machine-generated output and turning it into fluid communications, and this shortage is capable of slowing the uptake of the game-changing MT technology. Let's be honest: machine translation has never had an easy time of it. Back when I started overseeing deployments of MT by Lexcelera, the translation company I founded along with the MT services firm LexWorks, the reaction I received could be described as bemused scepticism. I was told that MT was five years away from being good enough – and always would be.

What has happened since then? MT has improved, but not as much as you may think. Progress has been made in a number of areas, particularly with the hybrid engines that combine the best of rule-based machine translation (RBMT) with statistical machine translation (SMT) techniques, but these changes have been incremental rather than groundbreaking. MT alone is still not capable of delivering fully automatic human quality translations.

So why, then, is MT on the roadmap of almost every savvy user of translation services today? If the quality of MT hasn't improved as much as we had hoped it would, there has been at least one significant change in the MT landscape: our expectations. We have stopped expecting MT to be perfect. Instead, we have realized that there is a place for imperfect MT, and when it needs to be perfect, a strong business case can be made for human rework.

This means that if MT is not perfectly fine out of the box, it's not an insurmountable problem. A linguist can improve the raw output more quickly than translating the same text from scratch – and this is where it gets interesting from an economic point of view. When a linguist, known as a post-editor in this context, corrects raw MT output, productivity gains are impressive. Considering that the results can be virtually indistinguishable from a traditional translation, using MT sounds like a no-brainer.

There are some caveats, of course. The MT engine must be the right engine. The content must be the right content. And most importantly, the engine must be properly trained for the content, language pair, domain and even, at a more granular level, product line. But the biggest caveat when you want publication quality output is that MT has to be a joint human-machine effort. Today, what is limiting MT more than anything to the early adopters is the lack of human resources. The issue echoed throughout the industry is that there are simply not enough post-editors willing to work with MT.

If my company has managed to retain a large pool of post-editors, it may be because we understand one basic truism: post-editors really hate poor MT output. They hate it so much that the one constant in the translation industry of late has been post-editor anger over being asked to mop up bad MT. And who can blame them? I believe the main reason for the shortage of post-editors is that too many companies show disrespect for their time and abilities by churning out poor quality MT and expecting them to work miracles and to give a sizable discount while they are at it.

In their haste to respond to cost-cutting demands, whether from customers (as is the case with language service providers) or from upper management (as may happen within the enterprise), inexperienced MT practitioners may be guilty of pressing into service the first engine they think will do the job. Lacking the expertise to know which engine to use and how to train it so it performs well, these inexperienced companies are inadvertently burning out the post-editors who are left with the clean-up jobs.

This inexperience also means that opportunities to train post-editors properly may be missed, and that post-editors may be regarded simply as end-of-chain workers rather than as key contributors to the process of improving MT.

It is incumbent on companies to make sure that post-editing isn't thankless drudgery with errors that don't stay fixed and lower pay for more work. Hence, here are some ways that companies can keep translators happy about post-editing MT.

Choose the right engine

For optimal quality, the first and most important question is not which engine to choose. The debate around whether to use a rule-based or statistical engine treats MT as a tool. MT is far from a single tool – it is a process. Part of that process is determining the best tool to use with a given type of content, language pair, workflow and quality requirement. You also have to consider the available resources, including human resources, technical resources and data.

There are cases when a rules-based approach works best, cases where a statistical approach works best, and cases where a hybrid of the two works best. The trick is to know which engine to use in which situation. Because the MT process has an impact on the quality that post-editors are given to work with, one best practice we use is testing.

Being engine-agnostic means that before starting any project we fully test our assumptions by running the content through an SMT engine, an RBMT engine and a hybrid. The best quality output is the one we put into the post-editing process. After all, we owe it to the people we entrust with post-editing to make sure they have the best quality to work on.

Train the engine right

An MT engine that is not properly trained, whether rule-based, hybrid or statistical, is going to waste post-editors' time as they correct errors that ought not to be there in the first place. It should go without saying that an engine that is inexpertly trained, or based on poor-quality data, will not encourage post-editors to take on another project.

When a rule-based engine is trained, it already 'knows' the language, so what it is trained on is terminology. With RBMT or hybrid systems, one of the advantages is that you can be sure that it will use the terminology it was trained on. This is why it is easier to post-edit RBMT or hybrid output. Today's SMT systems are still hampered by a lack of predictability, which means that translators waste a lot of time verifying terminology that ought to be already automatically verified. With an RBMT system that is correctly trained, the terminology has been hard-coded, so post-editors know it's the right terminology. They can see that a term came directly from the client, domain and even product-level glossaries. SMT post-editors, on the other hand, complain what a time waster it is when they have to constantly verify that the terms employed are the right ones.

Let post-editors improve more than the text

Post-editing may seem at first glance to be less fulfilling work than translating, because basically it means correcting some pretty dumb errors. To combat this, a best practice is to involve post-editors in the challenge of coming up with ways to not only improve the text they are working on, but to improve the system itself. While most post-editors aren't engineers, as qualified linguists they can certainly determine which improvements are one-offs and which ones need to be made in the engine to improve quality. Asking post-editors for feedback on improving the engine engages them more fully, increases their satisfaction and helps in the building of better MT engines.

Update the engines frequently

It can be frustrating for post-editors to be faced again and again with the same issue they've already fixed. When post-editing SMT, that next training cycle may be six months or a year away because you usually want a fair bit of new data accumulated before you begin the process of retraining. In this case, the post-editors are not empowered to make lasting changes and it typically takes until the next training cycle to see any progress at all.

The picture is different with RBMT in the sense that as soon as errors are identified, they can be corrected in the engine. Directly. Changes take just a few minutes and engine performance rapidly climbs. An area of improvement for SMT engines – and some are already doing this – is to make those training cycles shorter so post-editors can see that their corrections have been taken into account, and also get the benefit of everyone else's corrections on the same text. Implementing corrections quickly is key to improving MT quality and reducing post-editor frustration.

Train post-editors well

Post-editors do not necessarily need to undergo university training. On the other hand, setting them to work with no training at all is a mistake. Post-editing is not the same as editing, and MT output is different from translation memory fuzzy matches in some fundamental ways.

It's best to let post-editors know what they should expect from your MT output and how the errors may be different from a traditional translation. Depending on the engine being used, they will need to watch out for different types of errors. If the output is statistical, they should know not to be swayed by those fluid sentences and to be extra vigilant for a missed word that changes the meaning entirely (such as 'not'). Also, terminology will need to be verified. With RBMT, the post-editors will ideally work in an environment where they can see which terms came directly from the glossary, so they will not need to check them. But they will need to spend extra time on sentence structure because RBMT is generally more awkward than SMT.

Post-editors will also need to know what level of post-editing quality is expected. Light post-editing aims just to make the text understandable, while full post-editing results in quality that is indistinguishable from human quality. They'll need to know which level of post-editing is the goal. We find it also helps to set expectations for how quickly they should be working. For light post-editing it could be 20,000 words per day, while human quality is usually connected with a speed of 5,000 to 8,000 words per day.

Conclusion

The above are just a few of the ways to make post-editing machine translation a creative rather than a thankless task. Post-editors are essential to obtaining quality MT. To expand the pool of available post-editors it is necessary to respect their time by choosing the right engine, training it properly and updating it often; respect their talents by involving them in the process; and set their (and our) expectations correctly.

You'll know when your MT process is working. It's working when translators want to do post-editing work instead of complaining bitterly about it. Even better, you'll know it's working when they write you testimonial letters about how surprised they are by the quality and how fast it enabled them to work.

By the way, that has really happened.

Interview with Tineke Van Beukering

Tineke Van Beukering is an accredited freelance Dutch/English translator based in Brisbane, Australia. She has a degree in chemistry from the University of Groningen (Netherlands) and specializes in translations in the chemical field. She studied and worked in the Netherlands and lived in Germany for four years before migrating to Australia in 2000. Tineke and her family settled in Brisbane, and in 2008 Tineke established Dutch Translation Services. She translates mostly for clients in Australia, Europe and the USA. She has been working as a post-editor, i.e. checking machine translation output, since 2009 and has shared her post-editing experiences with a wider audience at conferences in Australia, New Zealand and the Netherlands, and given several workshops on the topic.

1) Tineke, what motivated you to add post-editing to your client service portfolio and what are your experiences with this activity?
Well, Nicole, back in 2009 I came across a post-editing job in the chemical field, which is the area I specialize in. I had never done any post-editing before and was rather hesitant towards it actually. I was very much in doubt whether or not to take it on. Back in those days, I still thought of machine translation as heralding the end of freelance translating and tossed up whether or not I would be 'digging my own grave' if I were to start post-editing. But when I talked about it with colleagues, I realized I should see it as a business opportunity, so I started taking on post-editing work.

Initially, it was quite a challenge. Post-editing requires a different mindset from translating. Rule number one is to use as much of the machine translation as possible. Rule number two is to only change what is incorrect or inappropriate. As a consequence, the resulting translation can be quite different from how a translator would have translated the text from scratch. That's the part I found hard to adjust to in the beginning – letting go of a translator's point of view and switching to a post-editor's point of view.

As long as the intention of the text is clear and all meaning is conveyed correctly, it doesn't matter that the document reads as though it's been generated by a machine. It sounds completely wrong when you're used to traditional translating, but it actually makes sense.

Not all texts need to be translated at the highest quality level. Certainly, documents intended for publication do. But for instance, when translations are needed only to get an idea of the content of large volumes of texts, so a decision can be made as to which documents are relevant and may require full translation, a lesser quality can be quite acceptable.

Once I had overcome my hesitation towards the different expectation and end quality, I started to enjoy post-editing. I like comparing post-editing with doing jigsaw puzzles. The words generated by the machine translation are like the pieces of a jigsaw puzzle and the resulting post-edited text is like the completed puzzle. The post-editor shuffles the words (pieces) around to make them fit. Of course, some people like doing jigsaw puzzles and some people don't. Similarly, not everyone might enjoy post-editing, but I certainly do (and yes, I do like jigsaw puzzles...)

To me, post-editing brings variety to my work. When I can alternate post-editing, translating and other tasks, it makes my work more interesting and I can focus better than if I was only translating day in day out.

2) What impact has post-editing had on your translation business, and does the income you generate from this service reflect the time and effort invested?
I had started my business only the year before when I came across this post-editing opportunity in 2009. Starting up a business takes time, and we all know you can't usually expect to run at full capacity in the first 12 months. My workload increased significantly once I started post-editing, and my business took off a lot faster because of it. There is a lot of work in this field, even though it is not as commonly advertised perhaps as translation jobs are, so that definitely opens up opportunities to generate income.

Post-editing pays a lower rate than translating, but taking into account the fact that post-editing is faster than translating, because more words can be processed in the same amount of time, the actual income generated doesn't have to be any lower than the income generated from translation.

However, all post-editing jobs are different, and care needs to be taken to assess each job prior to committing to it. If the initial machine translation is rubbish (situation A), it will take a significant effort and amount of time to post-edit it into something that can be used. When the machine translation is of reasonable quality to start off with (situation B), the process will be a lot faster. If paid the same rate per word in both situations A and B, a post-editor might face running at a loss with situation A, while generating a nice income in situation B.

3) Do you enjoy this diversification from the translation career you originally embarked on, or do you find it challenging?

I most certainly enjoy this diversification in my career. As indicated already, I enjoy the variety it brings to my everyday work. It means I don't do the same type of work all the time, which keeps my mind sharp. The diversification also provided me with a new challenge of a positive kind. Taking on something new is always a challenge at first. The challenge of having to master new skills and become proficient in a new field was very rewarding for me. I don't mean in terms of remuneration – we already talked about that – but in an intellectual way. I like expanding my knowledge and skills and I've learned heaps from doing post-editing.

And from one thing comes another. Since then, I've been involved in projects more closely related to the actual machine translation, which is fascinating work. I could never have imagined I'd be doing that kind of work one day. In the past couple of years I've also given presentations and workshops on post-editing in Australia, New Zealand and the Netherlands, something I hadn't done before either.

Post-editing has opened new horizons for me. What I'm trying to say is that trying something new can actually lead to even more new opportunities presenting themselves.

4) Where do you see freelance translators in five years' time in terms of diversification?

I think in five years' time, more freelance translators will have diversified and will provide services such as post-editing, as there is definitely an increasing demand in this area, but I think this will mostly apply to the younger generation. If we look at post-editing in particular, it requires first of all a positive attitude towards machine translation.

Recently graduated translators, who are just starting their career, have never known a world without machine translation. They are therefore more likely to be open-minded towards services such as post-editing. Other generations of translators, however, might be less accepting of post-editing machine translation, as it contradicts what they were taught to be the only way to do a translation properly.

With technology developing rapidly, the translation industry will keep on changing at a fast pace. Changes in the industry will lead to new developments, which will lead to an increased demand for new services. Those translators who diversify and follow the latest developments will be in a better position to take on new opportunities as they arise. New opportunities tend to generate more work, which in turn leads to a better income. In the current climate, when translation rates for freelance translators are more and more under pressure, diversification seems a great way to tackle the future.

EDITING OF NON-NATIVE TEXTS

Jeana M. Clark *is passionate about translation, technology, lifelong learning and promoting the translation and interpreting profession. She applies insights gained in her current MBA coursework to her roles as a business owner and as the treasurer of the Iowa Interpreters and Translators Association. In her 10 years as a professional translator and editor, she has been drawn to business, information technology, legal and real estate documents and to provide computer-assisted translation training. She was recently appointed to the Economics, Accounting and Management Advisory Council of Central College and plans to advocate for internships, the entrepreneurship programme and mentoring opportunities.*

I DO BELIEVE THAT DIVERSIFICATION plays a vital role in the success of a freelance translator. However, diversification simply for the sake of diversifying is not the answer. If successful diversification is defined as making more money by working with better paying clients on more interesting assignments, then translators need to appropriately consider their specialization, skill set and aptitude when taking any steps in a new direction.

Most professional translators and interpreters are specialized in certain fields of expertise. It is nearly impossible to be a self-proclaimed generalist or jack-of-all-trades who is not only ready and willing to accept anything that shows up in the inbox, but sufficiently competent to do so. Attempting to diversify by haphazardly venturing into a new subject area on a whim while trying to win a new direct client or land that bioweapons project we stumbled across is not likely to bode well for our reputation or the translation recipient.

Diversification at the expense of integrity or translation quality is not the kind of diversification we want to pursue.

On the other hand, diversification that allows translators to expand their business strategy in a way that capitalizes on our specialized knowledge, skill set and aptitude while ameliorating our weaknesses is definitely something worth pursuing. For example, if you have an insatiable desire to take on that bioweapons project, you could join forces with a colleague who has the appropriate expertise. Partnering with a knowledgeable colleague is a great way to expand into new areas of specialization. This concept can be achieved on several different levels: (1) a traditional mentor-mentee relationship; (2) a partnership in which you edit for your colleague and soak up all the knowledge you can; and (3) by using your colleague as a subject-matter expert to review your translation and answer any specific terminology questions while you are translating.

Expanding specialization areas is certainly one way translators can diversify, but diversification can come in many other forms. A person might build their skills and competencies so they feel comfortable adding another language pair or accepting assignments in the opposite direction. I personally only translate from German into English, but I know several colleagues who accept work in both directions. This expands their client base and helps even out workflow.

I was focused entirely on translating and editing when I started working as a professional translator 10 years ago, but I gradually branched out. Over the years, I have taught German language and culture classes, started offering on-site Trados training in my area, and accepted a position on the board of my local interpreters and translators association. I would love to say that all of these diversification growth spurts were carefully crafted components in my strategic plan, but the truth is that I simply capitalized on the opportunities as they presented themselves. The key is to develop and maintain a long-term strategic plan, but be diligently flexible enough to recognize and take any opportunity that will help you achieve your long-term goals.

Where do I see translators in five years?

Technology and technology tools are here to stay and will become increasingly integrated into our daily work over the next five years, with machine translation and cloud-based solutions most notably taking a prominent role. Translators will need to be chameleons and appropriately reflect the environment of this fast-paced, digital age.

Contrary to common belief, the chameleon cannot simply change colour on a whim; it changes colour as a result of an external stimulus such as temperature, danger or emotion. Likewise, translators must learn how to absorb and internalize the technological advancements in the translation industry in order to ward off predators and harness technology for their own strategic competitive advantage.

By predators, I am referring to price-dumping agencies, unprofessional or unskilled interpreters and translators, or any person or entity that seeks to undermine or devalue the vital services that professional interpreters and translators provide on a daily basis all around the world.

Even though these types of agencies and people are a threat to our profession, we should not necessarily ostracize them or viciously attack them in forums, blogs or personal encounters. I suspect that most of these people, especially on a personal level, are simply engaging in this predatory behaviour because they don't know any better or because they are convinced it is necessary for survival.

It is up to us, individually and collectively, to show them the tangible and intangible benefits of becoming high-quality translation agencies and professional translators in skill set and character. We won't win any hearts and minds by reciprocating nastiness, whereas befriending them on a mentor-mentee basis, giving them some helpful links or literature, or inviting them to training sessions or to join the local interpreters and translators association might be just the encouragement they are looking for. We need to be firm but professional in our approach to protecting our industry from people and entities engaging in predatory behaviour.

I want to make it very clear that I believe computer-assisted translation tools (also referred to as translation environment tools) and machine translation programs such as Microsoft Translator or Google Translate are not predators in our industry. The sheer magnitude of data that is zooming through fibre optic cables around the world makes it physically impossible for human translators to attend to all the information that needs to be translated.

According to American Translators Association President-Elect Caitilin Walsh, 'over two quintillion bytes of digitized data are created every day. Translation providers (individuals and companies alike) currently handle less than 0.0001% of that; even though the translation industry is growing at 12%, data volume is increasing at an even faster clip."[1] Information is power and translators have an incredible responsibility in this value chain to work with technology to produce the highest quality translations as quickly as possible.

The true battle going on in our industry today is not between humans and machines. It is between a new hybrid species of superior human and machine intelligence and any predator seeking to devalue the translating/interpreting profession itself. This modern day hybrid translator needs some fine-tuning and training to operate at optimum levels, but we can all achieve optimum output if we take the time to maintain our mechanical parts and keep up with the technology as it changes. If we can learn to use technology to our advantage while championing the cause of professional interpreters and translators, we will continue to gain the respect that we are looking for and the many associated benefits, such as increased pay, prestige and a seat at the negotiating table for rules and regulations, standards and continuing education mandates.

Translators ultimately need to change their colour to absorb and reflect this technologically advanced environment; however, our stimulus for changing should not be fear, but merely a response to something as natural as temperature changes. Professional interpreters and translators who are able to embrace technology and technological advancements in our industry, for example, by simply acknowledging that a machine translation plug-in is just another helpful tool available to us, will be in the best position to meet whatever challenges lying ahead, five years from now or 20 years from now.

Editing of non-native texts

As a freshman in college, I was convinced that I wanted to major in English because I loved to write. My love of writing probably dates back to my infatuation with reading in my formative years; I was officially hooked once I discovered Nancy Drew and the Hardy Boys. I moved from book to book in those collections like a locust in search of sustenance. Nevertheless, after I discovered that writing papers was

---

1 Walsh, C. A Lot Like Us. *The ATA Chronicle*, 2013 Jan, 42(1): 7.

a central component in every college class, my analytical-rational side became convinced that international business management would be a wise choice because it would broaden my job search net. I added German studies to the mix because I had always enjoyed my German classes in high school and had had the good fortune of participating in several exchange programmes to Germany. However wide I thought my net was going to be at that age, I can tell you for certain that I never imagined starting my own international business and becoming a professional German translator.

After digging into translation projects as they trickled in and taking continuing education classes on interpreting and translating at a local community college, I began to realize that being a translator was a natural fit for my interests, and the rest is history. My love of writing is more of a love for the actual craft that is translation. As long as we faithfully convey the message of the source text in an appropriate register without adding or omitting anything, we are allowed to be creative in how we actually express this message. It's like having the best of both worlds; we don't experience the crippling writer's block that can come from staring at a blank page, but the contextual frame is narrow enough to reign in that creativity so we don't wander off on our own little tangent.

Editing and translating have been central components in my service offerings since the very beginning of my career. I actually like to switch back and forth between the two. Autopilot takes over if I translate for too many consecutive days or hours. Diversity is the spice of my work life – I can literally feel my creativity gland shrivelling up if I don't vary things a bit. Editing for someone else jolts my brain back to active mode, engages the problem-solving skills, and gets my creativity flowing again. The ability to take this extra burst of creative energy and apply it to whatever translation that is currently awaiting my attention is the best inoculant against complacency and boredom.

I enjoy editing translations – regardless of whether the translation was produced by a native English speaker or a native German speaker. In fact, in our team, we prefer to have one of our native German speakers translate a text and then have it edited by one of our native English speakers who also references the source text. This gives us an appropriate check and balance for reducing the likelihood of any mistranslations. It also means that the final English version is thoroughly vetted for faithfulness, register, syntax, spelling and grammar so we are able to provide an accurate, print-ready translation that reads well and is suited for its intended audience.

Editing for non-native speakers is enjoyable and can be lucrative, but also poses some special challenges. It is definitely advisable to procure the source text if you are asked to edit a translation produced by a non-native English speaker. In my capacity as a native English speaker editing English translations produced by native German speakers, there are plenty of times when knowing and understanding where a German might be coming from on a particularly strangely worded sentence doesn't actually help me decipher what the translator wanted to convey. Referencing the source text helps me to figure that out and also make sure that I don't introduce a mistranslation in my attempt to fix the syntax, preposition choice, passive voice or some such issue that native German speakers often wrestle with.

The prevalence and use of Global English can also cause some difficulty when we edit for non-native English speakers. Global English (or 'Globish' as it is sometimes referred to as) is universally understood as English that is used internationally by non-native speakers; it is essentially simplified English that is stripped of idiomatic phrases, figurative meanings and ambiguities. It is completely natural for such a language to emerge as a lingua franca – a 'bridge language' between speakers who do not share a common language. But even though spoken Global English is completely acceptable in today's business and academic circles, it is not acceptable in written texts because it is considered non-standard English.

On one level, it might seem that an English text that is as stripped and concise as possible would constitute a well written text requiring less intervention from an editor. However, if the text we provide to the client ends up sounding like 'Me Tarzan – You Jane' or something Yoda would say on a *Star Wars* episode, then we have committed a mortal sin as editors of non-native texts.

Clients hire native English-speaking editors to ensure that the English target texts read well and flow naturally – they will not be very pleased if we deliver Genglish or Globish unless they have specifically requested it.

Editing for multiple non-native English translators on one project poses its own set of unique challenges such as managing terminology, style and the project itself. An editor's job will be much easier if the project and terminology have been managed in real time and the translators have been collaborating on a cloud-based platform throughout the project. It also helps if the editor is familiar with the writing styles of the individual translators and has edited for them in the past. Editors might want to consider all of these issues when deciding whether to quote the project by the hour or by the word. This type of project is not for the faint of heart, but having the opportunity to blend various sections produced by multiple translators into one cohesive text can be quite rewarding and another successful way to diversify.

From a personal development standpoint, some of the most interesting and challenging edits are those of texts that have been drafted in English by non-native speakers, that is, there is no source text. The most important thing in this situation is to clarify with the client ahead of time whether or not you will be functioning as a subject matter expert during the edit. Agreeing to function as a subject matter expert on an electromechanical component testing project might make perfect sense for an editor who worked as a mechanical engineer for 20 years before becoming a technical translator. However, if we have no experience in mechanical engineering and/or it is outside our area of specialization, we should make sure the client is fully aware of the situation before accepting the editing project. We can still offer a value-added service by editing the text for grammar, spelling, syntax and readability. The client in this circumstance might also want our native speaker input and ask us to flag anything that doesn't seem to make sense or sounds strange so they can ask their own subject matter expert to double-check that particular passage.

The added benefit of editing non-native texts, monolingual or otherwise, is that editors can gain valuable knowledge about the specific subject area. For example, someone who edits the same type of data sheets for a chemical additive company for several years might be willing to translate the same type of documents later if the client agrees to be available for any terminology questions that might arise. This long-term relationship and personal development opportunity can be mutually beneficial by providing additional revenue streams for the editor and continuity and consistency for the end client.

In my experience, diversity comes in many forms, but can always be successfully leveraged to our advantage as long as we stay true to our long-term strategy and in tune with the temperature of our surroundings, especially in terms of technology. Our profession is too fascinating to be conducted with a monotonous workflow and same-old-stuff-different-day mindset. As translators and editors, we might be a hybrid species of superior human and machine intelligence, but we are not robots. By diversifying our services, we can expand our bottom line, client base and knowledge while amplifying our creativity and gift of written expression.

Interview with Sheila Wilson

Sheila Wilson is a freelance French to English translator, editor and trainer. After a first career as an analyst-programmer in London, Sheila set off for Europe, arriving on the idyllic island of Fuerteventura via three years in the Netherlands and 15 in France. Needing to stay busy, she retrained as an EFL teacher and, much to her amazement, loved it. Specializing in business training, her native language became the focal point of her new professional life and, as her skills developed, she added translating marketing texts from French, revising, copy-editing and proofreading to her list of services.

1) Sheila, what motivated you to add editing of non-native copy to your client service portfolio?
When you leave your native country to live abroad, you automatically become something of an 'expert' in your native language, at least to your neighbours. When that native language is English, you're in the enviable position of having a skill that's much sought after. It's a skill that can be offered as a favour to friends, neighbours and the local community – there's never any shortage of people who'd like you to 'just take a look' at something they've written in

English – or it can be turned into a professional service, if you have good writing skills. I like to offer both.

In my case, I didn't have the level required for translating when I left England for France via a three-year stopover in the Netherlands but, to my great surprise, I found that the job of training adults to use English at work really appealed to me. My students in the south of France were primarily in the tourism and hospitality sectors, and I learned to my horror that it was often the responsibility of my intermediate-level students to write the English-version websites, brochures, leaflets and flyers and then publish them without as much as a spell check.

Later, as a translator specializing in tourism and marketing, I found I was getting very little tourism work: by and large, those companies will not pay for a professional translation. However, I did find some who were prepared to pay the lower cost of having their own texts revised. This has the added bonus of delivering copy that the writers can be proud of, yet which is essentially their own.

That's what I find most motivating about this service: you're working directly with the writer in most cases. It's a very personal service, and you can vary your service level to suit the client's wishes. Some only want to pay for correction of the real howlers (like the house being advertised as being in the bottom of a pit, when it was in a sheltered valley); others are looking for a totally polished version; yet others are interested in a longer-term collaboration, with one text's instructive remarks serving to improve future copy.

Those last ones are my ideal clients, although they're proving to be rather elusive at the moment.

2) What impact has this activity had on your translation business, and does the income you generate from this service reflect the time and effort invested?

This service dovetails very nicely with translation work, not being vastly different from bilingual proofreading. Some of my clients ask for both non-native editing and translating, notably communications agencies that may be developing multilingual websites from scratch, or reworking existing websites.

I generally quote per hour as, like all revision work, everything depends on the quality of the text and the requirements. So it's easy for me to be sure I generate an adequate level of income, and my long experience of this type of work (nigh on 15 years now) means I can work fast enough to keep the quote reasonable.

One problem is deciding when to stop work on a text. This is common to all editing jobs of course, but in this particular case, a very large proportion of the changes will relate to 'unnatural phrasing' – difficult to define exactly as errors, but certainly not fit for publication. Also, clients cannot be left to tidy anything at all themselves. Lastly, they often find it difficult to see why one phrasing is better than another – explanations have to be in very simple terms but still may not be understood. On more than one occasion, I've proposed English lessons, as a gentle hint that all demands on my time need to be paid for.

3) Do you enjoy this diversification from the translation career you originally embarked on, or do you find it challenging?

Both! I enjoy a challenge! If I'd wanted a safe and quiet life, I could easily have stayed in the UK, in which case I very much doubt I would ever have become an editor of non-native texts, or a translator, and most certainly not a teacher.

Once abroad, however, EFL teaching and subsequently translating became logical career paths, and this type of editing was an obvious offshoot from both. Although teaching skills aren't a requirement for the job, they certainly help, and can provide the client with a very clear bonus: their polished text comes complete with a rich learning experience. For me personally, this job draws on all my skills and interests: it uses my skill of producing effective English copy; my teaching skills – without the need to travel; my attention to detail and powers of concentration. I'm sure other translators can identify with those same strengths.

Is it too challenging? Well, it can certainly be difficult, and sometimes it's simply impossible. The client has to understand that. If a text is unintelligible – a tossed salad of English words and false friends with a dressing of foreign phrasing – no amount of work is going to turn it into a perfect text. An editor is no substitute for a mind reader! Trying to work with such texts is demoralising, and an editor has to learn where to draw the line, and which jobs to reject out-of-hand. Even if I accept a job, I always reserve the right to mark short or long phrases, or even whole paragraphs, for reworking – I refuse to spend time trying to work out what the writer might have been trying to say. The chances that I'll change the meaning are too high.

On the other hand, some non-native texts read really naturally and only require slight 'tweaking' before being returned with compliments to the writer – a very satisfying result for both parties. Of course, the majority of jobs fall between the two extremes: the usual non-native errors (L1 interference in word order, articles, tenses), oddly phrased sentences where sometimes more than one interpretation is possible, and the occasional incomprehensible line or two. Nothing would overwhelm a keen editor, but you do have to love the job – it certainly isn't a job for all translators.

4) Where do you see the freelance profession in five years' time in terms of diversification?
I hope to see it from a distance as I have plans to retire around then!

We're already seeing an explosion in the numbers of people calling themselves professional freelance translators. Students, even schoolchildren, the unemployed, bored housewives (and house-husbands) and retirees: if they can speak a foreign language, they can call themselves translators. Some of them may do a reasonable job, others may post-edit machine translation output and deliver total rubbish, but they're all happy with ultra-low rates. Why not? They aren't paying taxes or investing in their career.

Genuine career translators will have two choices: work long hours as non-specialist translators, delivering quantity at the inevitable detriment of quality, or find ways to distance themselves from these competitors. Unless the industry becomes regulated, the way to do that will be by providing excellence, for excellent rates, to discerning clients.

Specialization will become increasingly important in this focus on excellence but, contrary to what you might think, diversification will have a part to play, too. One person may translate in many subject areas but specialize in one language pair; another may specialize in legal texts but from several source languages; yet another may specialize in delivering convincing material in his or her native language. This is the niche market for the translator/trainer/editor, the translator/editor, and the trainer/editor.

I'm not sure how much work there will be in this niche market for native speakers of other languages, but for English native speakers I believe the market will grow steadily in the coming years, as non-native speakers feel the need to communicate their business effectively in English.

VOICE-OVER

Martina Heine-Kilic is a German freelance translator and voice-over talent currently living in Dallas, Texas. She grew up in Germany and moved to Mexico as a teenager. After graduating from high school in Mexico City, she lived in France, Italy and Germany before moving to the US in 1996. Martina received her master's degree in translation from the Ruprecht Karl University of Heidelberg, Germany. Today she is an experienced translator who specializes in medical and IT translations. Several years ago Martina tapped into the voice-over industry and is now offering voice-over services along with translation, editing, proofing, software testing and project management. Besides her commitment to the profession for more than 15 years, Martina is a member in good standing of the American Translators Association (ATA) and serves on the board of the Metroplex Interpreters and Translators Association (MITA) in Dallas.

DIVERSIFICATION IN MY OPINION happens in a natural, organic way as one's career progresses. The key is to be selective in your choices, to be receptive to new opportunities and to educate yourself along the way.

I believe it is not necessary to have a fixed strategy, but it is probably a good idea to assess your situation once a year. If you realize that you have been working mainly for one client you should think about adding a few new ones. In our volatile economy, it is not advisable to put all your eggs in one basket since that one client could all of a sudden be gone. I don't think there is a safe number to put on this, because every situation is unique, but I would say you should have at least a handful of solid clients/agencies.

At the beginning of their careers, translators tend to take all the work they can get to expand their client database. This is important in order to position themselves in the industry. However, over the years, as your experience and expertise grows, a natural weeding out process takes place.

The goal should be to eliminate the lowest paying clients and keep those clients who pay well and on time, care about quality and care about you. Along with this comes the opportunity to select the specialization that is of particular interest to you. This usually happens without much planning and is a natural process in a freelancer's career.

Even though we have access to unlimited resources to do research in all kinds of disciplines, diversification should not happen at the level of subject area expertise. While there are some translators who are true generalists, we can't all be all-round translators and know about everything. For most of us, it is important to have an area of expertise. I believe we naturally gravitate towards subjects that speak to us. By focusing on a few subjects, we increase our diversification opportunities in areas in which we are particularly adept. In other words, selectively diversifying can greatly increase your opportunities as you build your career.

Taking advantage of opportunities along the way

The translation business is so much more than TEP (translation, editing, proofing). There are so many opportunities for us out there. While some of us are perfectly content to sit at our desks and work in the classic role of a translator, others become antsy and need to get away from the traditional setting from time to time. Either way, I think it is important to get out of one's comfort zone once in a while to spice things up.

I ventured out into something new when I accepted a part-time project manager position after moving to Dallas in 2004. My translation business was going very well, so there was no pressure, but I found myself very isolated and needed to be among people. I ended up working as a part-time project manager for three years. I learned so much and now have the highest respect for project managers. However, when the balance shifted to the point that I was investing more time and energy in my project manager job than in my own translation business, I made the decision to go back to full-time freelancing. Capitalizing on my experience and new skills, I still offer project management services on a contract basis. This service can be very useful for smaller agencies that need help during peak times. Coincidentally, I am now a back-up project manager for a company providing translation services in my line of expertise. While my initial goal was simply to get out from behind my computer screen and meet new people, in the end it led to a great opportunity to diversify my skills.

Another opportunity presented itself about four years ago. More and more requests for voice-over assignments began arriving in my inbox. Initially I politely declined, saying that I did not offer that service. Since all the voice-over requests came from translation agencies, I thought there must be a connection and obviously other translators must offer voice-over services. So when one day a translation agency urgently needed a female voice for a fairly technical industrial reading, I decided to give it a try.

The recording was in a professional studio in Dallas and needless to say, I was pretty nervous. I didn't have any experience with studio equipment nor did I know the protocol of a recording session, but I did practise my script many times the night before. It was a great experience. A wonderful voice coach told me exactly what to do in the recording booth, what to say when I made a mistake, how to sit and how far to be from the microphone. I did well, the money was nice and I was intrigued by the industry.

What exactly is voice-over and what does it have to do with the translation industry?

Adding voice-over services was not part of a plan or a strategy for me. The opportunity presented itself and everything fell into place. After the initial experience in the professional studio, I decided to educate myself and read several books, including *Voice for Hire: Launch and Maintain a Lucrative Career in Voice-Overs* by Randy Thomas and Peter Rofé, and *Voiceovers: Techniques and Tactics for Success* by Janet Wilcox. Subsequently I took voice-over classes at STAGE, a local performing artists' organization, and attended voice-over weekend seminars.

Like a first-time attendee at an American Translators Association conference, I was amazed by the size and the opportunities of this industry. During the first few voice-over lessons I was a bit intimidated by the incredible voices of some of the participants. It quickly became clear to me, however, that simply having a 'great voice' is not enough. Among the many skills required of a voice actor are sharp reading skills and the ability to take direction. As in the translation business, these two skills are crucial to being successful.

One of the first things we learned was to interpret the copy. What style is it? Announcer style, hard sell (impersonal, rough, nasty, screaming), or announcer style, soft sell (gentle, low sexy voice)? Is it narration, storytelling (documentary) or an industrial reading (instructional, technical, e-learning)? Or is it a testimonial (the girl next door, a satisfied customer) or the voice of a spokesperson (representing a company, service, product)? Who is the target audience? Who, what, where are you? What is the mood? What is the message of the script? What is the purpose of the script?

Sound familiar? Don't we do most of this on a daily basis when we receive a translation project? I felt at ease very quickly and had a lot of fun with it. Another important focus was on the awareness of volume and loudness. You have more control of your voice at a lower volume and can do much more with it. The most difficult skill for me is the half-voice, a soft whisper often used for expensive products (like perfume).

We practised with all sorts of scripts. I found that I do well with instructional readings and technical texts (for example, medical). I realized that my niche was going to be e-learning in German. According to Voice-OverXTRA, the e-learning industry is growing so fast that there are countless production companies popping up all over the world, and Dan Hurst predicts 'As companies figure out the tremendous savings they accrue by training with e-learning, we'll continue to see this business grow exponentially'.

So if you are a translator or interpreter with the required business skills, enjoy reading aloud or telling stories, you may be a good candidate to tap into the voice-over industry. Joe Chavez, an agent in Dallas, said during a presentation at our local voice-over meetup that 25% talent plus 75% professionalism is preferred to 100% talent, as long as you are committed to practising and continually improving your skills. As an experienced freelance linguist, you have the 75% covered. We are used to the professional requirements of the business side – tight deadlines, fast turnarounds, business etiquette, etc. – which means we can fully focus on the art of voice-over.

How much do you have to invest and how do you get voice-over work?

From a time investment perspective, concentrated practice is needed to reach a professional level of performance. The financial investment is comparable to investing in a CAT tool. After a couple of voice-over jobs, the investment pays off. First, you have to invest in education such as books, classes, workshops, seminars and private coaching.

Next, you will have to invest in audio equipment. This can be very expensive, but as a beginner all you need is a good computer (you already have one as a translator), a decent microphone (a high-end USB microphone is sufficient at the beginning), a pop filter (protection filter for popping your Ps, Bs and Ts), a microphone stand, headphones and a simple audio editing software program (such as Audacity, a free, open-source, cross-platform software). Down the road you can upgrade to a cardioid condenser microphone with a large diaphragm (you will need an amplifier). You can also switch to professional audio editing software like Pro Tools or Adobe Soundbooth.

Finally, it is important to control the acoustics of your space. You can either buy professional acoustic materials to control sound reflections or simply use a closet as a recording booth. It is important that you are away from any windows and that there is no echo. The messier your closet, the better!

You will have to record a demo. This is a must in the voice-over industry. Without a demo, you will not be able to seek representation with an agent. A voice-over demo is a brief sample of your capabilities, showcasing your talent. It is time-consuming and must be done in a professional recording studio. Next, you should become a member of an online voice-over marketplace and try to consistently get bookings. You typically pay an annual fee to create a talent profile with voice samples. The voice-seeker posts a project for which the voice-talent can audition. The voice-seeker chooses the voice that he likes best and awards the job. I also receive voice-over assignments from translation agencies. After all, this is how it all started.

The rates for voice-over work are all over the place and range from ridiculously cheap to hourly rates that you can only dream of as a translator. I struggled a lot at the beginning with quoting jobs and had to rely on the advice of experienced voice-over talents for each project. I use the same approach now as with my translation business. Cheap stuff simply gets ignored and I am very picky about auditions. After all, I am first and foremost a translator. The voice-over jobs need to be fun and interesting. A recent hilarious assignment was to read numbers and price announcements for an online BINGO game in English with a heavy German accent. It was fun and I made more in 30 minutes than the rest of the day translating. Another completely different experience was an on-camera assignment for an instructional DVD for a medical device that required reading off a teleprompter. The recording session lasted over six hours and at the end your voice still needs to sound the same as at the beginning. It was exhausting, but a lot of fun!

A nice way to combine translation and voice-over is to offer proofing plus recording of the script. Often the German scripts are translations and have grammatical mistakes or simply don't read well. I correct the errors and politely make suggestions for improvement. If the mistakes are minimal, I do it for free. If the script is really bad, I ask politely to be reimbursed, which has never been a problem. Since I present translation services and voice-over on my website side by side, clients see that I am a language professional and are usually very grateful for this added value.

80/10/10

Over a period of one year I dedicate about 80% of my time to my core business: translation / editing / proofing / software testing. About 10% is dedicated to project management assignments and the rest is voice-over work. This might change in the future, as I consider adding private CAT tool coaching.

The possibilities are endless. There is no real plan and no strategy. I am simply trying to stay true to myself, recognize both my capabilities and my limitations and keep it all interesting. I will keep riding the wave and see to which shores it will take me in the future.

SUBTITLING

After completing a BA (Honours) in German and Russian and an MA in Slavonic Languages at the Australian National University, **Felicity Mueller** *lived and worked in Austria. Since moving to Sydney in the mid-1980s she has been a freelance translator, conference and community interpreter and teacher of translation and interpreting. She holds NAATI accreditation as a Senior Conference Interpreter and Translator and is a member of AUSIT and the International Association of Conference Interpreters. Felicity happily diversified into subtitling in 1987 and was a permanent part-time German subtitler/editor with the Special Broadcasting Service (SBS) until 2012. Still a freelance subtitler, she is currently lecturing in Translation Studies at the University of Sydney. Since 2010, Felicity has been teaching intensive interpreting courses at the Centre for Translation Studies at the University of Vienna and working as a contract translator at the Organization for Security and Co-operation in Vienna.*

IN MY CAREER IN LANGUAGES I have worked in translation, interpreting, subtitling and teaching, and have found that each area complements and builds on the others. The variety has been rich and rewarding for me personally and professionally. This has happened without any particular decision on my part to diversify. In other geographical and personal circumstances I may well have specialized in conference interpreting or an area of translation, or chosen to pursue an academic career.

I'd like to point out that I am not alone in this. Many of my colleagues work in translating and interpreting as well as teaching (although I don't know many who are also subtitlers). Well-known examples are Daniel Gile, a mathematician, conference interpreter and academic, and Ingrid Kurz, a conference interpreter and academic with a doctorate in psychology and interpreting.

My entry into the translation and interpreting profession and subsequent diversification into audiovisual translation (AVT) was not motivated by business considerations nor was it planned. Languages have always been my passion, and still are. I took opportunities that appealed to me and have always enjoyed my work. The fact that my Austrian husband

and I chose to live in Sydney in 1984 and that we have three children was also a major factor in my career decisions.

Despite (or perhaps because of) my BA Honours in German and Russian and my research MA on Russian and Serbo-Croatian grammar, my options were limited. After finishing my BA, I worked as a foreign language correspondent and office administrator/translator in German-speaking countries for two years. I also worked briefly as a translator and editor with the department of immigration and as a tutor in Russian-English translation in Canberra in the late 1970s.

After settling in Sydney in the mid-1980s, I gained accreditation with the recently established National Accreditation Authority for Translators and Interpreters (NAATI) and began translating and community interpreting, gradually moving into court, delegations and later conference interpreting. I found freelance translation work challenging because it was difficult to combine deadlines with family life, and because I missed contact with people. The big jobs seemed to come at Christmas or when we had house guests, and I found it stressful at times.

At that stage there was no postgraduate training for translating and interpreting in my language combination. The training I have gained has been through short courses, attending conferences in Australia and Europe and my own reading.

I began university tutoring in German-English interpreting and then lecturing in translation and interpreting at the University of Western Sydney in the 1990s, and later taught at the University of New South Wales. Note-taking for consecutive interpreting became a specific area of interest and expertise after working with many German delegations. I am currently teaching Translation Studies in the MA programme at the University of Sydney.

The Special Broadcasting Service (SBS) was established in Australia in the early 1980s to 'provide multilingual and multicultural radio and television services that inform, educate and entertain all Australians and, in doing so, reflect Australia's multicultural society'.

As soon as I saw subtitled films on television I knew I had found my dream job. SBS was showing feature films, documentaries and series in an amazing variety of languages, series like the hugely popular Mexican soap opera *Rosa De Lejos*, and detective shows like *Derrick* and later *Kommissar Rex*. Watching the subtitles of Edgar Reitz's first *Heimat* series, much of which was in the Hunsrück dialect, gave me great respect for the subtitlers and editors, and I was keen to get involved.

A vacancy eventually came up. I was tested at exhaustive length and found suitable, but the birth of my third child meant a wait of another two years for a position. People tend not to diversify out of subtitling because it is such enjoyable work. Thus a new and very happy chapter of my life began. My work at SBS gave me training and expertise in the work I loved, contact with colleagues from a variety of backgrounds, regular work hours and income, family time and the flexibility to continue with some freelance translation and conference interpreting assignments. In business terms it also gave me something that many freelancers do not have: compulsory employer-subsidized superannuation.[1] This became more important towards the end of my time with SBS. If I had continued as a freelancer this would not have happened. Combining a permanent part-time job with freelance work meant quite a bit of juggling. My solution was to focus completely on the task in hand.

I see subtitling as a point along the translating and interpreting continuum, somewhere between the two. It involves converting 'spoken' language (primarily scripted dialogue, that is, text that was written to be spoken) into written form to be read, but still with the idiomatic features of spoken language. Thus, a translator's skills of conveying the full meaning of a text are combined with an interpreter's ability to focus on the meaning of an utterance. Due to time constraints this means a great deal of omission and condensing.

The visual nature of film also has to be considered. The subtitles are at the bottom of the screen, and the audience is interested in watching the film and not particularly in reading as well, so readability is paramount. Coming from a translation background, I would have liked to fill the screen with a full version of the text complete with footnotes and detailed

---

1 Contributions towards a pension fund.

explanations of cultural concepts. It took me some time to adjust and to condense as accurately as possible while accepting the loss of meaning that generally involves. Once I overcame my initial frustration, I came to enjoy that process and find it more creative than translation.

Coming from an interpreting background, it was not a problem. It wasn't legal or conference speeches (at least most of the time), but entertaining, if often challenging, film scripts. If a film was not to my taste there would be another one in a week or two, so the boredom threshold was low. My only problem was that I hadn't spent enough time with criminals, drunks and detectives in either German or English-speaking countries!

However, our team was collaborative, and someone always knew the answer or knew where to find it. We had good access to research material and dictionaries and later the Internet, which came in handy for the seemingly endless series of Hitler documentaries produced by Guido Knopp which were one of the mainstays of our work. That meant learning the skills of documentary translation for renarration, which is very different from subtitling. The original version is not audible, and adaptation to the target audience is possible. A colleague with a musical background taught me to subtitle opera based on the rhythm of the music. I also subtitled a combined ballet/opera, a wonderful version of *Orpheus and Eurydice* choreographed by Pina Bausch, which remains an all-time favourite. The editor and I decided to place the subtitles at the top of the screen so that the dancers' feet were visible.

At the time I was unfamiliar with translation studies, but now know that subtitling involves walking a tightrope between what Laurence Venuti calls 'foreignization' (giving the audience the feeling of the foreign) and 'domestication' (adapting the material to make it easy for the audience to grasp).[1] Viewers may switch off if a film is full of italicized terms, but others may enjoy the challenge.

Another tightrope relates to the *skopos* or purpose of the subtitles. Should we be faithful to the film-maker's ideas or adapt them to make them easier and more relevant to our target audience? If in doubt,

---

1 Venuti, L. (ed.). *The Translation Studies Reader*. Routledge, 2004: 15-18.

readability and ease of comprehension generally win, as television needs viewers and they need to know what is going on. In film adaptations of literary works the subtitles are more likely to reflect the complexity of the author's original text. Examples of this are our team effort subtitling Peter Stein's 26-hour version of Goethe's *Faust* (Parts 1 and 2) and subtitling film adaptations of Thomas Mann's novels. In these cases there are close parallels with literary translation, with the added challenges of time constraints.

The editors of subtitles, who look at the film from the viewer's perspective, have an ability to find a creative balance between the filmmaker's intention and the viewer's response. A long struggle to find a pun that continued over several subtitles, or convey the humour of a joke with an untranslatable punch line or the rhythm of a song or poem was generally resolved at a 'conf', a discussion between subtitler and editor.

After more tests, editing became another area of specialization or diversification for me, and I was privileged to work on films in a variety of languages. I believe that work has helped me as a translator and reviser of my own translations and those of others.

These days, diversifying into subtitling on a permanent basis is not such an attractive option. Work is irregular and there are few permanent positions as television networks struggle for ratings in a highly competitive global environment. Many commercial subtitling companies offer low rates, impose unrealistic deadlines and may require subtitlers to purchase or lease their own software. This means that the pay can range from above that of a teacher through between that of a skilled labourer and policeman to below that of an unemployed person, as Danish subtitler Claus Stenhøj points out.[1] In fact, sometimes there is no payment at all. Crowdsourcing of subtitles has become popular. Fansubs is 'the (legally rather dubious) practice of amateur subtitling and distribution of films.'[2] Fanboys in countries such as Japan or Finland create subtitles of new movies or episodes of popular US series because they don't want to wait weeks or

---

1 Stenhøj, C. In Defence of Subtitling as a Profession. Presentation at the 'Media for All' 4th International Conference – Audiovisual Translation: Taking Stock. London, 2011.
2 Munday, J. *Introducing Translation Studies: Theories and Applications*. Routledge, 2012: 279; See also Cíntas, J. C. and Muñoz Sánchez, P. Fansubs: Audiovisual Translation in an Amateur Environment. *The Journal of Specialised Translation*, 2006,(6): 37–52.

months until the official versions are released. They make up for patchy language knowledge and lack of training with unbounded enthusiasm, and the viewers don't seem to mind.

Viki[1] adds crowdsourced subtitles to its movies and television programmes on its website, with mixed results. Anyone is welcome to subtitle and/or edit translations. That work is not paid or seen as a professional job, yet on the same website the company advertises paid jobs for technicians, etc. The message is very clear and, I believe, alarming: anyone can subtitle and there's no need to pay for it.

The Open Translation Project of the not for profit group TED[2] encourages volunteers to subtitle TED talks and provides helpful guidelines. This is an excellent cause, and may be useful for language students thinking of moving into AVT and fun for others for whom languages are a hobby. But if anyone can subtitle without requiring training or payment, what effect is this having on the careers of AVT professionals? It's not all bad news, according to Professor Aline Remael of the Department of Translators and Interpreters of Artesis University College, Antwerp and the University of Antwerp. The market for a variety of work including subtitling and documentary translation continues to grow.

In theoretical terms, no difference is made between subtitling that is interlingual (between languages) and intralingual (within a language). Intralingual subtitling includes captioning, audio description, audio subtitling and respeaking in areas relating to access for the deaf and hard of hearing and the blind and visually impaired.[3] This market is growing exponentially. Many trained professionals will be required in the future, for intralingual and interlingual subtitling and interlingual audio subtitling. The ability to subtitle corporate DVDs and Internet material is also a valuable additional skill for translators that may give them a competitive edge.

1 http://www.viki.com/community. Retrieved 20.07.2013.
2 http://www.ted.com/OpenTranslationProject. Retrieved 20.07.2013.
3 Remael, A. From Audiovisual Translation to Media Accessibility: Audio-Description and Audio-Subtitling: Challenges and Opportunities. Presentation at AUSIT Conference, Sydney, 1-3 December 2012. For a description of the situation in Australia, see also http://www.mediaaccess.org.au/about/about-us, retrieved 18.05.2013.

I hope I have shown that diversification brings professional rewards and personal enrichment. The skills we learn in every area of translation and interpreting work complement and build on one another. There will always be room for specialized translation, but I am confident that there is also a future for trained translation and interpreting professionals who are prepared to move out of their comfort zone and learn new skills when the opportunity arises. In my experience, just about every new assignment involves moving out of my comfort zone in one way or another, so why not diversify?

What do translators need today?

To succeed in the language industry in today's world, I believe the following is ideal:

- an excellent grasp of all levels of the source language, preferably gained through long-term study and residence in the country or countries where that language is spoken
- native-speaker level skills in the target language
- an undergraduate degree, not necessarily in languages, possibly in an area where specialization is planned, e.g. business, science, engineering or law
- postgraduate training in translation and interpreting
- IT, business and marketing skills.

If the language combination is in demand and there are clients willing to pay for quality, specialization works well. In that case a permanent job or regular contracts with the client would provide security and hopefully a reasonable income. This is not always the case. The market is changing all the time; there is downward pressure on rates, machine translation is popular and is constantly improving. Flexibility and a willingness to diversify to meet the needs of the market will also be required.

Interview with Melissa McMahon

Melissa McMahon is a freelance translator (and subtitler) from French to English, who has been operating full-time for the last six years. She started her practice translating academic articles while completing a PhD in philosophy, before getting her accreditation and leaving academia for more commercial pastures. As well as translating and subtitling for film and television, she has translated more than 20 titles for Murdoch Books, mostly cooking and craft books, and also works in the legal and business translation field.

1) Melissa, what motivated you to add subtitling to your client service portfolio, and what are your experiences with this activity?
The short answer is I was asked: the Special Broadcasting Service (SBS) needed some extra French subtitlers and I was fortunate enough to be in the right place at the right time. You often develop new skills in response to a call for it, rather than in advance. I had done some full translations of film scripts in the past and was interested in the field. I think anyone who watches subtitled films wonders about the process, especially if they are familiar with the language of the film. It is also an attractive idea to watch films for a living!

2) What impact has subtitling had on your translation business, and does the income you generate from this service reflect the time and effort invested?
SBS has been my only subtitling client so far, and they offer very good conditions that certainly reflect the time and effort spent. I think they are probably exceptional in this respect. As for other translation-related fields, the conditions for subtitlers on the local (Australian) market are much better than on overseas markets.

The main impact for me has been that it has got me out of the house! I mostly work on-site at SBS rather than at home, and it has been wonderful to be working around other people. It has made me realize what I missed working for myself at home, but also the advantages of being independent. I think the ideal is a mix.

4) Do you enjoy this diversification from the translation career you originally embarked on, or do you find it challenging?

I very much enjoy this diversification. It has been challenging in the best of ways. Subtitling is quite a different discipline to translation, not just because it is more condensed, but also because it's temporal and visual: timing and placement are important factors. You also learn how to use a new set of technological tools. It's not always as glamorous a job as it might sound, but at the end of the day, yes, you are making a living watching films, and you get quite intimate with them. It's a creative job; you are actually contributing to the finished work.

5) Where do you see freelance translators in five years' time in terms of diversification?

I think diversity is an inherent part of the work as a freelance translator. The variety is part of the attraction of translation, and when you work independently you don't have a job description, so you adapt to what's asked of you – as in the case of subtitling above. It's also of course prudent to have more than one string to your bow: if business is slow in one area you learn to develop others.

Technology has opened up the translation market in amazing ways, and has also made it possible for individuals to develop skills and provide services that used to be out of their reach, such as desktop publishing, or publishing in general. I don't know whether things will be significantly different in five years' time compared to the difference between now and 20 years ago.

TRANSCRIPTION

Karolina Kastenhuber is a young polyglot from Austria who was initially inspired to pursue a career in the language industry after a year-long high school exchange in Brazil at age 16. She went on to study translation at the University of Graz, completed another exchange, this time to Siberia, and worked as a student teaching assistant in Spanish and scientific writing. After a brief foray into teaching German as a foreign language, she recently started her own freelance business as a transcriptionist, editor, proofreader and translator from Russian, Spanish and English into her native German, while at the same time working on her thesis on co-operative translation processes.

WHEN THE TOPIC OF DIVERSIFICATION in the language industry is brought up, the image that usually comes to mind is that of a translator branching out into a new field solely out of financial considerations (or even necessity). Indeed, modern communication technology has contributed to the globalization of the translation market, fuelling competition among freelancers all over the world and driving some to explore business strategies such as diversification primarily as a means of survival. However, while the outlook of having an additional stream of revenue is certainly among the more common motivations for freelancers to expand their range of services, it is worth noting that increased financial security is far from the only argument in favour of diversification.

Diversification as a door opener

From my perspective as a relatively new freelancer, one of the most powerful benefits of diversification (and one that is often completely overlooked) is its potential to act as a door opener for young language professionals who are just starting their freelancing careers. Today, many talented and well-educated language experts aspiring to make their way into the business find themselves in a classic catch-22 situation: to get assignments, they need experience, but to get experience, they need assignments. This is not an easy cycle to break when you're competing against fellow freelancers all over the world. By broadening their perspective on the industry and exploring other language related services besides translation that their individual skill set allows them to provide, these hopeful newcomers can target a greater number of potential clients, thus enhancing their chances of getting a foot in the door and speeding up the process of establishing their business network.

Note that this is by no means to be understood as encouraging amateurs to diversify into areas they aren't qualified to work in. Obviously, not all working fields are equally suitable for getting a newly minted freelancer's business going, and some paths of diversification – like launching a business school for freelance translators, the example of another of the contributors to this book – are most definitely better left to those with at least a couple of years of solid freelance translation experience under their belt. This does not mean, however, that a newcomer should stick to 'traditional' translation as his or her only work area for years before daring to even think about adding another service.

On the contrary, I believe young translators need to be encouraged to find out exactly what their interests and marketable skills are and build their range of services accordingly, taking a broad view of both the industry and their own particular abilities right from the start. Why not, for example, use your super-fast touch-typing skills to offer transcription services? Why not take advantage of your extraordinary command of your native language to provide monolingual proofreading or write articles to be published online? Or why not take your passion for playing video games as an incentive to get into game localization?

As freelancers, we have the invaluable opportunity of designing our own individual job profiles, regardless of the boundaries suggested by the traditional separation of occupational titles like translator vs. editor vs. transcriptionist. For many newcomers, embracing that opportunity and putting their existing potential to maximum use – ideally with the help of a mentor to turn to for initial guidance – is all it takes to get the ball rolling.

Diversification as a preventive health measure

Another observation that can be made regarding the positive effects of diversifying one's business is as trivial as it is important: variation is healthy! Freelancers, and among them language service providers, are typically considered to be a high-risk group for developing work-related health problems like burnout syndrome due to a wide range of factors, including financial insecurity and job dissatisfaction as a result of monotony. Here, too, diversification may be a valuable strategy, both because it can be used as a means to achieve a smoother revenue stream, and because the added variety works wonders against job fatigue.

As a freelance translator who also provides transcription and monolingual editing and proofreading services, I have experienced after completing a large volume project in either of my specialties feeling disinclined to take on another of the same kind right away. In situations like these, having the opportunity to switch to another task that requires me to activate a slightly different aspect of my skill set comes as a huge relief. When deadlines allow, I even like to alternate between several projects at once, working on whichever I feel the need to tickle my brain cells with in order to stay focused and happy. I might not be able to reach my goal of working eight hours a day if all I have on my to-do list is transcription work, but splitting the time up between translation, transcription and editing or proofreading, it is not only doable, but usually also makes for quite an enjoyable workday, while at the same time allowing me to keep my overall productivity at a high level.

Diversifying the other way around: how I made my way into the language service business

When the issue of diversification is discussed, it is usually implied that freelancers who expand their range of services generally do so starting from their core specialty, that is, the profession they originally trained for or have the most experience in. In that respect, my own personal experience of breaking into the language industry can be described as somewhat unorthodox, given that I started out not by providing what I had studied at university – which is translation – but other language-related services, namely transcription and, soon after, monolingual editing and proofreading.

The first client to provide me with regular transcription work was a civil engineer whom I worked for as a side-job alongside university classes and whose secretary kindly showed me how to use foot pedals and transcription software. I had not been specifically looking for a job as a transcriptionist, but once presented with the opportunity, I considered that I might as well make use of the touch-typing skills my teenage Internet addiction had equipped me with. Since that time, I have completed freelance transcription assignments for clients from a wide variety of fields, dealing with different settings from dictated text to focus group discussions and covering fields as diverse as civil engineering, sports and social work.

Very often, when I tell fellow freelance translators that one of the three pillars I am currently basing my business on is transcription, their initial reaction is rather negative, many of them claiming that transcription is hardly intellectually challenging and can be done by pretty much any fast typist. However, while it might be true that one doesn't necessarily have to be a trained translator in order to be able to complete most transcription projects, to me, transcription has still turned out to be a surprisingly rewarding task. This is not least because my clients, in turn, have proven to be very appreciative of my translator's education and the added value it allows me to provide. For example, when it comes to handling of multilingual files like interpreted interviews, I can supplement them with notes in order to explain sections that would otherwise have been 'lost in interpretation'.

How transcription has influenced my business as a freelance translator

As said above, becoming involved in transcription has not been a classical experience of diversification, as I started taking on transcription assignments long before I began working in the actual profession I had been training for. Instead, I have made my way into the language industry from the other end of the path, gaining the confidence to market myself as a freelancer while doing transcription work first, then adding monolingual editing/proofreading as another service and gradually zooming in on my core specialization, translation, only after that.

Offering transcription as an additional service besides translation during these early stages of my freelancing career was a tremendously positive experience. Some of the clients I originally started doing transcription work for have come back not only for my transcription, but also for my editing and/or translation services, or have recommended my services to colleagues in their own fields, thus enabling me to establish a business network that has been providing me with a stable and diverse workflow.

Another great benefit that I have received from providing transcription is the opportunity to immerse myself in new subject matter while listening and typing. This way, I have gained familiarity with terminology used in civil engineering, I have learned about a host of public health projects in my area and I have even acquired basic knowledge of the maintenance of ceramic printing machines. Does this make me a civil engineer, a public health expert or a printing technician? Certainly not, but it is definitely a valuable addition to my skill set that I hope to be able to further develop and put to use in future translation assignments.

TERMINOLOGY SERVICES

Diana Brändle is the proprietor of dbterm terminologieservice. Following a degree course in translation at Saarland University in Germany (her final dissertation was on the subject of terminological entry structures), she worked as a freelance translator and later as a terminologist for Audi Akademie GmbH. Since 2005, her company dbterm terminologieservice has been supporting small and large businesses in all issues concerning terminology work, and offers training and advanced training for terminologists. She is a certified coach for the ECQA Certified Terminology Manager qualification, a member of the Loctimize team and on the advisory board of the German Institute for Terminology (DIT e.V.).

EVERY COMPANY AND EVERY organization, whether large or small, is characterized by its own terminology and language. Product names, names of functions, characteristics, etc. have to be decided upon in different languages. If language is to be used clearly and consistently both within and outside the company, professional terminology management is a must.

Not only is terminology management important for communicating with the market, it is also important for knowledge management within the company or organization – particularly where people who speak different languages work together, or where people from different departments need to work together (development, marketing, etc.).

In future, the success of a company or organization will no longer depend solely on the products and services it offers: access to structured knowledge will also play a strategic role. To ensure knowledge is available in a range of languages, you need translators who know how to deal with the smallest modules of knowledge management, which form the basis of successful multilingual knowledge management – in other words, with terminology.

Are you one of the lucky ones? Does your client define and specify terminology in the source text? Does your client use authoring tools in all source texts to check terminology, thus ensuring that only defined, aligned and approved nomenclature is used, and terms are spelt consistently throughout all types of texts and media? Does your client consistently provide you with up-to-date, comprehensive and reliable multilingual glossaries with definitions, references, images, etc.?

Or are you in the other – probably much larger – group of translators who repeatedly stumble over inconsistencies in source texts? Who come up against synonyms, homonyms, unexplained abbreviations or incomprehensible nomenclature? Who spend a considerable amount of their time researching terminology? Who have to keep asking the author questions to understand what was meant by a term in the source text, and then delve into a multitude of sources in the search for a fitting equivalent in the target language?

If you're in the second group, how do you proceed? Do you keep a record of the results of your research? If you do, where and how do you keep such a record? Perhaps you've already created a veritable treasure trove of monolingual and multilingual glossaries – in Word, Excel or even a professional terminology management system. Maybe your stock is imperfect, or incomplete. Have you ever thought about telling your clients about your terminology hoard, or showing it to them, or perhaps even offering it to them? Have you ever thought about turning terminology into a business enterprise from which both you and your clients could profit?

In this article I would like to encourage all those working in the fields of translation, interpretation and localization to get to grips with the subject of terminology, and to gain a more profound understanding of terminology work where necessary – not only in order to create a good and well-structured terminology database for themselves, but also in order to offer such to their clients as an additional service.

Why me?

Why are translators predestined to be involved in the terminology process? There are valid reasons for this. In contrast to a company or organization's internal departments or external service providers, translators often have the best overview of texts on all subjects from the various departments of the company or organization in question.

Translators are confronted with texts from a wide range of authors from various areas, texts which are destined for different purposes, produced in a wide range of formats, and belonging to different types of text and different departments. Thus translators have a far better overview of the range of documents created by a company or an organization than does anyone else.

This also means, however, that they'll be the first to spot glaring inconsistencies in source texts. Let's suppose you come across the following variants of Figure 3.1 in a source text, or in a batch of different texts you're translating for one client:

> Use the corresponding hotkey
>
> Use the corresponding hot key
>
> Use the corresponding shortcut
>
> Use the corresponding shortcut key
>
> Use the corresponding access key
>
> Use the corresponding accelerator key
>
> Use the corresponding keyboard accelerator
>
> Use the corresponding keyboard shortcut

Figure 3.1: Examples of inconsistencies in one or more source texts

Of course you'll ask yourself whether the terms in the right-hand column above really do stand for the same term – are synonyms, in other words – or whether they are used with different connotations, meaning that different equivalents need to be found for the target language.

Variants in source texts which don't catch the eye immediately will become apparent as soon as you try to use a translation memory system in translation – if variants are contained in a source language segment, you won't get a 100% match.

You might also find yourself spending time over homonyms, which only reveal themselves to be such when you try to translate them. The English word 'capital', for example, could refer to a city, a letter, the top of a column, or money:

- The capital is normally the seat of the government.
- Their knowledge is their capital.
- The capital forms the topmost member of a column.
- The Arabic and Hebrew languages make no distinction between capital and lowercase letters – a system called unicase.

A translator must understand the content in order to translate it. If terms are unclear, you either have to deduce the correct meaning from the context, or ask the author. So you're continually collecting information about the products, services, functions, parts, etc. of a company or organization.

If you keep a multilingual record of these, with definitions, explanations and images where necessary, it would be valid to say that you are engaging in multilingual knowledge management (see Figure 3.2).

A	B	E	F	G	H	I	J
Subject	English	German	Grammatical gender	French	Grammatical gender	Italian	Grammatical gender
Architecture	capital	Kapitell	neuter	chapiteau	masculine	capitello	masculine
General	capital	Hauptstadt	feminine	capitale	feminine	capitale	feminine
Finance	capital	Kapital	masculine	capital	masculine	capitale	masculine

Figure 3.2: Three entries in Excel for 'capital'

Translators have to find target equivalents which are appropriate for both the target audience and the target medium. They'll notice, in other words, if the name of a product would be inappropriate in a target market because it has different connotations there, or whether a particular number or colour is regarded as 'unlucky', or the pronunciation would not be conducive to sales.

Here are a few examples from the automobile industry:

- Toyota 'MR2': sounds like 'merde' in French
- Lamborghini 'Reventón': Spanish = flat feet
- Nissan 'Pivo': Czech = beer

Translators and interpreters are not only linguistic experts, they're also cultural experts. Their expertise brings with it the obligation to share their knowledge with others – in other words, to make their clients aware of possible linguistic inconsistencies or inaccuracies, or point out wrong or ambiguous terminology.

Just as when an employee confronts their boss with a problem, if a service provider intends to confront their client with a problem, it's always best to not only focus on the negative side, but also to show where possible how the problem in question could be solved. This is exactly what a translator can do: point out possible terminological problems to their clients, and show them how these can be resolved. We'll be looking shortly at how this could be done, and what tools you'll need for the job.

Anecdote

> A language service provider has been working for an internal client for decades, and receives no feedback – other than the odd complaint, and the even more seldom word of praise – on his wide range of translation services. But on the day this language service provider uploads a multilingual glossary as a 'company dictionary' to the in-house intranet, the phones ring ceaselessly, and his inbox is flooded with emails: compliments and enthusiastic praise from all departments in the company for the wonderful and helpful multilingual company dictionary!

Possible procedures

Let's assume that every translator – whether consciously or unconsciously – deals with terminology on a daily basis, and, ideally, records the information he or she has researched according to the basic terminological principles. Of course this information will be valuable to the client. On the other hand, it would of course be ideal for translators to receive terminological information from their clients in order to remain up to date. In my view, this could certainly evolve into a 'win-win' situation.

You would benefit, because you'd be paid for a job that you have to do anyway, or you could charge a higher word price because of improved (terminological) quality. You could rise above your competitors by specializing in a particular area and creating your own record of specialized terminology. You'd be more in touch with what your client wants, and by exchanging terminology, could ensure that information is passed on more effectively.

The advantages of terminology management for your client are obvious:

- more effective communication thanks to avoidance of variants and unclear nomenclature
- increased customer satisfaction thanks to clear language
- (unambiguous language; comprehensible, consistent language from manuals to aids to customer support)
- avoidance of misunderstandings, which can lead to operating errors by users
- conformity to norms and legal certainty
- strengthening of corporate identity by corporate language
- better communication and better transfer of knowledge (within the company and externally)
- strengthening of a consistent and individual company profile
- improved translation quality
- competitive advantages:
  - documents available faster, shorter publication deadlines for software and other publications
  - simultaneous shipping in x languages
  - global edge on competitors.

Preconditions

What preconditions will you have to meet in order to offer terminology work as an additional service? The most important precondition is to be convinced yourself of the use and purpose of terminology work and able to see the correlations. Basically, you should have mastered the basics of terminology work, and know, for example, how to research, record and enter terminology in a tool on the basis of concept orientation and term autonomy.

You won't necessarily need to master terminology management systems such as crossTerm, flashterm, MultiTerm, qTerm or TermStar. Well-maintained and correctly compiled Excel tables are completely sufficient to start with. The main thing is to understand the principle, and record data cleanly and according to the rules of terminology work. If you do this, you'll be able to import your terminology data at any stage into your own and/or your client's professional terminology management system, or add data which you receive from your client to your own system.

But where and how can you find out how to record terminology correctly, and how do you offer your client terminology work as an additional service? There is a wide range of options available for further training in the field of terminology. Find the further training option that suits you best and/or ask an expert for advice. Or use one of the followings:

- webinars and YouTube presentations (e.g. offered by terminology service providers, tool manufacturers [e.g. across, SDL, Kilgray, Star, termsolutions] and associations)
- workshops (e.g. offered by terminology service providers and professional associations)
- certified courses (e.g. ECQA Certified Terminology Manager as an on-site or online course)
- summer holiday courses (e.g. Terminology Summer School of the International Network for Terminology, TermNet)
- online courses (e.g. elcat and ECQA Certified Terminology Manager)

- advanced training, seminars, conferences, etc. offered by associations (e.g. Deutscher Terminologietag; BDÜ; tekom, International Network for Terminology – TermNet, RaDt)
- courses, advanced courses and degree courses at university level
- advisory services and training (e.g. from terminology and localization service providers such as Loctimize GmbH)

Conclusion

Get fit in terminology work! Find training, read up on the subject, take part in courses, workshops and webinars to learn the tools of the trade. Implement what you've learned, and gain practical experience in terminology work.

Do it right! Whether you're already engaging in terminology work, or want to start off with it, do it right – in other words, stick to the rules! This will ensure your database is interchangeable with others, and enable you to offer your clients well-maintained terminology databases.

Talk about terminology! Collect the facts, that is, how much time you spend on researching terminology; how many terms you record per project, type of text or order; what additional information (e.g. subject field, definition, source) you include in your terminological entry; and tell your clients about it!

Go for it! If you find mistakes in a source text, need to ask the author for clarification, or stumble over other terminological problems, keep track of these things. Keep a record of how much time you spend clarifying each individual issue, or what could have gone wrong and what the consequences could have been had you not noticed and corrected the issue in question. Don't be afraid to talk about it, and make sure you have some ideas for improvements up your sleeve!

Offer your clients support in terminology work for their languages and specialist fields!

TRANSCREATION

Percy Balemans *graduated from the School of Translation and Interpreting in the Netherlands in 1989. After working with a translation agency as an in-house translator for a few years, she served as a technical writer and copywriter, information designer, web editor and trainer for an information technology business. She has been a full-time freelance translator since 2007, translating from English and German into Dutch and specializing in advertising (transcreation), fashion, art and travel and tourism.*

WHEN I LOOK BACK ON MY CAREER, which now spans almost 25 years, it has diversification written all over it. After I graduated from the School of Translation and Interpreting in Maastricht, the Netherlands, I started working as an in-house translator for a translation agency specializing in IT texts. I spent some time working at the translation department of IBM in Amsterdam and some time working at the agency's office, for different end clients. After a couple of years, I decided I had had enough of IT translation and I found a job as a technical writer for a company in the IT business. I ended up working for this company for 14 years and during that time I got the chance to develop all sorts of different skills: in addition to technical writing, I worked as a web editor, web developer, trainer, copywriter and information designer, and I set up and managed the company's helpdesk. In the same period I was also certified as a scuba diving instructor and taught scuba courses. How diverse can a career be?

But after those 14 years I realized I missed translation. So I returned to the translation business and, based on my experience, I initially went back to IT translation. But even though by now CAT tools had made life a lot easier for the IT translator, it was not really what I wanted to do. I missed creativity in my work.

It was time to diversify again, this time in my areas of specialization as a translator. Based, again, on my past experience, I found translation clients in the scuba diving industry and among human rights organizations, the latter because during my study I had spent six months working at

Amnesty International's headquarters in London and later I worked for several years as a volunteer for the same organization. Although these new areas of specialization were not, in themselves, that creative, at least they gave me the opportunity to try my hand at different types of texts.

First steps in transcreation

Then one day I was approached by the project manager of an agency specializing in transcreation. I had never even heard the term transcreation before, but the small job he offered me to begin with didn't seem too difficult. I was asked to translate a couple of leaflets for digital cameras. Part of the work (the technical specifications) was fairly familiar to me, but having to write copy that wasn't just technical, but had to appeal to a specific target audience and seduce them to buy the product was new to me, even though I had done some copywriting work in my previous job. However, the client was happy with my work. I was offered more jobs and, through word of mouth, other clients found me. The rest is history: transcreation is now my main area of specialization and I also offer presentations and workshops on the subject.

The nice thing about transcreation is that it offers a lot of variety. The types of copy offered for transcreation vary from websites, brochures, and television and radio commercials aimed at end clients, to posters and flyers for resellers. They can be about any consumer product: digital cameras, airlines, food and drink, clothing and shoes, financial products and cars. And it's not just about the text: transcreators are often also expected to provide cultural advice: for example, clients need to know when a specific translation or image does not work for the target audience.

Transcreation and subject specialization

But it didn't end there. Specializing in transcreation as such is not enough. Transcreation is a type of translation (translating advertising and marketing material) rather than a subject (such as legal translation or medical translation).

In addition to specializing in transcreation, you will still need to specialize in one or more subjects, because you need to know what you are writing about: you need medical knowledge to translate a brochure about an MRI machine, you need technical knowledge to translate a leaflet with technical specifications about a car, and you need financial knowledge to translate an advertising campaign about a financial product. So if you want to diversify in transcreation, start with the subject(s) you already specialize in.

After doing a lot of transcreation for the digital camera brand, I was asked to work on copy for a fashion brand. I enjoyed it and it soon turned out that this particular client wanted to have more material transcreated and therefore the transcreation agency asked me to join the team for this client.

I discovered I enjoyed translating about fashion, which led me to delve into the subject: I read books about fashion history, made sure I kept up to date on the latest fashion trends, and started visiting fashion museums and exhibitions dedicated to fashion. This, in turn, led to other translation jobs on the subject of fashion: I have translated numerous articles for a fashion magazine and texts for an exhibition on Jean Paul Gaultier which was on display in Rotterdam in early 2013.

Transcreation versus translation: what's the difference?

But what exactly is transcreation? What makes it different from translation? Isn't transcreation just translation, but of a specific type of texts? Let's start by defining transcreation. This is how Ira Torresi, an Italian translator who has written a book on translating promotional and advertising texts, defines transcreation:

> A type of adaptation that involves copywriting and, possibly, prompting the creation of new visuals for the promotional material, rather than relying on the same verbal and visual structures of the source text. In this approach, the translator is seen as a creative professional with highly developed language skills and an in-depth understanding of social, cultural, legal and promotional conventions currently in place in the target community.[1]

---

1 Torresi, I. *Translating Promotional and Advertising Texts*. St Jerome, 2010: 187.

And this is how Common Sense Advisory described transcreation in its 2010 report on transcreation:

> The term 'transcreation' is now more commonly applied to marketing and advertising content that must resonate in local markets in order to deliver the same impact as the original. The term may be applied when either a direct translation is adapted, or when content is completely rewritten in the local language to reflect the original message.
> Most often, transcreation includes a hybrid of new content, adapted content and imagery, and straightforward translation. [...] Transcreation provides the freedom to address the cultural gaps. It allows the intent of the message to be communicated so that it is positively received by the intended audience, without requiring the local version to remain fully faithful to the words or images used in the original version.[1]

In other words, transcreation means recreating a text for the target audience: 'translating' and 'recreating' the text; hence the term 'transcreation'. Transcreation is used to make sure the target copy is the same as the source copy in every aspect: the message it conveys, the tone of voice, the images and emotions it evokes and the cultural background. You could say that transcreation is to translation what copywriting is to writing.

One could argue that any translation job is a transcreation job, since a good translation should always try to reflect all these aspects of the source copy. This is of course true. But some types of texts require a higher level of transcreation than others. A technical text, for example, will usually not contain many emotions and cultural references and its linguistic style will usually not be very challenging. Marketing and advertising copy, however, does contain all these different aspects, making it difficult to create a direct translation. Translating these texts therefore requires a lot of creativity.

---

1 Kelly, N. and Ray, R. *Reaching New Markets through Transcreation – When Translation Just Isn't Enough.* Common Sense Advisory, 2010: 2-3.

What makes a good transcreator?

As with any other area of specialization, transcreation requires specific skills. Some are the same as needed for translation, others are specific to transcreation.

First of all, and not surprisingly, a transcreator needs to have excellent creative writing skills: copy needs to be written in the correct style for the target audience and with the intended purpose in mind. This means that sometimes the style should be formal, for example when writing for business clients, and at other times it should be very informal, even leaning towards spoken language, for example when writing for young customers.

Often, the transcreator has to work within limitations of space or layout, or according to the requirements of specific media (television or radio commercials, Twitter, etc.), and a lot of creativity is required to write copy that fits within these limitations, but still sounds natural.

In addition to creativity, a transcreator should have an excellent knowledge of both the source language and the target language and a thorough knowledge of cultural backgrounds. This seems obvious for a translator, but advertising material often contains puns or references to local cultural knowledge or current events, and the transcreator has to understand these and know what to do with them in the adaptation: replace them with local puns/references, leave them out altogether or come up with an alternative solution. Some clients go so far as to demand that the transcreator lives in the country for which the target campaign is intended, to make sure that he or she is up to date on both language (which changes all the time!) and local culture.

The transcreator also has to be familiar with the product being advertised and be able to write about it enthusiastically; this is where subject specialization comes in. In addition, it certainly helps if the transcreator can handle stress and is flexible, since the advertising world is a fast-paced world and deadlines and source texts tend to change frequently.

Finally, as a transcreator you should 'dare to be different': let go of the source text, come up with completely different solutions. In many cases, clients will ask for alternative versions so they can choose which one they like best, so you are free to come up with a couple of alternatives that are truly different and original.

Transcreation also has its own, unique problems: unlike a copywriter, a transcreator often has to work with existing material, for example a finished advertising campaign with a set layout and visuals. This may mean limited space or tag lines which are split up over multiple lines or have a specific layout to highlight the content, all of which will have to be recreated in the target copy. And then there's the question of whether visuals or puns used in the campaign are appropriate for the target market: what works for one country might be too risqué or even offensive in another country.

Diversifying into transcreation

My main reason for diversifying into transcreation was because I like variety in my work: learning new skills and delving into new subjects. Although a lot of my work these days consists of transcreation, I still offer 'regular' translation as well. After all, sometimes it is hard to draw a line between transcreation and translation: an advertising campaign can consist of both creative copy and technical specifications, and a seemingly straightforward internal training document for a large international company may have to be adapted to reflect the cultural background of the employees in the target country.

Diversifying also makes smart business sense: it is never a good idea to put all your eggs in one basket and rely on one area of specialization. If, for some reason (an economic crisis, changes in government regulations on which documents need to be translated), the workload in one area drops dramatically, the diversifying translator will always have something to fall back on. This is also why I am constantly looking for ways to broaden my current subject areas. Based on my specialization in fashion, I have branched out into art, since a lot of fashion texts contain references to the art world. To this end, I read a lot about this subject, I visit museums and exhibitions and I have completed an introductory course in art history. I am now looking into expanding my knowledge of textiles.

However, the trick is to find the right balance: don't diversify into too many different, unrelated areas. I think there is a lot of truth in the saying

'Jack of all trades, master of none': clients don't tend to trust translators who offer too many areas of specialization or too many services. Instead, they prefer someone who focuses on a limited number of (related) subjects in which he or she truly is an expert. I noticed that once I started focusing my marketing on transcreation, I received fewer enquiries for 'general' translations and more requests for transcreation, and mainly from agencies specializing in transcreation.

If you like being creative, have excellent writing skills and don't mind the 'fast life' of the advertising world, transcreation might be a good way for you to diversify. It also seems a 'safe' area of specialization when it comes to technological developments: if there is one area of translation that will not be taken over by machine translation any time soon, it is transcreation!

COPYWRITING

Alessandra Martelli *is a native Italian freelance translator (from English, German and Spanish) and copywriter working in the industry since 2002. She offers specialized translation, transcreation and copywriting services in the fields of marketing and advertising, tourism, medicine and pharmaceuticals, working for small businesses and international brands alike. Additionally, she serves as a volunteer translator for local charities and non-profits. A conference speaker and professional trainer for the translation industry, Alessandra is also a lifelong learning enthusiast who strongly believes in the value of professional development. She holds a diploma in business studies and foreign languages and a diploma in philosophy, and has completed over 400 hours of specialized training in copywriting, pharmaceutical translation, marketing communication techniques and more.*

IN ITALY, AS IN MANY OTHER COUNTRIES, the profession of translators and language consultants at large is not regulated by law. This means that almost anyone can claim to be a professional translator and start offering their services as such, with no minimum requirements in terms of academic and professional background, skill set or qualifications. As a result, the translation marketplace is bursting with professionals and improvised translators alike. This overwhelming availability has resulted, over time, in a downward trend in translation rates.

Moreover, many translation buyers have only a limited understanding of the peculiarities of translation services. Translation is often seen as a commodity, as 'stuff' they need to get done but which doesn't provide any added value to their business. Given this, price often becomes the only parameter translation buyers take into account when choosing their provider.

To overcome the challenges of such a crowded and messy marketplace, professional translators need to find a way to stand out and build long-time relationships with businesses, companies and organizations. To do this, they usually implement one of two diffcrent strategies: specialization (i.e. gaining a comprehensive insight on a specific field of knowledge) or diversification (i.e. offering complementary or additional services).

Specialization vs. diversification

Both specialization and diversification present specific advantages and possible drawbacks, and can be successfully implemented in a freelance translation business. Before making a decision, however, there are a few aspects to consider.

Skill set and requirements

Specialization often comes as a natural step in a translator's career. As you gain experience, you find out more and more about a specific field of knowledge and learn to understand its technical language and the peculiarities of different document types. However, you still need to get specific training to refine your existing set of skills, or to learn more about some specific aspects of the field of knowledge you specialize in.

Diversification, on the other hand, requires you to create a whole new set of skills to perform new services effectively. As an example, to offer marketing material design services, a translator would need to learn about visual marketing communication techniques and how to use graphic editing programs.

Target market and business identity

Specialization gets the translator from standard choice to premium choice when it comes to their fields of expertise. This allows the professional to go after more desirable direct customers and become 'the expert' for their translation needs.

However, an excess of specialization can result in a smaller customer base of returning customers, thus negatively affecting business in the quieter times of the year. Otherwise, diversification works on the concept that more services mean greater chances of acquiring new customers, or cross-selling different services to existing clients. However, offering a variety of services with no direct connection with one another can result in conveying a 'me too' image to our prospective customers, which could make them doubtful about the quality of our services.

Differentiation in the translation industry

Industry experts have mixed feelings about diversification in the translation industry. Some say it is key, as you cannot live by translation alone. Others say diversification is just a fancy word for 'you're not good enough to live by translation alone'. To me, this is quite the wrong way to look at the matter.

Specializing in a given field of knowledge is already a form of diversification, which over time has become the standard differentiation strategy for professional translators willing to be recognized as such. I know more than a few translators who specialize in one or more fields of expertise and run a successful and healthy freelance business living by translation alone.

Our industry doesn't need diversification per se. However, there always comes a point in time when rules in your submarket change, and you can either adapt or slip down the choice pile. Markets look a lot like savannas – however, humans are keener than other animals to adapt to changing environment and conditions.

To survive in the market, business skills are just as important as translation skills for freelancers. As solopreneurs, we benefit from having more direct contact with our customers compared to larger companies and businesses. Understanding what the customer needs and evaluating if we can provide them with extra help by offering them a more tailored service is one of the healthiest ways to run a business.

In the battle between specialization and diversification, I found my own way in between. I call this virtuous circle continuous re-specialization. Continuous re-specialization is a process based on the concept that an existing set of core skills can successfully be adjusted to fit new requirements and generate new business opportunities. Core skills can apply to several tasks or activities, and often industry-specific activities have a common core skills professionals need to possess.

By analyzing a potential new service according to the skill set needed to perform the task at a professional level, freelancers can successfully identify what they already possess and what they need to study or integrate to succeed in the new activity. As professionals integrate their existing skill set with new knowledge, new combinations are possible, and new combinations mean you might be almost ready to offer a new service you hadn't even thought of in the first place. Ideally, this process can bridge the best of both worlds, as it allows professionals to provide a more qualified service to existing customers whilst attracting new prospects interested in the new service alone.

Copywriting: differentiation as customer service

My first contact with small businesses as direct clients came as something of a shock to me. A lot of small businesses in my area are still family-owned companies with a solid, down-to-earth business mindset which could successfully translate as 'I only work with people I can meet in the flesh' and 'word of mouth is my best friend'.

Bad news: it might take ages for you to gain the trust of a small business owner, as they prefer to work with people they already know or referrals. Good news: once you get into their inner circle, you're in for good. Best news: small business owners love it when you show (not tell) how you can help their company grow.

As a marketing translator and transcreation specialist, I come across every kind of promotional copy, from brochures all the way up to TV ads. Having studied marketing communication techniques it is pretty easy for me to spot whether a promotional text was or wasn't written by a professional. Small businesses often have a limited budget for marketing and promotion, and frequently write their promotional texts in-house. However, not all small business secretaries are copywriting or marketing experts. As I developed long-term relationships with small business owners, they recognized the value of the occasional comments I sent suggesting improvements in the original copy to get better results in the translation as well. Their appreciation became trust, and they started to actively ask for feedback on their copy, even where they didn't need it translated.

By building on the set of skills I had developed as a translator, I gained the trust of customers who were starting to see me as their communication consultant. As a result, they began asking me to write their promotional emails, a brief press release, or their company presentation. The opportunity was there – my customers had a need and I was in a position to offer them a solution. A new stream of income and better customer service: who could ask for anything more?

Leveraging the copywriting skill set

When the time came for me to think of copywriting services as a possible new evolution, the translation side of my freelance business was quite healthy. Over time I had specialized in a few fields of knowledge, combining practical experience and professional development opportunities to widen and refine my translation skills. This had resulted in a small but expanding base of returning customers, including both translation agencies and direct customers, who were now and then joined by occasional translation buyers. Bills were fully paid and work kept me going for more than the average eight hours/five days a week schedule. I was happy with my business results, but willing to take it to the next level – and the next level was copywriting.

Leveraging the copywriting skill set was actually easier than it could have been, as I had invested in professional development throughout my freelance career. Having studied marketing communication techniques on my way to specializing as a marketing translator, I had a comprehensive understanding of the typical challenges and pitfalls in marketing copy. As a transcreation specialist I already knew some tools of the trade (like creative briefs and style guides) and the typical creative project workflow. Classes I took on web writing, writing techniques and composition were a nice bonus. My personal interests in search engine optimization and multi-channel communication also helped.

However, copywriting comes with a peculiarity no translation project can have. In translation and transcreation, you take the customer's voice and messages to a new audience. In copywriting, you craft the customer's voice itself. To do so, you need to build a different relationship with the customer, especially when it comes to small business owners. Larger companies are used to working with PR agencies and freelancers, or have an in-house marketing department which caters for their communication needs. But small businesses are different, and in most cases they just don't think someone else could speak their minds more effectively than they could themselves.

To overcome the challenge, your customers have to trust you will craft their messages in a way that explains why they are different and valuable. They have to see you will not sell them the old 'the best product you could ever get' froth, and they need to know you understand their vision, needs and goals. Therefore, developing your ability to spot the customer's hidden needs is just as important as learning how to write sponsored blog posts or case studies.

A new marketing strategy

One of the main challenges I faced as soon as copywriting services were on the menu was that I actually needed a different marketing strategy to achieve an adequate level of recognition amongst prospective customers. As I decided to keep my MTM Translations website domain as a one-stop reference point for customers willing to work with me, I needed to leverage my marketing tools to this new version of my business.

This led me to a massively redesign my website, and to rethink my content marketing strategy to include copywriting and business writing in my discussed topics. I also had to rebalance my social media activities accordingly, and rethink all my marketing materials. As a result, I now spend around 10 hours a week on marketing and promotion activities, using different channels to reach translation buyers and copywriting buyers.

In addition, I had to think of a new headline that could sum up all the different sides of my business. A translation-related headline was no longer enough to encompass it all. Also, I wanted something that would work effectively in both English and Italian, as I wanted my non-English speaking local prospects to get the right message. After more than a few sleepless nights and hundreds of embarrassing options, I finally came up with something that captures the essence of what I've always wanted to be and finally have become.

Present and future

Looking back at it all, I can see that my first 10 years in the translation industry have been a continuous process of education, evolution and re-specialization. As a result, my business has grown, return customers have increased and new customers are added every year. Over time, I moved from translating single documents to providing one-stop business and marketing communication solutions. Differentiating and continuously re-specializing gave me the opportunity to expand my knowledge in the fields I was interested in, and to successfully integrate them into my business.

A few years later, copywriting has become more and more important as a source of income for my business. My offering attracts translation and copywriting buyers alike, and I recently included web writing training in my activities as professional trainer for the language industry. I would have never envisioned this back when I started out as a freelance translator, but somehow embracing the differentiation and re-specialization concepts unlocked my entrepreneurial spirit and let me build the future I wanted for my business. It helped me to adapt to the changes in my industry and keeps me looking for new challenges and opportunities.

CROSS-CULTURAL CONSULTING

Tea C. Dietterich is CEO of 2M Language Services and a NAATI Advanced Translator and Conference Interpreter in her own right. Through her firm 2M, Tea is in charge of providing translations of publication quality into 155+ languages. Further services include foreign language typesetting and desktop publishing, multilingual publications, website and software localization, apps, multilingual voice-overs, dubbing and subtitling. 2M also provides cross-cultural training and simultaneous conference interpreting for international events. Tea is a board member of ABIE France (Australian Business in Europe) and President of the Australasian Association of Language Companies (AALC Inc). A former chairperson of AUSIT QLD (Australian Institute of Interpreters and Translators), she still sits on the AUSIT QLD committee. She is a member of the NAATI RAC (Regional Advisory Council), as well as an active member of the Australian Export Council (AEC/AIEX), the Australian China Business Council (ACBC) and prime international industry organizations GALA (Globalization and Localization Association) and ELIA (European Language Industry Association). Tea is based both in Brisbane (2M Head Office) and in Paris (2M Europe Office) and is a regular guest speaker and conference delegate at translating and interpreting and export industry events.

FORMER GERMAN CHANCELLOR Willy Brandt once famously said: 'If I am selling to you, I speak your language. If I'm buying from you, dann müssen Sie schon Deutsch sprechen'.

I understood from the beginning that my love for languages and translation not only needed to feed my family but cater for my insatiable travel passion and provide me with financial freedom and a high quality of life. For this I need clients who are willing to buy my translation services and for this I need to 'hang around where my clients hang around'. This mantra has served me well from my freelance days to my current life in the corporate world.

Anyone who sells to foreign markets is a potential client for me and you, my translator colleague, and we need to reach them in any way possible. I started to infiltrate the export industry and international trade industry through chambers of commerce, international trade and industry associations and local exporter clubs. Later on I continued this through pertinent groups on professional social media networks. It's not easy to sell translation services, but using Willy Brandt's famous quote hits home in export circles, so don't forget to speak the language of your target audience to ensure they can relate to what you are saying.

It's not easy to sell translation services, because often there is a lack of understanding about our industry, about what is involved and what knowledge of the target audience, the translation project, the target language, and the source language is necessary in the first place. I discovered that clients often thought a mere conversion was required, so I found myself educating the client first. Many things we – language and cultural experts – take for granted are not clear to our potential clients. Don't assume anything. I often had to start with the basics about cross-cultural deliberations, linguistic implications and what can happen if you don't get the right message across.

And there it was – my diversification was something I had been doing anyway, which made sense and was a means to sell my ultimate product. Translations morphed into a new product to sell because it was in demand and necessary.

As a linguistic or cross-cultural consultant, I positioned myself as an expert, assisted clients with questions they had, gave talks and presentations where needed, and started to catch the attention of not only new potential clients who would ultimately buy my translation services but those who were willing to buy consultancy services from me in the first place.

This can start with very basic information, but the effect can be enormous. Just watch my interview on Sky News business channel, on the Business Class programme, where TV anchor Bridie Barry interviewed me on 'Doing business in Europe'. Any European in cross-cultural circles will immediately hear this is not rocket science I am telling the audience, but that's not the point. Who is the target audience? Australians who want to travel to Europe in this case, and for most of them this basic information was news!

Of course I will modify my message depending on the sophistication of my audience and the type of event. As an example, the following points are not new, but for many of our clients they are.

Understand the culture

To make sure your message is sensitive to the country's culture, have your English source material checked for appropriateness first. Failure to understand cultural differences can bear serious consequences, and whole campaigns have been pulled due to lack of research into cultural awareness. Last minute redesign and reprinting is not only costly but can be very stressful, so make sure that images and text are culturally appropriate first, before the translation process occurs.

Check to make sure the colours you are using are appropriate for the country. For example, blue is a popular colour associated with the sky and nature. But in Iran, blue is the colour of mourning, and in many countries it is a colour associated with authority and discipline. Green is a very positive colour, associated with good health and life in many parts of the world. In China, green is thought to repel evil, and in the Muslim world it is linked to spirituality, religion and God.

It may seem obvious, but ensure your product names do not sound offensive in another language or another culture. You may remember when Mitsubishi had to rename the Pajero for the Spanish and Latin American market, or Ford their Mist car for the German market. Body parts also play different roles in different countries. A film poster with a man sitting on top of a Buddha statue caused problems in Thailand where most people are Buddhists and the head is the most sacred part of your body.

Pick the dialect of your target market

Does your target market speak US, UK or Australian English? South American or European Spanish? North African or Gulf Arabic? Also consider whether you might want English for non-English mother-tongue readers. When forming your messaging, be specific and be sure to put yourself in the shoes of your target market. The more you can relate to your audience with language that resonates with them, the more easily you will be able to expand into the new market.

Use business cards to your advantage

Companies often spend thousands of dollars to have their websites and materials right, but relegate designing and preparing their international business cards to the local copy shop. When expanding into international markets, it is important to make a good first impression. The right business cards are amongst the most powerful means of communication to use.

One of the most important considerations for an international business card is the title, as this will define organizational rank. Foreign businesses and organizations want to assign people of the same rank to deal with you. In Japan, the business card is of paramount importance, with the handing out and receiving done in a ritualistic fashion.

The names of the person and the company must be transliterated as a guide to pronunciation, and middle initials are often eliminated for simplicity. However, some countries do not adapt English-like spelling in names, for reasons of readability. For example, Czechs expect women's names to end with –ova. Sharon Stone is known as 'Sharon Stoneová' and Nicole Kidman as 'Nicole Kidmanová'.

Be sure to arrange numbers in the country's format. Europeans are used to phone numbers running together, whereas in Australia we separate the area code and then group four digits together.

These are just some examples of cross-cultural and linguistic consultancy, which today is a high demand service you can sell or use as a foot in the door to sell your ultimate product and passion, which is, after all, translation.

For me, the diversification to language consultant not only provided an additional income stream and attracted another target market that eventually also partly became translation clients, but it also added another layer of excitement to my business activities. I discovered that I not only enjoyed presenting and consulting but I even seemed to be good at it. It was a welcome alternative to get out and exchange energy with people, when my usual translation or project management activities were often rather solitary.

So give things a go; just try them out and see if you enjoy them. Languages are your passion after all, and finding the right language to share your passion with your target audience can not only contribute to your income and open up new markets for you but be fulfilling as well. Nelson Mandela said, 'If you talk to a man in a language he understands, that goes to his head. If you talk to him in his language, that goes to his heart'.

Interview with Clare Gallagher

Clare Gallagher runs Vivid Meaning, a language and cultural consultancy based in London. Clare holds a BA in International Marketing, and was awarded distinction upon completing an MA in Translation and Interpreting Studies. She specializes in the translation of promotional texts and transcreation from German and Spanish into English. Clare has carried out a highly successful piece of research about how the quality of company website translation affects how potential consumers perceive the company and its products or services. Having spent almost five years living and working in Germany, she has in-depth knowledge of German business culture. She uses her linguistic and cultural expertise to consult clients on a range of language and cultural issues involved in the internationalization process. Clare also has over 10 years of experience working as a trainer and in management in the field of specialized language training and cross-cultural communication.

1) Clare, you are a German and Spanish to English freelance translator and cross-cultural consultant. What motivated you to add cross-cultural consulting to your service portfolio, and what is it all about?

I have always enjoyed a varied career and see myself more as a language and cross-cultural specialist than a translator alone. I enjoy working closely with people and have been a language and cross-cultural trainer for many years. Cross-cultural consulting goes hand-in-hand with my choice to specialize in the translation of promotional texts and transcreation. It is essential the client understands how best to promote their product to an English-speaking market and I like to have a hands-on approach to helping clients. My marketing background helps here, as does my research dissertation on the translation of websites.

On top of that, working as a specialized English language trainer for professionals and director of studies at a language school in Germany gave me a great deal of exposure to German business culture. My company, Vivid Meaning, uses this knowledge and expertise to assist UK companies to be more successful when doing business in Germany. Through workshops and one-to-one consulting sessions, clients are made aware of potential areas of differences in how both nations do business, which aids communication and negotiation, essentially resulting in a better business relationship.

2) What impact has cross-cultural consulting had on your translation business, and does the income you generate from this service reflect the time and effort invested?
Having this extra element makes my work more creative and rewarding. I'm a social creature and consulting involves more people contact than translation. Also, clients can see how the cross-cultural aspect has a direct impact on sales and profit in terms of both marketing and helping them to understand German business culture better. I am currently marketing these services and working on client acquisition, so the balance between time and effort invested and income generated is not where I'd like it to be yet. There's a workshop scheduled for the autumn, so I'm on the way to the balance tipping in my favour!

3) Do you enjoy this diversification from the translation career you originally embarked on, or do you find it challenging?
It is challenging, but I also find it exciting. I feel it makes my career more well-rounded and satisfying. I always intended having a diverse career in the language industry and enjoy being that step closer to my clients and their business.

4) What skills and/or qualifications do freelance translators need who are thinking of expanding into this field?

As linguists and translators I believe we all possess cross-cultural expertise and our clients often benefit from this knowledge and expertise. For certain specializations, developing the cross-cultural element further makes sense. There is a range of training courses in cross-cultural consulting out there that may suit some translators. Alternatively, perhaps they have gained expertise in this area during their career that they can further build on.

5) Where do you see freelance translators in five years' time in terms of diversification?

I imagine many translators will keep translation as their main income source and will hopefully be quite happy and successful with that. Specialization will be more important than ever, however. The industry does seem to be changing quite rapidly, and it would be wise for translators to consider potential areas of diversification that can help them remain competitive and be more comfortable financially. I see combining translation with other areas of interest and expertise becoming more and more common to differentiate ourselves from one another. Collaborating with other small businesses whose services complement yours, e.g. a web design business, is another way for translators to stay afloat in an industry sadly dominated by agencies and a downward pressure on rates.

Thank you for the interview, Nicole, and best of luck with your diversification endeavours, translators!

LINGUISTIC VALIDATION

Nora Torres is an English-Spanish translator, localizer, proofreader, quality manager and cognitive debriefer. She holds a BA in translation with a major in law from the University of Buenos Aires, and has been in the translation industry for over 30 years now. Initially an in-house translator for the largest publicly-held bank in Argentina and a classroom-based and distance-education teacher of English for international trade, she became a freelance translator in 1992. Nora was Vice-President of FairTradeNet (FTN), a worldwide, Geneva-based association of freelance translators and, as such, was part of the delegation representing the Association at the World Summit on the Information Society (WSIS) in December 2003. Nora's involvement in FTN opened up new career paths for her. She became a certified life sciences linguist in 2007 and is currently co-owner of trans-l'artisan, a translation studio specializing in biomedical translation under the motto of 'Traditional values enabled by cutting-edge technology'. Since the mid 2000s, she has diversified her business into the various steps of linguistic validation, and plans to become a full-time in-country investigator in a few years' time.

THIS ARTICLE IS INTENDED TO show how diversifying into linguistic validation has helped me widen and deepen my range of translation-related services, secure an additional source of income and open up new possibilities for my future career path.

My career started in the early 1980s and was greatly influenced by the tremendous technology advancements that took place in the following years, and by transformational political and economic developments adversely affecting my home country, Argentina.

The way I work today has little to do with the basics I learnt during my university years, or with how I worked in the first years after graduating. The metamorphosing ability acquired along the way has enabled me to cope with the deep changes reshaping the translation industry in the recent past and will hopefully help me deal with the changes expected to occur in the foreseeable future.

Working as a staff translator: the old way

As soon as I received my BA in translation with a major in law from the University of Buenos Aires, I got a job as a staff translator at the translation department of the major public bank in Argentina. We worked the old-fashioned way – face to face, in groups of three or four. There were no computers, no Internet, no CAT tools, no translation memories, and no desktop publishing resources either. Just plain, ordinary typewriters.

There was an extraordinary collection of dictionaries in the office, and every now and then we would cross the sadly famous Plaza de Mayo Square to browse the fantastic library hosted by the ministry of economy, or we would walk 10 blocks down Florida Street and treat ourselves to a couple of hours at the wonderful, now gone, US Lincoln Library.

The following years witnessed such formidable breakthroughs as the arrival of word processors (stand alone office machines combining keyboard text entry and printing functions) which were shared by several offices, and some time later, computer terminals at each desk. I had a steep learning curve to climb, and I loved it.

In addition to acquiring word-processing and computer knowledge, I developed a thorough comprehension of financial and economic subjects and terminology (especially in the field of international trade), also gaining proofreading, quality management, and glossary compiling experience.

Entering the freelance world

In 1991, after landing a few large translation projects from corporate clients, I felt ready to go freelance, relying on the experience I had built during my 12 years of employment. I divided my time and attention between translating and teaching. I managed to:

- create a small but strong portfolio of direct clients, all domestic banks and corporations; and
- begin teaching English for International Trade at the Argentine Chamber of Commerce and other local trade organizations. Over time, I wrote an extensive, thorough handbook for use in

my classes, and eventually developed a nationwide distance-learning programme.

Getting a foothold abroad

Everything went like clockwork until 2001, when a deep economic crisis hit Argentina, after a few years of severe recession. All bank accounts were frozen, and most banks and companies went bankrupt or reduced their expense bill to a minimum. My client portfolio vanished into thin air.

I did not despair. With lots of time available, and a newly-installed Internet connection at home, I soon discovered there was another world out there – translators from around the world clustering together around portals such as ProZ.com and translatorscafe.com. I signed up for several of them and started interacting, uploading my résumé, searching for jobs, submitting quotes and attending local Powwows.

That same year, I got to know about an ambitious project, FairTradeNet, a not-for-profit association based in Geneva, Switzerland, whose mission was to promote and advance the work of freelance translators and other professionals on the web, at fair rates. From the very beginning, this helped me get a firm foothold in the international arena. I came to see things from a different viewpoint and understand that even if I appeared to be over-qualified in the local market, going international required a whole new set of skills.

After a succession of trials and errors that lasted for a few months, I finally got my résumé properly drafted, an effective and appealing cover letter written and my rates well adjusted to the international market. I acquired new computer equipment, learnt how to use two CAT tools and other software and secured my first client abroad in late 2001. Very soon, I found myself working for some major agencies in the United States, Canada and Europe.

For the next few years, I had a steady workflow that consisted mainly of translation and proofreading assignments, mostly finance-related, from translation agencies in the United States, Spain and France, and proofreading and editing jobs for an online editing and proofreading company from Ontario, Canada. Also, after working for a couple of years on a pro bono basis for FairTradeNet, I became Vice President and HR Manager of the Association in 2003, and in this capacity I attended the Worldwide Summit of the Information Society (WSIS) held in Geneva in December that year.

Linguistic validation, a promising turn in my career's long, winding road

In the mid-2000s, I had my first encounter with linguistic validation when the life sciences department of one of the agencies I was working with invited me to take part in a long-term project involving the translation of patient questionnaires for use in clinical research trials in a number of countries globally.

Since then, I have participated in a myriad of linguistic validation projects, at all stages of the process, from plain translation to cognitive debriefing interviews, and the provision of a final deliverable. With time, this has proved to be a great opportunity to diversify my service offering.

What is the aim of linguistic validation?

The aim of the entire process is 'to achieve different language versions of an English instrument that are conceptually equivalent in each of the target countries/cultures. That is, the instrument should be equally natural and acceptable and should practically perform in the same way. The focus is on cross-cultural and conceptual, rather than on linguistic/literal equivalence'.

What is the present status of linguistic validation as part of the language industry?

The need for translation and adaptation of 'clinical outcome assessment' (COA) instruments for use in foreign languages has grown rapidly due to the increase in the internationalization of clinical trials of investigational drugs.

What kinds of instruments are usually subject to linguistic validation?

The expression 'clinical outcome assessments' usually refers to patient-reported outcomes (PROs), clinician-reported outcomes (ClinROs), observer reported outcomes (ObsROs), and quality of life (QoL) questionnaires.

These are called 'instruments' and include instructions, items (also known as questions) and response categories or response choices to those items/questions'.

What are the steps in a typical linguistic validation process?
The typical steps in the process are as follows:

1. **Forward (front) translation.** Two independent linguists render separate translations of the source material into the target language. For linguistic validation purposes, a forward translation should not be a literal translation of the original instrument, but one that is conceptually equivalent to the original and culturally acceptable in the country in which the translation will be used.
2. **Forward translation reconciliation.** The two forward translations are compared and reconciled into one version that combines the best of both. The reconciled version should be conceptually equivalent to the source.
3. **Backward (back) translation.** The primary purpose of a backward translation is to provide a quality-control step showing that the quality of the forward translation is such that the same meaning can be derived when the translated text is moved back into the source language.
4. **Backward translation reconciliation.** The backward translation is thoroughly checked against the instrument in the source language to identify any misunderstanding of concepts, or any mistranslations or inaccuracies in the forward translation. This often results in adjustments being made to the original forward translation.
5. **Cognitive debriefing (pilot testing or pre-testing).** At this stage of the linguistic validation process, the translation is tested (validated) in the target locations 'to determine how

intuitive, understandable, and relevant the items (questions) of the instruments are to patients".[1]

Finding appropriate respondents and getting their consent to be interviewed can be a challenging task for a linguist new to this process. A specific number of qualified respondents per target country and language, of various ages, occupations, and levels of education, needs to be identified. Most importantly, respondents need to have or have had the condition that is the subject of the instrument being tested.

A linguist working on this type of projects (usually called an in-country investigator) needs to use one or more recruiting methods, which may include: (i) setting up a network of physicians, nurses, and/or hospitals; (ii) placing recruiting advertisements in the media; (iii) placing posters and flyers in public spaces, businesses, universities; (iv) using Internet search engines to look for related forums and support groups; and (v) using social media.

Once an appropriate group of respondents has been identified, individual interviews are scheduled and conducted. During an interview, the respondent is first asked to answer the instrument (e.g. a patient questionnaire), and then the interviewer and the respondent go over the instrument together, item by item, in order to spot any terms or expressions that might be unclear, difficult to understand, or even offensive to the target audience.

6. **Cognitive debriefing analysis.** Upon completion of all interviews and once cognitive debriefing grids have been filled out with the information arising from such interviews, another linguist must analyze the findings and determine whether the instrument actually needs any adjustments.

At this stage, decisions to make changes to the instrument

---

[1] Cleeland, C. S. The M. D. Anderson Symptom Inventory User Guide (Last updated: October 4, 2010). http://www.mdanderson.org/education-and-research/departments-programmes-and-labs/departments-and-divisions/symptom-research/symptom-assessment-tools/MDASI_userguide.pdf. Retrieved 19.07.2013.

need to be carefully weighed and should be kept to a minimum. However, any changes introduced at this point are usually sound and relevant, as they are the result of field-testing the translation, a luxury not many texts can afford.
7. **Clinician review.** There may still be another step that consists of the linguist finding a local clinician specializing in the condition at stake who will make sure that technical terms and concepts have been accurately rendered in the target language, and that the instrument will be easily understandable for patients in the target country. The recruitment of clinicians for this stage of the process is often done using the same healthcare provider network established for the recruitment of respondents for cognitive debriefing interviews.
8. **Medical review analysis.** After the clinician has provided comments and suggested changes, if any, it is the linguist's role to express his/her opinion on whether or not such changes are objective adjustments that will improve the translation.

In general, however, the translation company's quality manager ultimately decides on these changes, usually working in direct collaboration with someone from the client's staff.

How many linguists does a linguistic validation project involve?

As you can see from the descriptions above, linguistic validation is a labour-intensive undertaking: at least eight linguists will be required per target country.

Step of the process	Linguists involved
Forward translation	2 front-translators
Forward translation reconciliation	1 proofreader + 1 quality manager
Backward translation	1 back-translator
Backward translation reconciliation	1 quality manager*
Cognitive debriefing	1 in-country investigator
Cognitive debriefing analysis	1 qualified linguist** + 1 quality manager*
Medical review analysis	1 qualified linguist** + 1 quality manager*

* May be the same linguist   ** May be the same linguist

Does linguistic validation require any special knowledge and/or skills?

Linguistic validation is definitely not for beginners or amateurs. All stages of the process call for mature, knowledgeable professionals, who will have the inner and outer resources needed to provide an outstanding service.

In my case, after 20+ years of experience, I was familiar with some aspects of these projects, but others were entirely new to me, and I had to prepare myself in order to step up to the challenge. I had been working on backward translations for a few years, and in order to improve my English writing skills I had studied for and obtained a Certificate of Proficiency in English (with an 'A' grade) from the University of Cambridge in 1993. However, I felt I needed to acquire content-specific knowledge and skills.

In 2007, I was certified as a life sciences linguist for translation of English into Spanish by the first translation agency for which I had worked on linguistic validation assignments. This certification covered informed consent forms, clinical research protocols, health questionnaires, health insurance forms and patient brochures.

In 2009, I took a clinical research training course with the National Institutes of Health, Office of Clinical Research Training and Medical Education. This gave me an overall understanding of how clinical trials work and helped me to see the whole process from a more solid perspective.

In 2010, I became a full member of TREMEDICA, an international association of medical translators and writers, which gave me access to an extraordinarily rich pool of resources.

In addition, as part of these ongoing training efforts, I have signed up for a six-week course on clinical terminology for international students, which is due to begin in November 2013.

Conclusion

Many linguists and non-linguists see machine translation, crowd translation and cheap ('peanut') translation as ominous threats looming over freelance translators. This does not need to be the case; the answer lies in specializing and diversifying. Linguistic validation is just one of the fields in which a well-established linguist can explore new possibilities.

Currently aged 53, I am not far from my old age, and I plan to become a full time in-country investigator. This would mean working fewer hours at my computer/desk, having more frequent contact with other people and being left with more time to take care of my garden.

There are many other diversification options out there; just open your mind and heart to them, and fear not the future.

ONLINE LANGUAGE TEACHING

Vanda Nissen *is a native Russian speaker with a BEd (Hons) Major in Russian and Russian Literature. She also has a PhD in Applied Linguistics from Voronezh State University (Russia) and has taught Russian as a foreign language to students of all ages. She is the author of a textbook on Russian speech etiquette. Vanda is a registered high school teacher in South Australia and currently teaches Russian at Year 12 and International Baccalaureate levels, and at the University of Adelaide. She brings strong knowledge and understanding of, and experience in, online language learning. Apart from Russian and English, Vanda speaks Danish, Swedish and Polish. She is a NAATI accredited English-Russian translator (professional level), and she also works with Scandinavian languages and Polish. Vanda can be reached at info@kaskelot.eu.*

WHEN NICOLE ADAMS ASKED ME to write an article on online teaching, I thought that it would be a great opportunity to share my experience as an online language teacher. Our rapidly changing world requires diversity of skills, and I advise you to diversify and not put all your eggs in one basket. Online language teaching is one of the available 'baskets' for translators, especially for those who, like me, also have teaching qualifications. Teaching languages online is becoming more and more popular due to its effectiveness, lower cost and use of new technologies.

My first online lesson took place in 2005. Back then I had not even been aware of online teaching. One day I saw a job posting on ProZ.com – a UK-based company was looking for experienced language teachers with some basic IT knowledge. The posting sparked my interest because I wanted to find a way to combine translation and teaching. The company was offering customized online language lessons aimed at business people. In my case most of the students were people who had business interests in Russia and Russian-speaking countries. Later on, the company got some private schools on board, and I received two groups of schoolchildren. Adult learners and children have, of course, different aims, and thus require different teaching approaches, but from the technological point of view the structure of the lesson was the same: a virtual classroom with a whiteboard, and the facility to upload PowerPoint presentations and Word documents, highlight and erase. The school used both commercial software (virtual classroom facilities) and freeware (Skype). At that time Skype was a new concept, and it had its drawbacks, mostly due to the poor sound quality.

The second school I worked for had been applying more or less the same principles: their own classroom and Skype/landline/mobile calls. Their target groups were different: businessmen, employees of international organizations, travellers and students. They all had one thing in common – a lack of time. That is why teachers were required to update their availability on a daily basis. The company had been offering lessons at short notice (making it rather inconvenient for the teachers) with the possibility of booking lessons six hours in advance.

After we moved to Australia from Scandinavia, where we had lived for nearly six years, this became too time consuming. The other reason I decided to stop was the time difference with Europe and the USA, where my most of students came from. However, teaching for these schools was definitely a valuable experience, not only because it was an extra source of income but also because it has helped to widen my horizons. I still offer online lessons, but rather irregularly, because I also teach Russian at the University of Adelaide and Russian at International Baccalaureate level.

Key competencies of an online language tutor

Online teaching offers more opportunities for students and tutors than traditional classrooms. Most online schools offer one-to-one tuition, small- to medium-sized groups, intensive courses, and kids' language clubs. You can choose how many hours you want to teach and set your availability. It is very convenient, especially for those freelance translators who are often fully booked.

Teaching language online requires different skills from the ones used in face-to-face classrooms. I am going to discuss the key competencies of an online language tutor and you will find that translators with a teaching background have certain advantages compared to traditional language tutors.

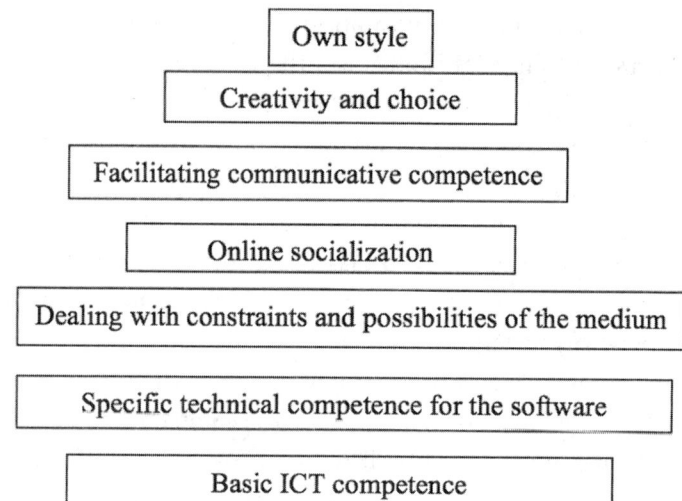

Figure 3.3: Skills pyramid (Hampel and Stickler, 2005)

1. As you can see from Figure 3.3 above (bottom line), the first level of skills for an online tutor relates to ICT competence. This includes the ability to deal with the computer equipment (keyboard, mouse, headsets) and familiarity with Internet browsers, plug-ins, etc. This competency is a prerequisite for a successful career in translation, too, so translators already have some advantages there.
2. The second level of skills requires understanding and knowledge of specific software applications for teaching languages online. These applications may include freeware and open-source (Yahoo Messenger, Skype) and commercial software, or a combination of the above. From my experience, online language schools often create their own virtual classrooms, and teachers should familiarize themselves with communication tools such as electronic whiteboards, chat rooms and electronic mailing lists to support the students' learning through computer technologies. On top of this, online teachers need to know about other applications, from applications that specifically facilitate CALL activities to course management applications.

3. It is not enough just to familiarize yourself with a particular application – a successful language tutor has to understand the constraints and possibilities of the medium (third level). Skype, for example, is a great tool for online teaching with the possibility of approximating real life experience, but it requires a fast Internet connection (and back in 2005 this was a big problem because only a few countries could offer fast Internet connection at that time). Poor Internet connection will significantly limit task design. This is a constraint.

On the other hand, Skype offers a lot of possibilities for online language teaching. Using the basic messaging function, the student develops writing and reading skills, while audio and video functions help with listening and speaking skills. One of the major difficulties for second language learners is learning to communicate fluently with native speakers of the language. Regular classroom students are more limited in their opportunities than web-based students. Skype (and other similar software) allows students to communicate with native speakers and gain insight into the target language's slang and cultural aspects. As I mentioned earlier, Skype is a way of communicating in real time. Unlike writing emails, instant messaging reflects a student's skills in using the language being learnt 'right here, right now'. It allows the teacher to constantly assess the student's ability to manage in real situations.

I would recommend always checking sound and video quality prior to your lessons. Sound quality is a crucial element in online teaching. Telephone interpreters know from experience how poor sound can interfere with successful communication. Another tip is to prepare PowerPoint presentations. In my opinion, this is the best format for online language learning. You can use them with virtual classrooms, Skype and Yahoo.

4. The fourth level of skills, online socialization, requires establishing relationships between the tutor and the students. Due to the limitations of online learning, students often need more encouragement; miscommunication can lead to tension.

Interpreters are familiar with the socialization requirement – in certain settings (e.g. hospitals, police stations) successful interpreting is not possible without established relationships between the parties involved.

5. The fifth level of skills is represented by the teacher's role in facilitating the communication process between all participants in the classroom, in our case the virtual classroom. It involves a number of strategies.

6. Creativity and choice present the sixth level for online language teachers. Creativity is associated not only with the design of tasks and materials but 'also with finding new uses for online tools' (Compton, 2009, p.8). Here, again, translators have certain advantages because we are used to dealing with different online tools and are often much more proficient than typical computer users.

7. The last level is about developing your own style. It requires the online teacher to master all the previous levels of skills. Even experienced language teachers may find it difficult to adjust their teaching style to a new, virtual reality. A good example is the lack of non-verbal means of communication. Before I started teaching online, I could not have imagined how important facial expressions and gestures could be. Teachers subconsciously note and analyze acts of non-verbal communication and react in accordance with them. It took me a while to figure out how I could deal with this lack of non-verbal cues. In my case, I encourage students to verbalize their feelings and I pay extra attention to markers such as intonation and tempo changes.

Another example is moments of silence. While in normal classrooms teachers can easily see whether the reason for silence is that students are engaged with an educational activity such as reading or writing, or whether it is that they are struggling with a task, moments of silence during online lessons can mean anything from problems with the Internet connection to a student's unwillingness to answer. These are only a few examples; the list is endless, as is your ability to develop your own style.

Since this article is just a short review of the most obvious skills and competencies required to become an online language teacher, I have tried to highlight situations common to both translation and language teaching online. I encourage you to try teaching online as one possible way to diversify.

Bibliography

Coburn, J. (2010). Teaching oral English online – Through Skype (VOIP). In *Acta Didactica Norge,* vol. 4, #1, art.1.

Colpaert, J. (2006). Pedagogy-driven design for online language teaching and learning. In *CALICO Journal,* 23(3), pp. 477-497.

Compton, L. (2009). Preparing language teachers to teach language online: A look at skills, roles and responsibilities. In *Computer Assisted Language Learning,* 22(1), pp. 73-99.

Hampel, R., Stickler, U. (2005). New skills for new classrooms: Training tutors to teach languages online. In *Computer Assisted Language Learning,* 18 (4), pp. 311-326.

McHugh, C. (2010). Classroom facilitated tandem language learning through web based video conferencing (Skype) to augment fluent conversation and student motivation. Position paper.

Russel, V., Curtis, W. (2012). Comparing a large- and small-scale online language course: An examination of teacher and learner perceptions. In *Internet and Higher Education,* 16 (2013), pp. 1-13.

Stickler, U. (2011). The DOTS project: Developing online teaching skills. In *Language Teaching,* 44, pp. 403-444.

Interview with Laura Ball

Laura Ball is a translator and language trainer working in German and English. She holds a first class degree in German and linguistics from Oxford University and a research master's degree in Mediaeval German from Newcastle University. Her professional qualifications include the Diploma in Translation awarded by the Chartered Institute of Linguists and a TEFL certificate from Cambridge University. She spent three years living in Germany, where she studied philosophy and musicology in Tübingen, worked as a language assistant in Halle/Saale and taught English and German as a business language trainer in Essen. Now based in Newcastle upon Tyne, UK, she offers language training services both in person and online via Skype.

1) Laura, you are a German to English freelance translator who also provides online language learning courses. What motivated you to add language teaching to your service portfolio, and what are your experiences with this activity?

I have always done bits and pieces of language teaching since qualifying as a TEFL teacher in 2008. Even before then I had worked as a language assistant at Der Lernladen in Germany and helped out at several summer schools. In 2008, I moved to Germany and taught English and German full-time through a company called EasyEnglish. During my master's year in 2009, I did some private teaching of German, English and even Latin. When I became self-employed, it seemed only natural to continue offering language training services in addition to translation. Knowing that working from home can become very isolating, I also saw language training as a way of allowing me to meet new people, to focus on something other than myself and, quite simply, to get out of the house once or twice a week. To begin with I taught private individuals and business classes at some of the companies in the business parks. It was all face-to-face, with nothing online at all.

However, having worked in both Germany and the UK, I felt there was generally more of a demand for the type of language lessons that I provide in Germany. The problem was how to supply that demand whilst living in the UK. Like many people, I use Skype to keep in touch with friends and family in different countries, so I asked myself, why not use it for language lessons as well? The first opportunity to test this approach came when one of my students relocated to Germany but wanted to carry on lessons with me. We agreed to continue meeting at the same time each week, but via Skype rather than face-to-face. Since then, I have had a few opportunities (although not as many as I would have liked) to refine the process of teaching online. As I use a lot of open-source material from the Internet, instead of giving my students a copy of the exercises to complete, I direct them to the relevant site online so they can download it for themselves. I also send them Word documents via the 'send file' function instead of printing out and handing them a hard copy. I use the chat function to guide my students to the relevant pages and exercises in the course book – both student and teacher each need their own copy – and I ask them to talk me through their answers rather than handing me the book for marking. Occasionally, using the 'share screen' function can be very useful to illustrate certain points more clearly.

In my experience, online teaching offers several advantages over traditional lessons. The main one is that using Skype necessitates much more communication, automatically giving the students a chance to practise their skills in a way they wouldn't otherwise be able to. Secondly, there is no need to travel to the lesson or hunt for a room to teach in. Finally, because the students access the resources themselves instead of being given handouts, they soon reach a position where they have all they need to continue learning independently. Paradoxically, this is actually the ideal outcome of any language course, as it means that the student is enabled to continue learning their whole life long and to adapt their skills to other situations as well. One potentially problematic feature of online teaching, on the other hand, is the Internet connection. It is important that both student and teacher have a good Internet connection, as video conferencing is vital, and when you only have a one-hour lesson, the connection must remain perfect for that hour or the student is effectively paying for nothing and everyone's time is wasted.

2) What impact has online language teaching had on your translation business, and does the income you generate from this service reflect the time and effort invested?
Teaching German and English online has certainly widened my client base when it comes to translation. Not only does it provide me with personal contacts

at the companies I teach at, which puts me at an advantage if they ever need a translator or if I am looking for new clients, but it also means that I am more likely to be recommended as a translator. In my experience at least, word-of-mouth has played a greater role in language training than in translation. Language students are far more likely to recommend me for translation than are translation clients. It is also more usual – perhaps because of the interactive nature of language training – that one of my students will later ask for a translation than it is for a translation client to then ask for language lessons.

Another, perhaps more subtle, impact of language training is the effect it has on my overall linguistic ability. When planning lessons and teaching, I tend to refer to my grammar books and university notes far more often than I do when translating. As a result, my language skills are much more finely honed than they would be if I were a pure translator, and this helps me to translate even more accurately and efficiently. Online teaching is also a refreshing change from translation, as it uses my brain in a different way. This helps me to maintain my interest in translation and the motivation to keep going, particularly on those dull days when nothing seems to go right.

In terms of the income generated by this service, it is probably somewhere around the middle of the scale. Unlike face-to-face teaching, there is no need to factor in travel time and costs for the lessons, so that represents a saving for both me and my students. My experience with Skype has so far only been with one-to-one lessons, and I take care to tailor the courses and lessons specifically to my students' requests and needs. This means that I sometimes spend an inordinate amount of time and thought planning each lesson, so when I add up the final charge for the lesson divided by the total number of hours spent teaching and planning, the overall hourly rate can come out as disappointingly low. This is certainly something to think about in the future.

3) Do you enjoy this diversification from the translation career you originally embarked on, or do you find it challenging?
Having always blended language training with translation work, I appreciate the diversity it offers. I value the contact with people that it brings, the different skills it requires, the fact that I can use my love of grammar directly and the thrill

of trying out something that is often innovative for my students. There is also an exhilarating sense of power in being able to carry out a variety of different jobs from a single computer, potentially from any location in the world!

The challenge lies in mixing language training, with the preparation it involves, with translation work. Both activities are time-consuming occupations that involve juggling several different deadlines at once. I find that blocking lessons together can relieve some of this time pressure. For example, teaching three or four lessons one after another is much easier to manage than teaching the same three or four lessons spread out over a week. At the moment, I teach on Thursdays and Fridays only, with either Friday afternoons or Mondays blocked out for preparation. This makes it much easier to decide whether to accept or turn down translation work and how to fit everything in. By way of contrast, just a few months ago I agreed to teach a series of English lessons which meant I was teaching on Wednesday evenings, Thursday afternoons and Saturday mornings. Finding time to plan lessons, complete translation work and relax in between the classes was exhausting in itself and I am much happier now I have re-arranged my classes.

4) What skills and/or qualifications do freelance translators need who are thinking of expanding into this field?
My top recommendation would be to go on a TEFL course, ideally a CELTA (Certificate in Teaching English to Speakers of Other Languages) course as these are run in association with Cambridge University and enjoy worldwide accreditation. They can be more expensive than other courses, but are certainly worth it in my view. Although the focus is on teaching English, the course covers general teaching techniques, planning skills, classroom management and much more, all of which can be applied to other languages. For German, the DAAD (Deutsche Akademische Austauschdienst) offers teacher training and there are numerous other DAF (Deutsch als Fremdsprache) providers, too.

Secondly, nothing can beat practical experience. Anyone who has already spent some time working as a language assistant as part of their foreign language degree will already have some idea of what teaching is like. Experience in a real, rather than a virtual, classroom will expose you to the teaching environment as well as to the course books and resources that are available. You will benefit from being able to exchange ideas with more experienced teachers. Having first gained some experience in didactic methods and found out in advance what kinds of problems your students struggle with, you will find it easier to adapt your lessons and teaching style for Skype. I could otherwise imagine it being somewhat overwhelming to start straight out with online teaching.

A third prerequisite is being IT literate and having a good Internet connection. As mentioned, a slow or weak Internet connection can prove disastrous for a lesson. Familiarity with Skype, with whichever operating system you use and with MS Office (or equivalent) also goes without saying. As the teacher, your students will look to you for guidance, and that includes dealing with IT issues! You don't have to be an IT expert, but being able to keep the lesson running smoothly from a technical point of view is also an integral part of offering online services in the first place.

5) Where do you see freelance translators in five years' time in terms of diversification?

With what seems to be increasing pressure in the market to work quickly and for low prices, I see translators reacting to this by becoming increasingly specialized and looking for niche markets where they can still charge rates that reflect the professional services they deliver. With global marketing potentially available to everyone, one of the ways it is possible to distinguish yourself is by offering particular specialisms and by being outstanding in those fields. I therefore suspect that diversification will go down the route of developing specialist knowledge within one or two languages, rather than diversifying out into translating from several languages.

Another recent development is the advent of PEMT (post-editing machine translation). However we as translators may feel about this, I believe that it is here to stay. I don't think it will mean the end of translation as a viable profession, but I do expect it to change the way in which we work, and I feel we could see a lot of translators adding PEMT skills to their portfolio over the next five years.

AN INTERPRETER'S STORY

With over 20 years experience in the language sector, **Eva Hussain** *is a sought-after linguist, consultant and trainer. Eva's background also includes IT, project management and systems development. She holds NAATI professional accreditation in interpreting and translating in Polish and speaks several European and Asian languages. Currently the CEO of Polaron Language Services, Eva's previous roles include management of an international telecommunications service provider. She has also worked for local government, large corporations and community organizations. Throughout her career, she has addressed conferences and seminars and worked with non-profit organizations and community groups as a researcher, facilitator and educator. Her voluntary roles have included deputy president of the Australian Institute of Interpreters and Translators (AUSIT), President of the Polish-Australian Chamber of Commerce and Industry (PACCI) and President of the Australian-Polish Community Services (APCS).*

I DON'T CONSIDER MYSELF TO BE A great interpreter. I never trained as one and, like many of my colleagues, ended up in the profession accidentally by sitting a three-hour test. Sadly, most of my learning happened on the job and on the run. I no longer do much interpreting but when I did, from the get-go I used to receive some unexpectedly positive feedback from clients. It ranged from 'excellent' to 'the best interpreter we've ever worked with' and led to more confusion in my already confused head. How could that be? Was I really that good? What were the other interpreters like then?

Luckily, I had enough sense and had received enough professional training in other contexts to fill these 'excellent interpreter' shoes eventually, but my journey was unnecessarily stressful and shaky. I'm here not only to tell the tale, but also explain how I turned it into a great business idea. There are four essential ingredients: find a problem that enough people find frustrating, develop a solution to it, package it, and promote it, preferably with the help of industry friends and colleagues. Here is the story of how I did it.

The problem

My hands-on experience as an interpreter taught me that when it comes to interpreting, you just have to think on your feet and make it up as you go along. A door opens, you get pushed in and you're expected to perform and guide other participants through the language maze. There are many schools of thought, styles and methods of how to deliver interpreting services, but in most instances, the interpreter is the only person who understands the goings on. Everyone relies on him or her not only to help people understand each other, but also to shape the communication, putting the interpreter in charge of the discourse. Clients often feel out of depth – and is it any wonder? With an incoherent range of approaches, there are gaps, risks and many inconsistencies in how interpreting services are delivered and received. If the interpreters can't get it right, what hope do the clients have?

Somehow, as soon as language and culture come into play, standard professional exchanges seem to become unclear and disorganized. Over the years, I have watched experienced doctors, lawyers, judges, physiotherapists, nurses, accountants and policemen lose their cool and go into a chaotic spin. In those instances, I simply had to take charge and put everyone at ease – and in their place – to ensure that communication via interpreter happened the way it should, seamlessly and logically.

One of the cardinal rules of interpreting is for the interpreter never to offer cultural advice, especially when it's unsolicited. That's the theory. In practice, many interpreters are asked and expected to provide insights into their clients' culture, traditions, norms and behaviours that fall well outside of their brief. It is difficult to separate the linguistic and cultural components of the interpreter's job. Are we truly just a conduit to verbal communication, or is it also our duty to minimize cultural faux pas and disasters? And what is communication anyway? Surely it is not just about the oral component. What about body language, tone of voice, facial expressions? And how many interpreters can resist stepping in when they can clearly see that it's not the language that's contributing to the communication barrier but something in the cultural approach of one or more participants that can easily be explained and solved instantaneously?

Many professional interpreters simply make it a rule never to express their personal opinions on anything, including culture and language. They subscribe to the view that they've been hired to assist with the linguistic facilitation of a dialogue by parties who do not speak the same language, and nothing else. They consider cultural brokerage and advocacy a minefield, and prefer to stay well away from them. Others use their professional judgement to decide if and when they might interfere with the discourse.

Another school of thought, especially prevalent in the community interpreting domain, says that it is the interpreter's duty of care to step in and assist in the capacity of a cultural broker when needed. With millions of dollars spent on interpreting in Australia, this is a pretty cloudy picture. I thought so, but for a long time felt powerless to change it, other than making sure that I did a good job. I kept notes of all the challenges I faced, hoping that one day I could somehow use this anecdotal evidence. I didn't know it at the time, but the idea of developing a training package out of my experience was germinating all along.

The solution

Turning my knowledge and frustration into a business idea took some time and, again, happened by accident. I was asked to participate in an interpreting role play back in 2004 by a colleague of mine, Sarina Phan, who had developed a training module with the Victorian Transcultural Psychiatry Unit designed for clinicians working with interpreters. This was my first opportunity to show professional clients how to work with interpreters, something I was simply dying to do.

Around the same time, I was approached by Ljubica Petrov from the Centre of Cultural Diversity in Ageing (CCDA) and asked to deliver a number of diversity training sessions at aged care facilities across Victoria on CCDA's behalf. This led to a long-term relationship with Mayfield Education, where I delivered cultural diversity workshops for their Certificate IV in Aged Care and Patient Services.

At this stage, I was also burning out from doing up to eight hours of interpreting and travelling per day and felt that sharing my knowledge with others might be a better use of my skills and resources. I had lots to say, but rather than complain, I wanted to use my energy to create something positive. As my translation and interpreting business was growing, I had increasingly begun presenting at conferences and running ad hoc workshops for clients and colleagues, so I decided that I would like to include training in my suite of services on an ongoing basis.

The package

My market research indicated that there were many providers of how to work with interpreters, cultural diversity and cultural competency training packages. I looked at the competition, their pricing and their course structure to see if there were any gaps. What did I have that the others didn't? What did I know that was new, fresh and interesting? Can working with interpreters, diversity and cultural competency be combined? Did I really have something unique to say? Where could I acquire clients? How could they benefit from my experience? My head was buzzing.

Prior to setting up a translation business, I had worked for a local council and an ethnic community organization and as a bilingual educator at the Cancer Council of Victoria. I had a pretty good understanding of how local councils and not-for-profit organizations worked, and thought they'd be a good place to start.

I was right. At this time, Hobsons Bay City Council was tendering their cross-cultural training out and we convinced them to give us a go and allow us to present one free session. I spent countless hours thinking, preparing and analyzing their local statistics and needs. I knew that to succeed, I had to present something that was outstanding: interesting, relevant and informative. The purpose was to help people do their jobs better. Having sat through many conferences, workshops and training sessions, I knew I had to make it engaging and fun. There is nothing worse than yet another boring presentation.

So what did I do? I made the session about me. Yes, humble me, a migrant woman who came to Australia with no English, no education, no money and no idea and turned her life around. Instead of talking about diversity, I showed them diversity. I started believing my own publicity and celebrating my own success. Everybody could relate to that and the feedback I received was phenomenal and surprising even to myself. People talked, shared and laughed. I was learning and very much enjoying the ride, too.

When it came to bidding for the contract, though, I wasn't so sure that I'd get it. I redesigned the original session and took all the suggestions for improvement on board. I came to the tender presentation with a box of little cakes that I had bought from various bakeries around Melbourne: Chinese, Greek, Italian, Polish and Vietnamese. Again, I wanted to show diversity to the tender panel. Talking about it wasn't enough. They got it. I was ecstatic when we won the tender. Since then, I have delivered nearly 30 sessions to the Hobsons Bay staff and management, always with great feedback.

I faced another challenge in 2010, when I designed and delivered over 20 cross-cultural awareness and language services training sessions to the New South Wales Department of Ageing, Disability and Home Care. These were full-day events, rolled out across the entire state between 2010 and 2012. Some workshops attracted over 50 people per session and were hard but rewarding work. I travelled to the furthest corners of New South Wales and met some incredible knowledge-hungry people. These workshops are still running in the metropolitan Department of Ageing, Disability and Home Care regions.

The promotion

In any industry, you have to have a keen eye for the opportunities and grab them as they arise. Once you have paid your dues, I believe it is your duty to mentor others, help improve the standing of the profession and share your knowledge. This is one example of how you can turn technical knowledge into a packaged service that benefits others. One important thing I found through the process was that people were happy to promote and endorse me, and also give me opportunities and constructive feedback.

In my journey, I came across many people, mostly women, who would go out of their way to give me a chance. They must have seen something in me that I didn't, and I very quickly learned to say yes to everything that was thrown my way. In my business, I have always subscribed to the idea that you say yes first, then work out how to deliver it, within reason of course. The fact that other successful people believed in me when I didn't helped me to build confidence and trust in my own abilities. In highly competitive and volatile markets you have to look out for openings and see problems as challenges, not obstacles. If a door closes, you get through the window!

4

Extra-linguistic diversification
DEVELOPING NEW BUSINESS STRATEGIES

WHEN DIVERSIFICATION IS discussed among freelance translators, *extra-linguistic diversification* often causes the most controversy. Some of the concerns mentioned initially ('Diversification is only for bad translators. I'm successful and make a lot of money from translation alone, so I don't need to diversify'; 'I'm not an outgoing person; I'm not comfortable selling or putting myself out there'; 'I have no time to diversify because I don't want my core activity [translation] to suffer'; 'I trained to be a translator; why would I want to do anything else?'; 'I'd rather improve my existing translation business and become a better translator.') relate to precisely this type of diversification – *extra-linguistic diversification*.

There is no doubt that the freelance translation world has evolved significantly over the past 10 years. The Internet and technological developments, including CAT tools and machine translation, have changed the job profile of a translator beyond recognition. Freelancers have had to adapt or risk getting left behind. Thanks to globalization and technological progress, we live and work in a tightly networked world, where an increasing number of services are outsourced to freelancers around the planet. A number of translation companies have, for example, started to outsource their project management, and I know a number of freelance translation project managers who work for several agencies around the world.

Similarly, social media networking and marketing were dismissed as a fad a few years ago, but it is now obvious to even the harshest critic that they are here to stay and have become an integral component of running a small business. Here, too, there is huge potential for freelance translators who are not currently using the opportunities presented by social media.

Next, I would like to make a bold assertion: while it is usually assumed that a freelance translator has to make a choice between specialization and diversification, I define specialization as a type of *extra-linguistic diversification*. Interestingly, several contributors also take this view of specialization as diversification. If you currently consider yourself a generalist (encouragingly only 12.4% of freelance translators surveyed do, see Figure 4.1), it is advisable to consider specializing in one or more areas in order to position yourself as an expert and command the higher rates that your clients will happily pay for your expertise.

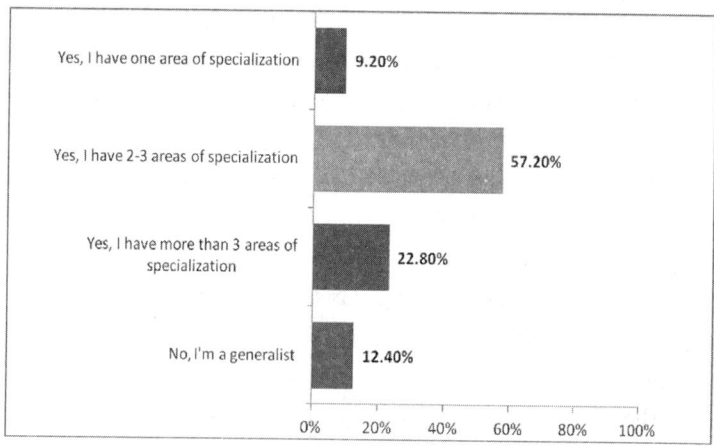

Figure 4.1: When it comes to translation, do you specialize in a specific field?

Any change you make to your existing business structure that impacts on your service portfolio is diversification. I firmly believe that it is not a matter of choosing between specializing and diversifying – far from it. Developing from generalist to specialist means diversifying. Switching from specializing in a field that is highly competitive to a niche market is diversifying. Adding a second area of specialization to your existing one is diversifying.

I also consider developing or changing your client base a type of *extra-linguistic diversification*. Although choosing to work only with select agencies is a very valid business model that can have outstanding financial rewards, and I know colleagues who do this very successfully and by choice, many freelancers endeavour to add direct clients to their client base. If, for example, you are currently working only with agencies, you may want to diversify into working with direct clients or developing a mixed client base. Perhaps you are a new freelancer in the process of establishing your business and are taking on low-paying assignments that happen to come your way because you feel pressured to accept in order to pay the bills. Consider taking a proactive approach and targeting smaller and more specialized agencies which pay better – another way of diversifying your client base. In this chapter, Judy Jenner, who has worked only with direct clients since going into business, tells us about the benefits of this approach, while Inge Boonen shares some valuable tips for freelance translators wishing to become a preferred supplier of reputable agencies.

I think it is crucial to understand that adopting *extra-linguistic diversification* in the current climate will hugely benefit a freelancer's business. As when CAT tools were introduced more than a decade ago, those who dither and refuse to embrace change are likely to be soon left behind. This chapter showcases colleagues who have successfully maximized the opportunities that come with *extra-linguistic diversification*, from freelance project management and strategic alliances made possible through global networking, to social media marketing and specialization.

PROJECT MANAGEMENT

Meike Lange *is a freelance translator, writer and project manager. Meike has developed her project management and administrative skills in the hospitality industry, in the air traffic industry, in concert and theatre management and in language education. Along with that she has been exploring the world of translation since 2004, which led her to apply her combined interests to managing translation projects. When not in the office, Meike can be found talking with friends and colleagues face-to-face, sailing regattas in an all-ladies team or scuba diving with her husband.*

COMPANIES IN ALL KINDS OF fields are outsourcing in order to flexibly adapt to changing market requirements. This trend brings many job opportunities for freelancers or people looking for a sideline. Most people I know in the translation industry, especially freelancing colleagues, offer multiple services. It seems to come naturally and is not necessarily the result of precise career planning. They just end up doing a variety of things because they can and because they enjoy doing it. The talents and abilities of most people enable them to do more than just one thing, and their experience and expertise allows them to take on different jobs. This is not only an advantage in terms of having different sources of income, but also adds a lot to personal satisfaction, avoiding boredom and getting stuck doing the same thing day in, day out.

However, not all individuals seek multiple tasks and there are some specialists amongst us who very successfully focus on their own niche and master it. Diversification therefore is not a must for everyone in the industry. It is, however, a way to make use of your full set of abilities, a way to explore and develop new skills and a way to offer your clients extra value.

Agents – the people who organize translations and what they do

The administrative tasks that need to be done in an agency are various. Some agencies assign them all to the description 'project management'; some choose a narrower term. I have experienced a few of freelancing-for-translation agencies; following is an overview.

A translation agency needs a solid base of trusted translators. They can be working in-house or remotely, with fixed contracts or freelancing, or a combination of both. Whatever the concept, these good people need to be found. In some cases initial test translations will be conducted, which is an interesting field where you get to learn a lot about your peers' understanding of quality translation; at times it can be shocking, but much more often it kicks off a fruitful co-operation. Communicating with 'your' translators, giving advice on how to use CAT tools, planning training and providing help on any open issue are other important functions. Sometimes you are in the role of translators' advocate within the agency and require diplomatic sensitivity. In addition, you become a communication error detector – when the same question hits you for the tenth time, you know that this information must made more accessible to your translators.

Project management requires strong nerves and trust in your business partners. In the end, you are responsible for someone else's work and their ability to meet deadlines. Most agencies have well-planned processes to guide the project along. If everything goes smoothly, working in project management is a piece of cake, but in a high number of projects, somewhere along the way something happens to challenge the project manager's coordination and improvisation skills. For those who enjoy problem solving, that is when the fun begins. It can be the document itself with tricky formatting or the un-user-friendliness of translation tools. It can be a client continually changing their mind. It can be a translator falling sick, delivering late or delivering poor quality. It can be a technical issue that gets in the way.

Processing multiple projects at a time in a number of languages provides many possibilities for pitfalls. Although an active team of project managers might be able to finish all projects with no damage done, finding ways to prevent the pitfalls is essential. Generating solutions and providing smooth project management that enables growth is the ongoing exercise of business development.

Developing ideas on what to tweak for better performance is a fun and creative process. Consulting with the people involved, like translators, software developers, project managers, clients and company owners to find out which ideas are useful and can be implemented reveals different views on your mutual production. Testing of the freshly implemented changes, be it prototype online processes or internal administration of projects, is part of the steady movement of 'plan-do-review-plan' growing companies go through.

As this all would not happen without people in need of translation, there is also the sales team, which is in charge of acquiring clients and keeping them happy. Traditionally this is done by in-house staff, but there are some sales talents in the community of translators. If clients approach you with job requests that would be too big to handle by yourself, you might consider co-operating with a corresponding agency on this. If you serve good projects on a silver tray you might as well get some commission out of this. The sales part is a path I have not yet entered, but it is tempting.

How has remote project management affected my freelance translation business?

My freelance translation business has never been a full-time job. I have followed different careers at once for most of my professional life. Working in different industries, the projects I worked on usually had me coordinating and organizing things. Translation was always around, as I mostly worked for international companies, surrounded by English native speakers, and I liked using the language. When I started supporting a translation agency I was also working for a language school and freelancing as a translator. By adding translation project management to my activities I had to cut down on the time I spent on other things. One of them was freelance translation. Currently I only translate of a handful of texts from my favourite clients per year. Although my freelance translation business has shrunk to a minimum, there are a number of side effects that I find very positive.

Expanded networks throughout the translation industry. Coordinating projects usually involves a bunch of people. These include translators, consultants, software specialists, project managers and editors. Working together gives us an idea of each other's abilities and a feel for how we conduct business. Building new relationships in your industry can lead to fresh ideas and new business options. The author of this book is one example. I got to know Nicole Adams through translation projects where she was the freelance translator and I the project manager. We always had a friendly and reliable working relationship and although she has not met me in person (yet), she seems to trust my abilities enough to ask me for a contribution to her book. For me, this is a great opportunity to write and publish, a field I have only recently entered and want to explore a bit deeper.

Experience and knowledge that can be transferred to other aspects of business. Working for translation agencies has provided me with insight into various aspects of the industry. I have learned a lot about how differently companies and translators approach text and translation. I also had to learn more about different CAT tools, an effort I procrastinated when I was translating. The new impulses in software helpers and in project handling have shifted my whole business to being more organized. The overview of what other translators deliver and what they earn lets me see my own positioning more realistically. I believe that seeing different agencies and platforms for translators, seeing how others do it and seeing what clients ask for will enable me to find business more easily should I decide to look for more translation work.

Money and enjoyment are my main motivations for working. Since I began working in project management, my financial situation has not changed a lot. It is not a way to rapidly generate large amounts of money, but I am earning enough to support myself. A recent calculation showed me that I would make slightly more from translating. The reason I keep doing the administrative work is the enjoyment I get out of coordinating projects, working with people, learning new tricks and finding solutions.

Approaches

There are different ways to find jobs in translation project management. If there are translation agencies nearby, it is a good idea to connect with them and see how they work. It can be a nice change from a solitary home office to drop into a more populated work environment every now and then. If you think you are great at coordinating projects, but have never done it, you might need to learn more and to convince people of your abilities. This could be done by completing an internship. That would be an investment of precious time, but it would be worth it to learn useful skills. If you would like to work from your own office, look out for agencies that mainly work online. Their infrastructure and setup is likely to facilitate connections to remote workplaces. If you have a good network of translators and clients, you might consider becoming an agent. Depending on the amount and size of your projects, you could quickly find yourself involved in management.

Interview with Alberto Ferreira

With over five years of experience in the localization industry, **Alberto Ferreira** *is a localization project manager with key interests in usability and content optimization technologies and processes. His extensive professional background encompasses project management for an ERP/CRM system deployment, as well as linguistic services such as desktop publishing, copywriting and proofreading. He is currently heading a machine translation implementation and usability research project in the localization department of Avira Operations GmbH.*

1) Alberto, you are an experienced project manager and currently work in-house in that role. What's your take on the emergence of remote project management offered by freelancers?

Remote project management presents its own set of challenges and, certainly, in a globalized world where business is spread across countries and continents, coordination and communication are more essential than ever. Remote project management helps to fill the void in certain areas concerning smaller manageable projects, which works well when they are short-duration and deliverable-based. For situations where several players are involved and continuous delivery is required, it is certainly harder to ensure the successful outcome of an enterprise. Remote project management can bridge gaps that are often present in internal company culture, however. External project managers are budget- and deliverable-oriented, which means they are not blind-sided by the conventional way a company works and also bring a fresh dynamic to a situation.

However, remote project management works best when all the roles are well defined and the team has experience of working together. Otherwise, productivity and goal alignment can be compromised. Remote project managers should take the time to understand the cultural differences in their team and work out pragmatic solutions as challenges present themselves. Developing these sensitivities in a high-pressure environment is key to the success of freelance project managers.

2) What skills and experience do freelance translators need if they want to diversify into project management? How should they go about it?

If you rely on online communication (as we all do these days) and have a keen sense of responsibility, remote project management might provide you with a viable professional solution. Some would argue that project management is best exercised by methodical and pragmatic individuals who enforce a standardized methodology, but true communicators who see the big picture often come up with the most creative solutions in the nick of time. Whether you are a left-brain or a right-brain thinker, or a combination, just ensure that results are delivered on time. If the results are not delivered 100% on time, ensure that you go the extra mile and deliver 110% to the client at the next opportunity. An additional tip: never promise the impossible, because you are the one who will have to make it happen.

3) As a certified translator who now works in project management full-time, do you enjoy this diversification from the translation career you originally embarked on, or do you find it challenging?

Moving into project management often happens to senior translators whose training encompasses a wide array of processes, collaborative software and a deep knowledge of linguistic services in general. In my case, it was a choice that came naturally from wanting to deal more directly with the translation project as a continuous process and knowing the typical expectations and challenges of the industry. Every new project poses a different set of challenges, but if you are motivated, you revel in these opportunities to learn. And that is one of the secrets: keep evolving by way of your own experience. Never treat project management as a mechanized activity.

4) Where do you see freelance translators in five years' time in terms of diversification?
Freelance translation is evolving towards a completely assisted activity and with the recent advances in machine translation, the volumes of translation in the near future will be much higher and much more likely to be processed automatically. Contrary to popular belief, this will not make professional human translation obsolete in any way, but it will increase the skills necessary to stand out in a very competitive field. Translation is only one of the possible linguistic services that are relevant to companies today, and translators should move into working more directly with the source content instead of focusing on the target. With companies producing so much content for online and technical purposes, this content needs to be linguistically adequate and its structure controlled. Translators should look more into the emerging fields of information architecture, technical writing, and content structuring and refactoring. The simple days of 'text in, text out' are gone; there are new dynamics at work in the market and the translator must seek out these new opportunities in a proactive way with proper training and hands-on experience.

STRATEGIC ALLIANCES

Writer, publisher, teacher, businesswoman, mentor, translator and motivational speaker, **Sam Berner** *conducts workshops for small businesses about knowledge management, effective use of IT for growth, time management and business intelligence. She also gives talks on work/lifestyle choices, going solo, and creativity in work, and seminars on business ethics and professionalism. She regularly presents workshops for the Australian Institute of Interpreters and Translators, community groups working with refugees and other non-profit organizations, as well as presenting academic papers at local and international conferences. Sam is the Managing Partner at Arabic Communication Experts.*

IN A BOOK ABOUT DIVERSIFICATION such as this, the reader would rightfully expect to find ideas on how to generate more wealth from activities complementary to translating and language. I will try, however, in my chapter to show how my core work – translating – can generate that additional income without diversifying into new areas of entrepreneurship.

I have grown a freelance business from a solo practitioner to a partnership, and built a globally dispersed team of translators to meet the increasing demand on our services. Admittedly, a lot of the process was in the form of organic growth, and to begin with rather unplanned. The lessons learned were valuable, however, and as the adage would have it, 'all's well that ends well'. To start with, let's look at the limits imposed on my ability as solo practitioner to generate additional income actively while remaining sane, and how I circumvented these limits while still concentrating on my core business of translating, because that is what I am passionate about and do best.

Limits on translator income

Time. A translator can only work a specific number of hours before they are forced to take time off. Exhaustion and prolonged working hours reduce the quality of generated output, not to mention taking their toll on one's physical and mental health. From personal experience, the maximum working time per day should not exceed 10 hours, with at least one day of rest per week in which no translation work is carried out.

Burnout. I started translating in 1984. In 1995, I faced major changes to my work, having to re-establish myself in my new home country. It took me six years of adapting, testing the market and finding my way, but by 2001, I was in business as usual. The six years of re-establishing myself also planted a seed of insecurity – I became a control freak. The increasing workload, administrative burdens imposed by bureaucracy, and perpetual external changes to technology and niche-market demographics meant that for many years I was too busy to be able to explore other things in life that I wanted to learn or enjoyed doing.

Output. On a good day, with the help of CAT tools, I can generate 2,500 words alone. I have heard of colleagues who brag of 8,000, and as envious as I am, I would rather not go that way. My maximum output is 4,000 words per day (eight hours) but that sort of stress cannot be maintained, because it affects quality. However, by 2008 my services were so much in demand that I had to find a solution or leave clients unsatisfied. Let go of clients, or let go of doing everything by myself – the dilemma was not easy, because I am such a control freak.

No translator is an island

Loneliness suits some, but most people are social, and working alone has been proven to be difficult despite all the benefits and freedom of 'tele-existence'. Translator associations, online fora, social media and networking sessions are all proof we need to stay in touch not only professionally, but also psychologically. I enjoy the congress of like-minded colleagues; in fact, most of my friends are linguists. Yet an increasingly heavy workload and long hours of staring like a hypnotized rabbit into the screen of my laptop left precious little time to participate in continuing professional development sessions and networking events. Worse still, I found myself unable to write – an inherently important part of my marketing strategy.

Re-thinking goals

By 2006, I had burnt out. The only motivation to keep running my solo show was the churning in my stomach generated by any suggestion of having to work for an employer. The limits mentioned above also meant that no matter how many more 'productivity tools' I used, or how disciplined I was with every moment of my waking existence, I was hitting a financial glass ceiling. So I re-thought my goal – from 'making more money' to 'making more money without total burnout'. I wanted to take on only meaningful material to translate, so I could maintain my language skills and engagement with the industry, not just hole myself up in the office doing whatever came my way. I also desperately craved time for my other interests: photography, music, travel and study. However, I told myself, none of this could happen if I kept hitting the financial ceiling.

Getting there

So how did I solve the dilemma? It was a very steep learning curve. I made an inventory of what I did not know, and found out it was quite a bit.

Business skills. This was particularly hard, because I prided myself on being a businesswoman. But the world outside my window was changing rapidly, while I was stuck in the mindset of last century, hammering away at the keyboard. Self-sufficiency and growth are not good partners, and I wanted to grow. I started reading books on management, and thinking of expanding.

Implementing technology. Translation memory, text-alignment tools, OCR, term extractions, automated word count and machine translation all played a huge role in speeding up my translation output. I started keeping an eye on everything new, with the single leading thought of how it would make me more productive.

The important lesson I learned is that no tool makes you immediately more productive, and no tool fits all translators' circumstances. I read an inordinate amount of manuals, and watched endless webinars explaining technology. I downloaded demos that worked, or crashed, or simply just irritated. I spent long nights fiddling with new software, always thinking of possible scenarios where they could be used. It was well worth the investment.

Collaboration. This is the crux of my success story. In 1999, well before any inkling of burnout, and at the height of my control mania, I 'met' on a forum a young Syrian colleague whose language skills left me breathless. We became e-friends, and eventually friends in 2001, about the same time as I 'met' an Egyptian medical translator for whom the whole process was one of 'churning' and who opened my eyes to the uses of technology. Then in 2005, on the eve of the big re-think of where my business was going, a translator on ProZ.com sent me a frank email asking for advice. After I had looked at her portfolio, and mentored her for over a year, a huge project provided the opportunity for all of us to work together. A year later, another Egyptian translator in the UK crept into the team, on account of her specific domain knowledge, which was needed for another project.

Building a team. In 2008, I met my current business partner through our professional association, the Australian Institute of Interpreters and Translators (AUSIT). We collaborated on a few ad hoc projects, building trust and understanding. When she joined me in 2010 full-time, she brought with her not just academic credentials but also a fresher perception of how we could run Arabic Communication Experts. For the first time, the haphazard team of friends and e-friends had a proper project manager.

In 2012, the team acquired yet another specialist translator who is also a competent terminologist. By now there was enough work not just to keep us all busy, but to enable us to invite three more colleagues to occasionally lend a hand. The team spanned North America, Europe, the Middle East and Australia. Arabic Communication Experts could work 24 hours a day, turn around 8,000 to 10,000 words, proofread them and even typeset them ready for print. The financial glass ceiling has lifted, and I (as well as my team members) can do other things in life besides translating.

Teething issues

One of the major issues that faced me, and is now facing us as a partnership, was trust – how to vet the proposed team members in regards to quality of work, commitment and professional ethics. So my business partner and I agreed on vetting procedures for new team members that include researching them online, speaking with them and starting them on small projects. We prefer team members who come with word-of-mouth recommendations, and we also actively look for talented potential, which we mentor.

When scouting for colleagues, we look for complementary skills: all of us can step into another team member's shoes in translation and editing, but some have skills in desktop publishing, various CAT tools, specific fields of expertise, language direction, or project management. This versatility also means that we learn from each other, enriching each other and growing as professionals.

The second issue is how to keep one's team from falling apart. At Arabic Communication Experts we call it the SAC method (sharing-and-caring). Be it civil unrest, divorce, illness or death of a family member, we go through it together, standing for each other and taking the load off when necessary. We also communicate a lot outside of the projects, and are friends online and in real life when possible. Leadership and motivating each other is also very important to the stability of the team. It is crucial to have a team leader who leads by example, not just a project manager. Otherwise, the team structure is pretty flat. We found that having clearly set expectations and procedures in writing helps ensure that everyone knows what to do and when, even in contingencies.

Thirdly, we looked into the legal and financial aspects of our team. Most of our team members are business entities in their own countries; one even runs an agency. All subscribe to codes of professional ethics. We all sign non-disclosure agreements for each other's projects, since any of the team members can bring a large project to the table to share. Initially, we worked as a co-operative: we would take on a project, split the work and split the pay.

Lately, however, different team members have specialized: getting the work, building corpora and term bases, translating, proofreading, managing the project. We still share the income, because we find the co-operative model more equitable to all team members than commission-based subcontracting. We also ensure that the team is part of the quoting process by negotiating with them when possible, keeping communication open and transparent.

Benefits

A team brings with it more reliability – clients are happy that more than one pair of eyes look at their work, enhancing quality assurance. Clients perceive a team as more trustworthy than an individual – after all, if something happens to one member, there are still others who can pick up and deliver.

A team spread around the globe, from the US to Australia, via Europe and the Middle East, means we can work in shifts. It also means we have more insight into the cultural aspects of the audiences we translate for, with a number of team members being *in situ*. Coming from diverse countries in the Arab world is also of great use when collecting business intelligence.

A team can take on larger projects – we now translate up to 8,000 words a day, and proofread an equal amount. Clients like that, because it means they don't have to spread the text among a number of translators and chase them one by one. A team that has diverse skills can be a one-stop-shop, and can offer clients more services than an individual. This attracts larger a client base, not just those needing translation proper.

Conclusion

The above approach to increasing one's income begs the question: are we becoming an agency? The resounding answer to this question is 'No'. Playing with language is my profession and vocation; I would feel bereft without it. But remaining the 'Steppenwolf' was beginning to undermine my bottom line and pushing me towards an inevitable burnout. Building a team of like-minded people benefited all of us, was fun, and made more financial sense, while allowing me to continue doing what I love: hammering out words on my keyboard.

Interview with Attila Piróth

*While working on his PhD in theoretical particle physics, **Attila Piróth** had the opportunity to translate one of the highest profile texts a scientist can dream* of: Einstein's groundbreaking articles from 1905, in which the foundations of relativity and quantum physics were laid. The satisfaction of making such outstanding works accessible in another language steered Attila to scientific translation, where he collaborated with several renowned publishers. In 2007, Attila passed the certification exam of the American Translators Association (ATA) and later became an exam grader. He has mentored early career translators since 2009, placing special emphasis on the intelligent use of translation tools. In 2010, he joined the International Association of Professional Translators and Interpreters (IAPTI), a worldwide organization promoting ethical business practices. He is a regular conference speaker and has given talks and workshops in 10 countries.

1) **Attila, you are an advocate of freelance translators forming strategic alliances with the right partners, both clients and colleagues, to grow their businesses and offer top-notch service. How did you first become involved in operating with strategically chosen partners rather than as a lone freelancer, and would you say forming such alliances can be considered a type of diversification for freelance translation professionals?**

Many years ago a high-profile English to Hungarian translator, Katalin McClure, asked me whether I would be interested in sharing a massive and complex technical project with her and two other colleagues. Working in that precise field and language pair, she could hand-pick her collaborators with more care than any project manager of a huge multi-language vendor. She chose the team carefully, selecting translators with an appropriate scientific/engineering background and a proven track record in technical terminology, who were also easy to communicate with.

This set-up was very different from the usual one where the project is managed by an agency that goes out of its way to keep the translator and the reviser anonymous to each other. In Katalin's project we discussed a lot among ourselves – I still recall some of the delicate terminology issues we tackled. We were all in different countries, but the experience came closer to working in a shared office than the usual isolation freelancers are used to. I felt I was working under less stress and with real colleagues.

Over the years, Katalin has become my regular translation partner. Such an alliance has several important advantages. It eliminates translator-reviser conflicts – which often originate from preferential changes – and the need to justify one's choices to a third party (the project manager, who may even not speak the target language). For us, it is quite different. We have become used to bouncing the file back and forth several times, until both of us are entirely satisfied with the result. I recall a translation contest with a generous deadline where the file moved to and fro 12 times. We tried to dissect every detail, with no hurry. It was a rare pleasure.

Several clients leave it completely up to us how we work, for example, who translates and who revises. This also has advantages for the client: faster turnaround, as communication is not slowed down by passing through a project manager; peace of mind, as the translator and the reviser won't start blaming each other; and superior quality, as all points have been approved by both of us.

If necessary, we can also include other trusted colleagues, so our capacity is, to some extent, scalable – unlike that of a single freelancer. I can direct some of my clients to her while I am on holidays, without fearing that she will snatch my clients.

In short, finding regular partners eliminates several drawbacks of the usual freelance way of working, while it enhances the freedom that goes with freelancing. If I had to give a single piece of advice to translators who are seeking to become established, it would be this: network a lot so that you can find good partners, both in your language direction and the reverse. They will be among your most valuable business assets in the long run.

2) What impact have strategic alliances had on your existing translation business, and does the income you generate from these partnerships reflect the time and effort invested in finding the right partners and nurturing the relationships?

Let me start with another type of strategic partnership that I have built over the past few years. In 2007 I founded a translation team called Solidarités with the double aim of providing linguistic aid to a French humanitarian organization

(Solidarités International) and of creating a unique workspace where freelance translators could network and collaborate around worthy projects.

Volunteer work is quite common in the humanitarian translation field, and complete demonetization is often promoted using arguments such as 'each dollar saved on translation is a dollar that can be spent on field action'. For several reasons, I find such arguments fallacious. I think it is a bad idea to turn this segment into a volunteer-only sector, as it paves the way to deprofessionalization, and I am lucky that Solidarités International has been a partner in trying something else.

Together, we created decently paid internship positions for early career translators. The interns work in close collaboration with volunteer team members (all of whom are professional translators) on translations for the organization, and they also attend a series of 10 to 12 two-hour training webinars about various technical and business aspects of our profession. (The webinars are free for all volunteer team members as well.)

Up to now, eight interns have benefited from this possibility, and according to their feedback, the internship has considerably accelerated the take-off of their businesses. My role in the team has been managing the projects and the terminology, as well as providing the training sessions and mentoring the interns.

This collaboration has brought me (and many members of the team) considerable relational capital. It has also allowed me a sort of diversification into training and mentoring, as well as project management. I can experiment with different workflows, manage joint terminology work and see at close quarters how to resolve conflicts as a project manager. I have come to the conclusion that working conditions are at the core of translator-reviser conflicts. When two isolated freelance translators, often completely anonymous to each other, communicate via impersonal email, their differences of opinion are magnified compared to two colleagues who can sit down in an office and discuss the same text over a coffee.

It is not easy to answer your question about the income generated by this partnership. The word 'strategic' applies well to this alliance. I have indeed invested a considerable amount of time in it, with the aim of creating a work environment that will be beneficial not only for myself but for colleagues as well, where we can exchange some of our best business practices.

What I have learned has certainly had an impact on my daily business. Putting on the reviser's, terminology manager's and project manager's hats has certainly given me a more comprehensive view of our profession. My experience with conflict management has enabled me to hold workshops on this subject and to handle translator-reviser conflicts with much less stress and more self-confidence than before. It is hard to quantify this as an income figure, even though it has definitely brought new business.

3) Quite a few freelance translators openly admit that they like to work alone and may have reservations about working in teams with others, outside of their comfort zone. Do you personally enjoy this diversification from the translation career you originally embarked on, or do you find it challenging?

Freelance translators are very much used to leaving their primary comfort zone. They have to take care of all different aspects of their business, from prospecting clients, negotiating terms and haggling over rates to handling software issues, chasing outstanding invoices, doing their accounting and much more. If you can burn the midnight oil over sorting out yet another bug in your CAT tool, you may be able to take on these challenges, too:

(i) Try non-anonymous revision – and fight anonymity in general. As an excellent colleague, Lefteris Kritikakis put it: 'If you can't stand behind your work, by name, you're not a professional, period. If lawyers were anonymous, they wouldn't be able to charge $300/hour.'

(ii) Attend some in-person events where you can meet colleagues. Blend talking shop with having some fun. Once you have played pool with a colleague until 5 am, or have fallen in the water from the same canoe, arguments about a split infinitive take on a different dimension.

(iii) Attend some in-person events where you can meet potential clients. If you need to be convinced about the usefulness of this tip, read Chris Durban's book, *The Prosperous Translator*.

(iv) Try, at least for an afternoon, working with a colleague in a shared office.

Even better, try to produce a snappy translation of a challenging text together.

When asked about the cons of freelancing, working in isolation is mentioned most often. Shared offices help overcome the inherent isolation home-based teleworkers face, and are becoming popular in a number of countries. If that's too radical a change, try at least steps (i) and (ii).

At the very least, speak to colleagues who have regular business partners, and listen carefully to the benefits. If you can find a way to have those benefits with less invested effort, be sure to send me an email.

4) Where do you see freelance translators in five years' time in terms of diversification?
As a brilliant Aussie colleague, Vivian John Stevenson, put it, 'Lawyers and doctors diversify by buying real estate, truffle farms and racehorses.'

When talking about diversification in the translation profession, post-editing rough third-party machine translation regularly comes up as a backup activity that the translator can fall back on if the translation income starts to dry up. One side provides the tools (and amassed linguistic data), and the other the skills. This alternative is most often promoted as a new niche for translators by those who own the tools.

In a typical scenario, strong emphasis is put on productivity, and some concession is made on quality. Qualified translators may then find that they do not need to use all of their precious skills. This should be a clear warning sign. It means they have to compete with less skilled translators on speed and rate, and that they depend on the infrastructure owned by the other party. Translators become interchangeable resources, which is of course highly desirable for certain stakeholders in the translation industry. But this is diversification downwards, towards a lower-profile activity. Those precious skills that remain unused become less and less sharp with time, so this is definitely not a business plan that I could recommend to freelancers.

Let's look at something that does not turn a white-collar translator into a blue-collar language technician. Revision, proofreading and quality assessment are services that many translators start to offer after a number of years in business, and for good reason: in the more interesting segments of the translation market the four-eyes principle is applied as standard. The skill set of these services greatly overlap with that of translation, but each requires separate training. Among those who categorically refuse to proofread others' work, most report previous bitter experience in an anonymous translator-reviser relationship. This hardly comes as a surprise to me.

The kind of diversification that helps you provide more comprehensive services paves the way to a more comfortable niche. Being able to ensure independent proofreading through a partner is the obvious first step. Being able to handle (by yourself, through a partner or via outsourcing) the typical file formats of the specialty fields you work in is the second. In many cases, you may then be able to handle the entire project in your language pair, which means that you don't need to outsource your marketing services to the entity that would coordinate the project in your place. You can directly deal with the end client – if you have the necessary sales skills.

So, what's my take for 2018? I expect less isolation, more peer-to-peer networking, less anonymity, and more teams offering comprehensive solutions, even in multiple languages. I expect that translators who are active online or in various associations will start to put their relational capital to better use. This will help eliminate unnecessary middlemen in the supply chain, and thus increase the income of high-profile professional translators. So, when asked about their diversification plans in five years' time, they will mention real estate, truffle farms and racehorses.

BLOGGING AND SOCIAL NETWORKING

Catherine Christaki has been a full-time English-Greek freelance translator since 2001 and co-owner of Athens-based Lingua Greca Translations since 2012. She holds a BA (Hons) in Modern Languages (French and German) and a Diploma in Translation (English-Greek). Her specializations include IT, medical and technical texts. She has been a proud member of the American Translators Association since 2008 and the Chartered Institute of Linguists (UK) since 2007. She is active in social media, especially Twitter @LinguaGreca, which has been voted among the Top 25 Twitterers three years in a row (2011-2013) in the Language Lovers competition organized by bab.la. She writes a popular translation blog called Adventures in Freelance Translation *and regularly talks about social media and blogging for translators in interviews and conferences.*

THE NOTION THAT NOWADAYS translators need to have a diversified set of abilities far beyond good language skills has been gaining momentum for the past five years. A freelance translator also needs to be a good marketer, social media user, blogger, bookkeeper, networker and so much more. Most of us finished our university degree in languages or translation and launched our businesses right away. Most universities don't teach you about the daily life that lies ahead of you as a translator, neither do they provide you with the necessary skills (although many translation institutions have started to make an effort to provide more 'hands-on' training and lectures).

If you're not online, you don't exist. Really?

I've read in many articles and heard many marketers say that if the clients can't find you online, they won't find you at all. In our day and age, I think both of those statements are true. I found my accountant, our logo design company, my web designer, even our handyman online. I know several translators who don't have a website or blog, nor do they participate in social media, and they still have plenty of work and successful careers.

That was me three years ago. A simple profile on Proz and a Gmail account was all I needed. My business was thriving and new translation agencies contacted me every month. Why would I change that?

If it ain't broke, don't fix it. Or maybe not...

That doesn't work when you are a freelancer. There are no set rules and no magic recipe for success. You have to keep evolving and improving your business in the way that suits you. Another saying that I heard when I was younger and keep repeating to myself is, 'If you don't move forward, you start moving backward.' Keeping things as they are forever is not an option. That's where diversification comes into the picture. Find out the additional things you are good at and share them with both your colleagues and your potential clients.

In this chapter, I will tell you how blogging and social media can help your translation career and show you the numerous advantages they both have for translation professionals, not merely as a source of added income, but also as a great way of finding new clients, free advertising, branding and so forth. Let me start with my story and what prompted me to join the wonderful online communities of translators.

Life before social media

I've always wanted to be a translator. I started studying foreign languages at the age of seven and even tried to translate a book (*Little House on the Prairie*) a year later using a small dictionary. Naturally, I failed miserably and stopped after the first few pages, but I was fascinated by the whole process!

Before discovering the world of social media and blogging, I had enjoyed being a full-time translator for nine years. My only contact with other translators was with my husband, also a translator, at home, and a few locally based colleagues by phone. I translated 12 to 14 hours a day with tiny breaks to reply to emails and call my accountant a few times a month. No online interaction whatsoever (not even Facebook; I was a late adopter and even now I only use it to connect with other translators), no networking outside the house, and no contact with colleagues from other countries save for a few translation blogs I subscribed to. Sounds sad and lonely? I was loving it, wouldn't have changed it for the world.

One of the things I had planned to do for years but always delayed because of too much work (never a good excuse) was creating my website. That was the only thing in my 'marketing plan' apart from some good ideas for finding potential direct clients that I knew I would never implement because they involved getting out of the house.

And then came Twitter

That all changed during the American Translators Association annual conference in Denver in 2010. Whatever the presentation topic, the speakers kept insisting that translators should have their own website, a blog and a Twitter account.

Right then and there, I decided to step out of my comfort zone. My husband was also attending the conference and we came up with our business name, Lingua Greca Translations, and I created our Twitter account (@LinguaGreca). During the next few months, we had our logo created and hired a web designer to create our website. Copywriting for the website was tricky, as I had no experience in anything remotely similar, and it is still a work in progress (as is my resume, which I keep changing every few months).

By that time (summer of 2011) people were responding very well to my Twitter activity. It wasn't easy. In the first few months, I was spending too much time on Twitter. I thought that I had to read every single tweet of the people I followed and I sent two or three tweets per hour (too many). Fortunately (for my and my followers' sake), I got better at it and we launched our website and blog in August 2011.

A new blog is born

My plan was to publish two posts per week: one every Monday with the content I had tweeted about the previous week (our 'Weekly favorites', which have become quite popular) and one every Thursday about translation, freelancing or any other topic that would be of interest to translators. Three years later, I still follow the same blog 'calendar'. There's never a shortage of ideas for blogging topics. When you read as many blogs as I do and interact with colleagues on Twitter and Facebook, there's always something to write about. Of course, there's not always enough free time to write an article each week and that's where guest posts from other bloggers come handy.

We have received great feedback about our blogging and social media efforts. The word people use most often in their comments is 'prolific', which I love and I think is very accurate. I try to be very careful about what I share and write about, but I'm also all for quantity, something for everybody, diversification in sharing too. The topics I focus on sharing are not only translation and languages, but also freelancing, marketing, networking and business.

Beyond the 'shiny new toy' syndrome

I love to share, whether it's useful posts other translation bloggers have written, a lesson learned from an experience, or what a conference was like for people who didn't attend. Before having the opportunity to use social networks or blogging to share useful tips, I used to do it with Greece-based colleagues on the phone. Not very productive, let me tell you, neither for me nor for them. A lot of time was spent talking and emailing templates and only a single person could benefit each time. Now, I can just write a blog post and share my experiences with lots of readers and followers all at once.

Before you share an article, you read it. I can't even begin to describe the things I've learned in the last three years from other translators through their blogs. I thought I was a good translator before. I think I'm a great one now because of all the extra knowledge I've gained.

When I was starting out, I had no mentor to help and the only online resources available back in 2001 were about translation theory. No tips about translation tools, famine and feast periods, how to get paid, or any of the other situations a translator faces daily.

Want to be a translator blogger?

Translators have great writing skills, but not all of us are great writers. Translating something is different from writing it from scratch. Even if you are a good writer, do you enjoy writing? Will you create a nice new blog, write some interesting posts and get people excited, only to let it wither away after a few months? Do you have the drive and ideas to sustain a frequent posting schedule? Are you passionate about sharing tips and experiences with your colleagues and potential clients?

Will you blog in your native language (highly recommended) or another language (e.g. your source)? If you choose the second, are you confident enough in your writing in another language other than your native? What will you write about? Do you have or plan to make enough time to write posts, reply to comments and maintain a blog?

What does it take to be a good social media user?

I'll focus on LinkedIn, Twitter and Facebook. You'll have to like sharing and interacting in all three networks. Each one has its own style and purposes. You shouldn't automate your updates, that is, when you share something on Twitter, it also appears on LinkedIn and Facebook. They all take time; it's not easy to come up with insightful things to say and useful stuff to share every single day. For newbies, it might be a good idea to focus on one social network and then join more if you have time and enjoy it. An important part of social media is reading other people's updates and commenting on them. Do you think you have the time and drive to get into it?

If none of the aforementioned questions and facts scared you away, read on for some of the many advantages of blogging and social media for translators as means of diversifying and growing their business.

Networking

This is the most important one as far as I'm concerned. You get to interact with colleagues and meet people from other fields, too; not only potential clients but also people who might come in handy later in your professional life (writers, bloggers, social media consultants and so on). The advantages of networking with colleagues are obvious: you learn from them and they fully understand your daily trials and tribulations. What about word of mouth? Apart from the fact that one of them might someday offer translation services in your language pairs so they might become your client, when they get to know you better they are also in a position to recommend your services to their clients. And that happens a lot.

What about potential clients? Will they read your blog? Karen Tkaczyk says no: 'They read about their subject and want me to handle the translation so that they don't have to think about it.' That's true to some degree, but there are ways to interact with potential clients through your blog or social media accounts.

Example 1: You attend a social media conference and notice spelling mistakes in the conference brochure. Write a review about the conference in your blog and invite the organizers to read it via email. Don't mention the spelling mistakes in your post (or do it in a nice way), but tell them in the email. What are the odds of them calling you for editing before their next conference? Don't want to go the blogging route? You can also contact them via Twitter. Congratulate them on a well-organized conference and mention the spelling mistakes (remember, nicely).

Example 2: You specialize in gaming translation. Write a review about a gaming application that hasn't been localized in your language and then contact the developer to tell them about the review and offer your translation services.

Example 3: Write a post about translation buyers. How to choose the right provider, mistakes to avoid, etc. Then, contact your local chamber of commerce and ask them to share the article with their members. You will get where I'm going with this. Potential companies might not stumble on your blog or LinkedIn profile on their own, but they are always interested in anything written about them or their products. Use your blog as the perfect excuse to contact them via customized and personal emails instead of cold emails starting with 'Dear Sirs'.

Boosting your online presence

Remember what I mentioned above about clients finding you online? You have a website or maybe just a good Proz profile. Will your clients find you easily and quickly enough? Probably not. They'll look for 'Source-Target translator' in Google and you probably won't appear in the first few pages of results. Would you look further than that? When you post regularly in your blog and you are active on social media, Google appreciates it and puts you further up in the results pages. Get your name out there and promote your brand. Let people discover who you are and what you have to offer.

Highlighting your expertise
Social networks allow you to follow the latest news in your field of expertise and blogging provides you with the right platform to talk about your specializations. There's only so much you can say on your website about your experience and projects you've worked on. Writing about them in your blog also allows you to talk and interact with colleagues who share your specializations.

Research your potential clients and generate leads
When translators talk about contacting direct clients, their main problems are what to say (see examples in Networking above) and whom to contact. Twitter and Facebook are great for finding out more about your potential clients and events they're organizing or planning to attend. But to find out whom you should contact to offer your translation services, LinkedIn is the ultimate tool. Search for the company and have a look at its employees. You'll be able to identify (or guess) who is the best person to talk to. If you don't have a common contact to do the introduction, then at least you have a name. Find a nice excuse and send your pitch via email.

Direct financial benefits of blogging and social media
When I first became involved with social media and blogging, I thought the ultimate goal was to reach and gain new clients. It never crossed my mind that the time would come when I would be asked to talk about them and that they would involve financial benefits. Obviously, there are direct ways to monetize your blogging and/or social media expertise.

You can offer paid webinars and training to colleagues. You can speak about these topics at conferences (they usually don't pay you to speak, but you get discounts or they may pay for your accommodation.). You can write paid reviews of translation, freelancing, social media products and applications. You can write e-books or books about social media and blogging for translators. You can write blog posts for translation companies (most of them outsource this to writers and social media marketing companies). You can add ads to your blog. You can work as a translation company's social media expert (part-time, obviously, unless if you come to like it so much that you give up your translation career).

Indirect financial benefits of blogging and social media

This is where it gets interesting, because the possibilities are endless. First and foremost is the word of mouth I mentioned under Networking above. That has helped my business significantly. Colleagues recommend me or send me work when their clients ask for Greek. Followers and blog readers who aren't translators ask questions involving Greek and then contact me for work when a translation project arises.

Let me give you an example. The author of a social media book contacted me via Twitter a few years back. He wanted tips on getting his book published in the Greek market, publishing houses he should contact, etc. I provided him with the information he wanted and that was it. A few months later, he contacted me again asking if I was interested in translating the book.

By boosting your reputation and online presence, more people get to know you. That can lead to exciting opportunities, like contributing to books written by colleagues and giving interviews to appear in translation journals and translator blogs. You can also be nominated for awards, like the Top Language Lovers competition that takes place each year.

Bonus benefits

I mentioned above the possible financial benefits of attending conferences to present on social media and/or blogging. How about attending a conference for free as their live Twitterer? I had that opportunity back in 2011 during the European Language Industry Association's Networking

Days in Athens and loved every minute of it. I attended all the presentations and the networking events, learned new things about my profession and met new colleagues and potential clients; all for tweeting away happily!

Time spent = money I could have made translating?
Definitely, and I haven't taken full advantage of either social media or blogging as I still prefer to spend most of my time translating. I've become a better translator because of them. Every day I learn something new; ways to translate faster and/or better, how to claim money from non-payers or how to avoid them altogether, and so much more. I've become a better marketer and networker due to social media. I've become a better writer and improved my English immensely through blogging. Most importantly, I get to help other translators. That is the biggest reward of all.

Diversify: option or requirement?
Nowadays, I think it's a requirement. You can still be a successful translator by focusing solely in your translation activities, but how long will it be before you're upstaged by other colleagues working in the same language pairs in the same fields but with great social media skills and/or blogs? We all need to work constantly on our online image and presence to show what makes us special.

Looking back at my experience as a translation blogger and social media user, I'd say it's been worth every minute of my time. I've met amazing people, learnt more about our profession than I could begin to describe and all in all become a better translator because of both blogging and social networks.

It's not only about finding new clients, nor is it just about showcasing your talents. The most important advantage for me has been networking with colleagues, because of what you learn from them and share with them.

Interview with Corinne McKay

Corinne McKay is an ATA certified French to English translator based in Colorado, USA and specializing in international development, corporate communications and legal translation and non-fiction books. She is the author of two books for freelance translators: How to Succeed as a Freelance Translator (2006 and 2011) and Thoughts on Translation (2013). Her blog, Thoughts on Translation, is a lively discussion forum for freelance translators from around the world. Corinne served for four years as the President of the Colorado Translators Association and is currently a director of the American Translators Association (ATA).

1) **Corinne, you are a renowned blogger for the translation industry and have even published a compilation of your blog entries in book form (*Thoughts on Translation*). What motivated you to start blogging for fellow translators?**
Like most translators, I love to write. And it's nice to have a forum for my own writing, in addition to translating other people's writing. Also, I really struggled to find good information about the business aspects of freelancing when I started my business, so I like to put that information out there for people who are starting in the industry now.

2) **What impact have blogging and your publications for freelance language professionals had on your translation business, and does the income you generate from these activities reflect the time and effort invested?**
I think it's important to identify your target audience. My blog and my books do not really bring me any direct business from translation clients, because I don't write about topics that translation clients would want to read (or at least not many of them!). However, I feel that my blog and my books are undoubtedly the best marketing tool I've ever used for the work I do with other translators – teaching and consulting about freelance business strategies – and I've also received numerous referrals for translation work through people who read my blog and my books.

3) Do you enjoy this diversification from the translation career you originally embarked on, or do you find it challenging?
Both! Overall, I really enjoy it. I find that having multiple revenue streams helps protect me against the 'feast or famine' cycles that strike a lot of translators, and I enjoy having a lot of variety in my work. However, it can be hard to 'keep all the balls in the air' when I have a full session of my online course, a large translation project and I'm trying to get a book manuscript out the door.

4) Where do you see freelance translators in five years' time in terms of diversification?
I think that there are a lot of opportunities to diversify if you want to: one on one training for translation memory tools, specialized glossaries, translation business books, preparation materials for translator and interpreter certification exams – the possibilities are almost endless. But I think that in reality, very few translators are willing to put in the time to develop diverse business lines, because it's a lot easier to just take the work that lands in your inbox!

SOCIAL MEDIA AND ONLINE MARKETING

Olga Arakelyan *is a professional translator from English and German into Russian and a certified EFL teacher. She also has experience teaching Russian as a foreign language. She works in close collaboration with foreign business owners wishing to expand their services to the Russian market. Olga is also head of Sharp End Training Russia. The company has a very special mission to help freelance translators enhance their marketing, business and networking skills and achieve success in their freelance career. That is the main reason why Olga is so passionately working on various training courses and webinars and co-hosting virtual events for freelance translators, such as online speed networking sessions, virtual conferences, and interviews with established colleagues. Olga runs two personal blogs, one in English called Your Professional Translator and the other in Russian called Freelance Business Tips, and a young, but quickly growing an active LinkedIn community called Marketing for freelance translators.*

FIRST OF ALL, I AM DEEPLY grateful to Nicole Adams for her kind invitation to participate in this wonderful project. I think that the book will be highly useful for many language professionals, including teachers, translators, editors and localizers.

I've witnessed some pretty heated discussions recently on the subject of income diversification. I used to be pretty judgmental about it, too. When I heard about it for the first time I thought, 'Why bother? I am a good translator; I don't need to diversify my income. Only mediocre translators have to think about additional sources of money!' I hear similar opinions about diversification from my colleagues even now. But the reality is that we all strive for financial stability, and that's exactly what diversification can help us achieve. It has nothing to do with us being bad specialists. In fact, based on what I see in the industry, it works in a totally opposite way. The more successful a translator is, the more eager he or she is to embrace the concept. I guess part of the reason is that it helps us to grow and become even better specialists, plus it gives extra visibility, which is always good for our business.

I came across the word 'diversification' a few years ago, before I even started using social media. I 'bumped into' Joy Mo's website called Translators Biz Secret.com while looking for some other information. I found her website rather interesting and subscribed to her newsletters, so she was the one from whom I heard this word first. At the time the concept seemed weird and rather unreal, so I decided that it wasn't for me. It was several years later when I finally realized that this idea is actually quite realistic and started applying it as well as I could.

I would like to share about my early freelance years, so you can learn a bit more about me and how I came to the decision to start diversifying my income as a freelance translator. I became a freelancer in March 2007. My very first year was pretty tough. In fact, I landed only one or two jobs during that year. Then I met the first two agencies who were satisfied enough with both my experience and quality to work with me on a regular basis. I got about 90% of my translation work through them and was completely satisfied with that situation.

That was a big mistake! A couple of years later I realized that I still had an employee's mentality, and that this mentality didn't serve me well. In 2009, the situation changed and I started getting a lot less work from those agencies. I realized that I had made a mistake somewhere along the way. I quickly joined a Russian company involved in teaching English through Skype to make up for the income I used to earn from translation. I soon realized that I couldn't physically tolerate working for eight hours a day with a headset on. I suffered awful headaches because of it. Besides, the income was far from what I wanted. After a year I had to give up teaching through Skype, but during that year I used all my free time to surf the web and find information on how other freelancers look for clients and projects, what kind of rates they consider reasonable and how they build their schedule. I came across the word 'marketing' so often that I decided to find out all about it, no matter how frightening the concept sounded.

Like many freelance translators, I am more of an introvert, so anything that involves interaction and getting out in public makes me panic. In my early days as a freelance translator, I used to associate marketing with a very aggressive 'salesy' approach involving meetings with strangers, handing them my business cards and convincing them that they needed my services. It sounded so scary! I never wanted to be a saleswoman, not just out of fear. I had tried selling cosmetics when I was a student and worked out that it just isn't part of my personality. I knew that in order to succeed I had to approach marketing from a totally different angle.

In 2010, I accidentally came across an invitation for freelance translators to attend a webinar about Facebook marketing. I had already been using Facebook for connecting with friends and family members, so I was interested in the subject and registered for the webinar. It was a real eye-opener. I learned a lot, not only about marketing on Facebook, but about social media marketing as a whole. I realized that having a profile on some freelance portals and directories was far from being enough, that I needed to make myself visible for prospective clients and that I needed to learn how to attract direct clients, not just agencies, because that's where the best business is. I also learned that social media marketing is not about being 'salesy'. On the contrary, it's about building relationships and nurturing them. That's what I wanted! So I started a blog, created a fan page on Facebook and opened a Twitter account. Later on, I added accounts on LinkedIn and Google+.

It took me some time to learn to use social media. At first I only read what others were publishing and reposted or retweeted stuff I liked. I didn't have a clear goal or a marketing strategy. No wonder my attempts didn't bring any spectacular results. But gradually, as I kept learning and reading, I developed my own strategy and my own vision of what I wanted to accomplish through social media. I started publishing relevant and targeted content and seeing real results!

As a result of my social media activities I made some very interesting connections with fellow translators, agencies and direct clients, and started getting more work. I learned a lot from those people I followed and I continued to learn and grow as a professional. I was also able to widen the scope of my work. Now I don't just translate and proofread or edit translated texts, but also write articles for a blog in one of my specialty fields, and I have served as a writer for a couple of other clients.

By 2012, I realized that I wanted to share my experience with fellow translators. At that time I met Jonathan Senior, the founder of Sharp End Training. I loved the vision of the company and thought that it would be a great chance to help those of my colleagues who want to change their mindset to that of an entrepreneur and develop their career. The first thing we did was record a free webinar about five business mistakes made by startup freelance translators and ways to avoid those mistakes. After that I held a series of written and audio interviews, all of them now published at Sharp End Training Russia. In February 2013, we held our first virtual conference for freelance translators which went a lot better than I had feared (you remember I always panic?). I am now running a growing LinkedIn group called 'Marketing for freelance translators' where we discuss a lot of things connected with marketing and business.

The Sharp End Training team was up for the next challenge as we tried to break the Guinness record for the longest webinar on 25 and 26 June 2013. We built a team of great speakers including some well-known translators and interpreters. As one of our fans pointed out, it was a real 'learn till you drop' experience. I still don't know if the Guinness team acknowledges it as a successful attempt. Even if it does not, we still had a terrific time. If you use Twitter, please search for the #lwwr hashtag and you will see the tweets people were sharing during the event. That will give you some idea of the excitement, and the passion participants shared with one another. It was a fabulous experience.

I have also started training Russian-speaking freelance translators on the subject of social media and have already delivered one webinar through ProZ.com and am preparing more sessions. My first course received some highly favourable feedback from the participants and is now available as a replay. The next webinar for Russian fellow translators took place in July 2013, and I really enjoy interacting with my colleagues and having fun together, teaching them something new and learning from them.

Has diversification been good for me and my business? Surely yes! It keeps me alert and motivates me to continue growing as a professional, and it gives me more financial stability and freedom. It increases my visibility among my colleagues and potential customers. It is also teaching me to come out of my introvert shell and interact with people.

I am often asked by fellow translators if social media marketing takes too much time. My answer is that, like many other things we do, it can be optimized. The key is to understand that it's a vital part of your business and treat it as such. Then, almost miraculously, you will find the time for it. As an example, I have just spent about 30 minutes scheduling my Twitter messages for the day. I know some people schedule their messages for weeks in advance, but I prefer sharing current information, so I schedule my Twitter posts for one or two days in advance. With Facebook and LinkedIn it's a little different. Here I may schedule for a week in advance and it works well. Every month and every quarter I sit down and plan my activities for the next month or quarter. I think about my strategy, and analyze my recent activities to see what went right and what needs some correction. I try to stick to the plan, though I have to admit I often do more than planned. I also spend a little time answering people who are talking to me in social media, who mention my posts and tweets. It really doesn't take long. This aspect of social media marketing can't be ignored, because social networks are meant for interaction, and we need to remember that.

Still in doubt about whether you need to diversify your income? Feeling fear? Look at me: I am probably the worst coward in this world and I was still able to do it. You just need to find out what fits your personality best.

DIVERSIFICATION THROUGH SPECIALIZATION

Valerij Tomarenko started doing translations when he was still a student of English philology in Russia. He also studied music composition and worked as a composer for theatre, film and television. Since settling in Hamburg, Germany, in 1991, he has been working exclusively as a freelance translator and interpreter (German to Russian and English to Russian) specialized in marketing, corporate and technical documentation, having been the owner of a boutique Russian translation company named Tomarenko ever since. Valerij is a member of BDÜ (German association of translators and interpreters), tekom (German professional association for technical communication) and IAPTI (International Association of Professional Translators and Interpreters). He is active as a contributor to publications on translation issues (e.g. on the EN 15038 standard) and as a blogger (Translator's Notes or Anmerkungen des Übersetzers, in English and German). His special interests in connection with the translation business lie in the area of translation quality and marketing communications.

ONE OF THE MUSIC TEACHERS I had in my formative years was a very peculiar person. Apart from being a composer with a degree from Leningrad Conservatory and a fabulous self-taught jazz pianist, he had a real passion for philosophy. His was a rather odd mixture of classical Indian texts in scientific editions and the great German thinkers of the early 19th century like Fichte and Hegel. Boris was a true Hegel freak. He always had a dog-eared and battered volume of Hegel's *Philosophy of Mind* in the Russian translation with him, from which he could recite whole passages, if not pages. However, it was never boring, since he had a very idiosyncratic, typically Russian way of making fun of everything, including Hegel and himself. Boris was extremely popular among his students; he was a legend. For us teenagers, it was fun listening to all his weird stuff.

Among all the random quotations that I have remembered ever since are some of Hegel's appallingly difficult, abstruse and obscure definitions, for instance, that of a method. I don't really know how it reads in the German original (Hegel himself thought his concepts were untranslatable and should never be translated, but that is another story), but the back translation from the Russian would be something like 'form of self-movement of intrinsic concept'. I did say it was odd stuff, but in my formative years it sounded sort of cool.

The true meaning, as my music teacher used to explain, was the 'intrinsic' (his favourite word) connection between a method and the subject matter that the method was to be applied to. For a methodology to be right, it should always reflect the subject matter, should be derivative of the purpose of the matter itself. Today, we would probably use the term 'compatibility'. What does this have to do with the subject of this chapter, that is, diversification and specialization? It was a fancy definition, but the idea stuck: a method is linked to the nature of something more substantial; it originates from the subject matter.

What is the nature of language and translation? According to most definitions that I know, it is a means, seldom an end. That is to say, we use language to explain, argue or persuade. It is a means of communication and thinking. We use it to get to know who did it when we read a thriller or to drive down the price when haggling at a bazaar (they do it in old books, at least). One way or another, language is instrumental. So is translation – or in most cases (I would leave aside poetry or literary translation), this is how it should be.

When language and translation become our area of expertise (and our way to earn money, by the way), we translators tend to forget that both are a means, not an end in themselves. Our clients order translations not for the sake of translation, but because they need us to get their message across. That is something that is worth remembering when working on a translation, I think, and something which helps to get a better idea of what a translator's specialization and diversification are about.

A piece for one-man band without music

In the late 1990s, one of my major clients was a German publishing house specializing in trade fair catalogues for the Russian market. At that time, the German publishers were in charge of the whole spectrum of relationships with international exhibitors, clients of the major Russian trade fair company, ZAO Expocentre – International Exhibitions and Conventions, in Moscow.

The texts that I received to translate were on different subjects, depending on the exhibition under way. Most events were industry-specific and business-to-business, but there were also some popular fairs aimed rather at the general public, like Consumexpo, for consumer goods, and Prodexpo, Russia's no. 1 food industry show. Regardless of the wide range of themes, most exhibitors' texts – articles and contributions for directories, catalogues, exhibition magazines and other media – had much in common. Many were in typical PR style, meandering between factual, objective information and outright advertising.

The German publishers did a lot of editorial work, compiling, preparing, correcting, modifying and otherwise shaping what many exhibitors managed to put on paper only at the last moment before the deadline. My task was mostly to translate this into Russian, since the majority of exhibitions took place in Moscow, occasionally into English or German for Russian exhibitors or presenters at symposiums, later on into other languages, a part that I outsourced. Though my formal task was primarily to translate all this scattered and highly diverse material, it was quite clear that translation was only one element in the editorial work. You didn't need much knowledge of Hegelian dialectic; plain common sense made the purpose of a typical magazine article quite obvious.

In many cases, it was clear that the exhibitors who ordered a translation actually wanted, and needed, a lot more. Their need, which I defined above as to bring the message across, boiled down to persuading the target group in another country to buy their products. I think this example illustrates clearly what I meant by instrumentality of translation and language in general.

As soon as I realized its purpose, translating exhibitors' articles became instrumental in my development as a translator. To achieve the internal or, to use Hegel's terminology once again, intrinsic, purpose of a particular text, a translator needs to interpret it and, being essentially an interpreter, to improvise. It is a method which is more than compatible with the subject within certain areas of work. I don't make a case for taking liberties with the source text in general. The method originates from the subject. It all depends on the particular purpose, client and target group. In my case, I think, certain liberties, typical for a journalist's or an editor's approach, were not only justified, but also methodically necessary and expected.

I don't want to go into all the details of a translator's work when translating and editing texts for publication in trade fair catalogues or industrial magazines. Into the bargain, I also took on the desktop publishing part of the processing later on, adapting the layout in QuarkXPress and organizing the whole prepress production. The final product that the German publishers received from me for each trade fair project was a set of high-resolution colour separations on film, ready for the printing of catalogues, magazines and, in several cases, even large format posters.

My work as a translator for this publisher was fairly specialized and diversified. It was fun, similar to working in a rather frantic, but cool and vibrant, advertising agency. It had nothing to do with music, but I felt like a one-man band. I diversified into being a translator, copywriter, editor and art director in one person. I still remember my creative attempts to find several Russian equivalents for 'plain vanilla' in an advertisement for some high-tech product, all of which I had to chuck away when I finally saw the photo of the product to be used in the ad. (I thought about suggesting another shot, but the client already had their article with their photo in other languages.)

I still have a very special and very diversified relationship with the people at the publishing house. (In case you are wondering why I describe my experience in the past tense: today, ZAO Expocentre, the major Russian trade fair organizer, has its own publishing and printing facilities in Russia, so the German publishers don't get as large a portion of jobs as they used to some 10 years ago.)

Nevertheless, such a relationship can also have a flipside. Above all, it is extremely difficult to find a replacement if things go wrong. The more special something is, the less chance of finding a substitute. This applies to both sides. On the other hand, to put a positive spin on such a setup, you are really hard to replace if you are doing a good job. Ideally, you have created the Blue Ocean with no competitors around. I don't think there is anything more desirable for a company or a serious and committed professional than this. It is also both interesting and rewarding, if you manage to cultivate your specialty and make the best use of your unique position.

Needless to say, you can always use your special experience elsewhere. Ever since, I have regularly worked on assignments and projects where translation goes along with copywriting and creative editing. This special experience with the publishing house also helped to shape my professional understanding and skills. Whenever people ask me about my profession and I say 'translator', I feel inclined to add: 'Well, not only'. It is not quite accurate to describe what I frequently do as a typical translator's work. Instead, I think of myself as a journalist (and sometimes even a PR manager) who prepares, processes and adapts the material provided by the client and takes care of the client's communication with a specific target audience in a particular country.

You don't have to invent anything

In terms of methodology, there are two basic ways to achieve a certain uniqueness, become something special or develop a USP (unique selling proposition) for the customer.

The first way seems to be quite natural and stands to reason. If there is something that you enjoy, or are passionate about, or have always taken an interest in, you already have your area of specialization. Again, the language serves as a means of developing and expressing what you are inherently interested in or passionate about. Your language skills could perfectly complement your subject of interest to land translation projects in this particular field and, quite possibly, you would find direct corporate clients among those who pursue your common interest in a professional way.

If you are 'just' a good translator with exceptional writing skills, the second way to specialize would be to follow your client. This is where the definition of a method (it is about compatibility, remember) stands us in good stead once again. A translation is a kind of copy, a reflection of a certain source. If you want to have a really good copy, you should engage with the original. Logically, if you pay attention to or take an interest in the source, in the original subject matter, you will find out that it is something special. It is something special for your client, and if it can become special for you as well, it certainly helps. The chances are that this specialness will rub off on you, so eventually you will have a special area of expertise and will be regarded as an expert in this or that particular field by your clients.

In any case, either you can draw on your special interests and skills and let them develop into your area of specialization as a translator or you can follow your clients, including your potential clients, as a translation follows the original, adopting the perspective of your client as regards the subject matter and arriving at your possible area of specialization.

Here we encroach upon another vast subject, that is, customer orientation. But it is all linked together. Translation is instrumental for our clients. Its purpose is to reflect and convey what is relevant for our client, that is the initial purpose of our client's communication. Once we realize that what we do serves as a means to achieve our client's purpose (and I think client orientation is to a large extent derivative of this), our task is to learn our client's priorities and interests. Adopting the perspective of our client can help our translation become a better copy of the original and can help us get a better idea of what kind of diversification and specialization is in line with the expectations of the market.

What do you mean you still don't buy it?

So what is the initial purpose of our client's communication? Granted, haggling in a bazaar would probably be way too special and not much in demand on today's business-to-business market and, hence, on the market for our translations. My example with companies preparing themselves to participate in industry trade shows may sound too straightforward or even blunt (persuade the target audience to buy the client's marketed and advertised products), but, to tell the truth, much of what we usually get to translate is about selling.

I could go even further and perhaps divide the stuff we translators usually receive to translate into 'pre-sell' (corporate brochures, presentations, contracts and agreements) and 'post-sell' (operating manuals, user guides). It all depends on who our clients and consequently we ourselves try to sell something to.

Just think about the words 'buying' and 'selling' in many idioms like 'I don't buy it' (especially if you don't 'buy' my arguments here). Even cold numbers, in case you are a financial translator, are possibly meant to convince people: the board of directors, shareholders, a purchasing manager or a tax inspector. If we are storytelling animals, as Jonathan Gotschall (*The Storytelling Animal: How Stories Make Us Human*) wants us to believe, it is worthwhile considering anything that we happen to translate a story. And, believe me, then it is more fun to translate it – even stories with numbers.

In any case, if we agree that the purpose of our clients' communication and information is, at least partially, selling (including selling in a figurative sense), it is worthwhile thinking about how our clients try to achieve their goal. They also resort to specialization and diversification to have a skin in the game.

Today, even commodity companies strive to be different. They don't want to be perceived as faceless sellers of interchangeable goods, who are forced to compete on price only. They are searching for and promoting innovation. They are looking for unique selling propositions. They develop brands and build customer relationships to enhance their specialness, to get a competitive edge, and to set their products and themselves apart from the competition.

I won't bore you with common knowledge and commonplace observations on the strategy of differentiation. I just think that it is worthwhile to bear in mind that it is directly linked to specialization – and diversification. If a method depends on the subject matter, if a translation is a copy and reflection of the original, and if we believe in customer orientation, we are best advised to follow the example of our clients.

As customer-oriented service providers, our task is to incorporate and convey our clients' specialness that they try to communicate to their target audience. They expect us to bring this message across and, quite often, adapt it to the specifics of the target culture. For our own professional growth, I think we can learn a lot from our clients in terms of differentiation, specialization and innovation.

The opposite is standardization. Hence my mistrust of all the known attempts to standardize our profession. Yes, I know that is mostly about processes and workflows. But if our clients strive to be special and take pains to express it in their brands, communication, corporate wording (for which we as translators are supposed to create a replica in the target language), and their own processes and workflows, I don't think it is helpful to emphasize a one-size-fits-all approach. It is best avoided if we, like our clients, value specialization and diversification. It is customization, not standardization, that goes hand in hand with client orientation in our business. Especially in reference to the definition of method that I started my reasoning with, and considering what language and translation are about (a means, not an end).

You're so special, you know

In my most creative days when I was translating and doing layout for trade fair magazines as a one-man band, I invented a couple of slogans for myself. *'Alles aus einer Hand'*, the German for 'everything from a single source' or 'one-stop shop', is rather trivial. It captures an idea of diversification though. Another slogan which I actually consider to be far superior, but totally unusable on account of the risk of never finding new clients, was 'Better than the original'. But even if we curb our ambitions and don't pretend to know better than our clients, specialization is a way to get on par with our clients in terms of knowledge and expertise. It is a very constructive way of customer orientation.

If you translate technical or marketing content for your corporate clients, you cannot not be specialized, because specialization, to a large extent, is predetermined by your clients' products and services, by the very content that you get to translate. It is a given. As more products and services become interchangeable and risk being copied and commoditized, as brands have ever more difficulties to find a distinction and secure a competitive advantage, our clients are increasingly looking for specialization. This concerns not only their own products and services, but also all the available resources and the whole production chain, including service providers. In other words, us.

Although a single product or service may not be necessarily special, a certain combination might become unbeatable as a unique innovative package. A part of this equation is your personality, which makes your work unique, especially in a creative field such as translation.

Having recalled my earlier music teacher when I started working on this article, I gradually come to a conclusion that his being both specialized and diversified made him so peculiarly inspiring. Since we as translators deal with such a wide variety of special subjects, all the makings for becoming specialized are staring us in the face. The Blue Ocean strategy (which suggests that an organization should create new demand in an uncontested market space, or a 'blue ocean', rather than compete head-to-head with other suppliers in an existing industry) for creating market opportunities or developing a specialty in a niche market may help with the rest. I even think we cannot do without fancy definitions or any twisted quotes from Hegel or whoever else. Specialization and diversification opportunities are not far to seek. From the viewpoint of methodology, at least.

Interview with Fernando D. Walker

Fernando D. Walker is an English-into-Spanish language mediator who specializes in the fields of renewable energy and sustainability. He makes use of his proactive attitude, motivation and passion to help individuals, groups, organizations and businesses involved in these sectors deliver their messages clearly and consistently throughout the Spanish-speaking countries. Fernando holds a BA in Translation and a Diploma in Interpreting. He is one of the founders of the International Association of Professional Translators and Interpreters (IAPTI), where he currently holds the post of Voting Member on the Board of Directors. He is a contributor to the North American Academy of the Spanish Language (ANLE), an association that honoured his achievement as a language mediator by offering him the opportunity to participate in the revision of the Dictionary of Americanisms.

1) Fernando, you are a successful translator who specializes in a very

specific niche and offers your services to a very narrow target audience. Were you ever a 'generalist', and can you tell us how you ended up offering 'linguistic services from English into Spanish to eco-friendly individuals, groups, organizations and businesses who want to communicate with Spanish-speaking communities effectively and in a culturally sensitive way so that they can increase their competitive edge in a globalized market while spreading their green ideas and contributing to saving the planet Earth'?

In fact, I was a generalist translator for quite a long time. At the beginning I didn't ask myself which topics I was most interested in, since the only thing I wanted to do was to translate. I was more focused on doing my best every time I began a new translation project than on analyzing how I felt when translating the material.

Without doubt, I preferred translating psychology to mathematics, but what really caught my attention was the translation process in itself. I am not saying that I am no longer interested in the translation process, but rather I enjoy it in a different way. After some time, I started feeling that my lack of marketing tools, together with my frustration at not being good at something in particular, of not being a specialist, was definitely leading to career stagnation. Apart from that, I felt that something was missing, that my work was not fulfilling all my professional expectations.

So, along with my business partner, Luciana E. Lovatto, I attended an online marketing course that gave me the possibility of analyzing in depth different aspects of my professional life, and one of them was 'specialization'. As I am very passionate about renewable energy and sustainability, I immediately thought: 'Why not offer translation services to these particular sectors which are not only gaining more and more importance, but could also help me join the dots between translation and my passion?'

My specialization is a way of differentiating myself from English-into-Spanish colleagues, but for the most part, is a way to accomplish my mission in life, that is, to communicate the messages of people whose work consists of protecting the environment and proposing ways to live more sustainably.

I truly believe in the importance of finding what you're really good at because it is key to giving meaning to what we do as linguistic mediators of different cultures.

2) What's your take on the concept of 'diversification through specialization'?
In my opinion, it's an interesting concept, although I don't quite agree with it, in the sense that I don't include specialization in my range of services. I am, in fact, a specialized translator who offers other services, such as editing, transcription, creative writing, and scientific writing for the sectors I am concentrated on. In my case, I decided to specialize for two reasons: to differentiate myself from other colleagues who work with my pair of languages; and, most importantly, to combine my passions of translation, renewable energy and sustainability. My specializations gave me the opportunity to be focused on certain sectors so as to really know and understand their specific needs. I think translators must understand that they can't be good at everything. It's important that we master a certain specialization in order to provide an excellent service for clients who value our work, respect us as professionals and care about quality. I used to think that being a specialist was a disadvantage, but time has proved me wrong.

3) What impact has your very narrow specialization had on your existing translation business?
It has had a very good impact on my translation business because not only clients but also colleagues know what my specializations are, so they remember my name more easily when they are looking for collaborators or translators in my areas. As regards clients in particular, since I participate in blogs and groups where my prospects are, this allows me to be present there, to show them my expert knowledge and to let them know what I do by interacting with them. For example, several clients who work in the renewable energy and sustainability sectors contacted me after reading my comments or visiting my website. Becoming a specialized translator is one of the wisest steps I've taken in my professional life because it has helped me fulfil my passions through translation and gain confidence in talking with potential clients.

4) Do you personally enjoy this diversification from the translation career you originally embarked on, or do you find it challenging?

Although I find it quite challenging and even difficult, I personally enjoy it a lot. Nothing is easy, so we must work hard if we want to achieve our set goals. I believe that challenges allow us to keep on learning and growing professionally and personally, so we have to look for ways to overcome them without being overwhelmed by them. It's important to see any challenge as a way to learn something new, as something that helps us put our creative side to work. I am constantly thinking how I can reach the clients I want to work with and how I can catch their attention, so as to offer them my professional services. My specializations give me both the energy and the satisfaction I need to continue looking for new clients.

5) Where do you see freelance translators in five years' time in terms of diversification?

I don't think that freelance translators will diversify much more than they are doing nowadays. Obviously we can't offer too many services properly without the help of other professionals. What I believe (or would like to believe for the sake of our profession) will happen is that we will see more and more alliances between translators who work with other language pairs and specializations. This will allow us to establish more versatile networks of collaborators as an alternative to big translation agencies where the relationship with clients is more distant and less personalized. I don't mean competing with large translation agencies, but offering a variety of alternatives to other types of clients who prefer to work closely with the professionals they hire. From my point of view, it is really important to stop seeing our colleagues as competitors and to start considering them as possible business partners with whom we could win interesting projects. Surely, trust must be the first ingredient in this relationship if we want it to prosper.

DIVERSIFYING YOUR CLIENT BASE

Inge Boonen has been active in the localization industry for 15 years. She is currently a senior business development manager at Arancho Doc focusing on providing value-added language services and solutions to her customers. Prior to joining Arancho Doc, Inge held various positions at a world's top 20 language service provider, including project manager, account manager and sales manager. With an academic background in languages and translation, and practical experience as a translator and proofreader, Inge is passionate about all aspects of the translation industry.

WHEN NICOLE ASKED ME TO contribute a chapter regarding diversification in the language industry, I was reluctant to participate, as I am not actually a translator. I started my professional career with a translation degree that I obtained in the late 1990s, but I actually never practised the trade. However, I have worked in the translation business since then. I have always been employed by translation companies, first as a project manager, then as a sales person. I was more than happy to contribute from that point of view.

Even then, while contemplating the question 'To diversify or not to diversify', my first reaction was that I first needed to understand what diversification means in this context. This question is being answered in other chapters. I will avoid it, and focus not on 'How to diversify' but on 'How to differentiate', and specifically how to do so in your relationship with a translation company.

When witnessing certain technological trends, translators understandably worry that they will be pushed out of the market. Small- and medium-sized translation companies actually share the same worry, as they may not have the necessary budget to invest in certain solutions. But there is a difference. While the translator's primary objective is to correctly convey a message from one locale to another, a translation company's objective is to manage the translation process correctly. Both tasks are being threatened by automation. Translating, however, even if automated usually, still requires some highly qualified human intervention, while project management can be extensively automated.

So, will a translation company still be needed as an intermediary between direct customers and translators? For the next decade, I think yes. There are still so many different requirements out there, which will allow both the profession of the translator and of the translation project manager to continue to exist. In a business-to-business setting there are several different possible scenarios. There are companies that decide to insource all translations. Sometimes they use employees who are subject matter experts without any qualifications as translators; in other cases they contract expert translators.

Translations may also be outsourced directly to freelance translators. This might happen through a translation management system, by requesting translations through the cloud or a wide variety of other possibilities. Then there is the scenario where a translation company coordinates the entire translation process. It takes the management out of the hands of its customer and in order to succeed it must partner up with translators. With more than 26,000 translation companies active around the world, this is an often seen scenario, and will be here for a long time yet.

In the translator-translation company context, the translator is the vendor, or seller, and the translation company is the buyer. As in any business, it is the seller who should try to differentiate himself from the crowd in order to acquire and retain his client. Selling seems to be an arduous task for some translators. The romantic idea still persists of the translator as a lone person sitting at his home desk for hours and hours, barely speaking with another human being, but making sure that at the end of his working day hundreds, thousands or even millions of people can understand each other better thanks to his effort. This is probably not the picture of a person who would go out and sell. But even if this is you, there are some easy tips and tricks that you can apply in order to be more successful. If you know the translation business, have an understanding of how translation companies view things and know yourself, you will go a long way in differentiating yourself from the crowd.

Know your business

You are reading this book, so you have already understood that it is fundamental to keep abreast with what happens in your line of business. Good for you.

If you have the budget for it, you might also subscribe to an industry-related magazine, or attend a conference once in a while. This will help you understand what translation companies are struggling with and what direction they are going in. It will of course also help you to understand what your fellow translators are up to.

If you feel you cannot afford the money, or you prefer investing it in other tools, try to have an open conversation with the translation companies you are currently already working with. For instance, if you are not convinced about the rate you are charging, whether you feel it may be too high or too low, ask whether it is competitive. You might be surprised with the answer you will get; a translation company might be more than willing to share its thoughts with you. It is in both the translator's and the translation company's interests to offer reasonable pricing, and to raise awareness about the value of translations.

Know 'the boss'

With the industry being under huge pressure to lower prices, the relationship between translators and translation companies is quite a tense one. Actually both parties are in the same boat, so make sure you know your fellow passenger. Once your knowledge increases, you may not consider the translation company as your temporary boss anymore, but as a true partner.

The two main people that you should know are the vendor manager and the project manager. A vendor manager is the person that you will agree the general terms and conditions with, regarding the tools you are willing to use, the process that they expect you to apply, and the rates and payment conditions. The vendor manager maintains contacts with the translators – or vendors – continuously monitors their quality, and attracts new vendors when necessary. This person or team might have other titles, but they are the decision-maker for you.

To sell to a vendor manager is a tough cookie. This person can be compared to the procurement or purchasing manager of translation services at a translation company. Their main task is to keep costs down as much as possible. But there is a positive note to this. Often vendor managers have previously had another position in a translation company. Often they were a project manager who then moved to this position, and prior to that they might have been translators themselves. So, even though they have a financial objective to respect, they do understand the work of a translator.

On a day-to-day basis on the other hand, you will have to deal with, typically, several project managers. These are the people who manage the entire translation process. They might be coordinating hundreds of people per day. They will be the ones asking you to use specific tools; they will set up the schedule and will monitor the quality of the project that you are collaborating on. They are extremely busy and often under considerable time pressure. Many of them will have a translation or related degree, and do understand how you view things, but they might not always have the time to show you. Typically they will give work to the translator that they feel most comfortable with. Often they will not make decisions based on price, but on past experiences. They want to feel confident that no hiccups will occur in the translation process, and will thus select the people who have not created problems in the past. Make sure that at any company that you will work for you know who covers these two roles.

Know thyself

Last but not least, make sure that you know yourself. Look at how you have been working in recent years. Are you more of an individualist or are you a team player? In the former case you might feel comfortable with short- or medium-term assignments that you can work at on your own. In the latter case, you might not shy away from some cloud work.

Do you prefer to work part-time or full-time? If part-time, you might like to plan your work well in advance and ask for regularly occurring jobs, while if you are a full-time worker, you may be fine with receiving the odd rush job.

Do you love to work at night or are you an early bird? In both cases you might try to collaborate with translation companies that are based in another time zone and thus get a competitive advantage over your fellow colleagues.

Do you hate stress, or on the contrary, does it give you an adrenalin surge? In the first case you might opt for translating a long manual to be delivered in a month, in the other, why not go for press releases that must be delivered within the next four hours?

Many other characteristics are possible. Once they are mapped, they may help you to better understand what kind of translation company you want to partner with, and they will help you to decide upfront which projects you should accept, and which you would be better not doing. Your translation company will be very grateful.

Sell thyself

Now you are almost ready to sell yourself. You know who you are and what kind of company you would like to partner with, and you have a fair understanding of where that company will probably want to go. It is good to refine this knowledge further and to ask yourself what you are good at. That will be your unique selling feature to transmit both to the vendor manager and to the project manager. The question is not which subject matter you already know best (this should be answered upfront) but what you can do during a translation project that someone else will not do. How can you differentiate yourself?

Let me give you some examples:

- If you love translating technical documentation, make sure you emphasize that you understand the importance of the correct use of technical terminology. Don't wait for the project manager to ask for a list of terms; send it yourself and ask for confirmation.
- If you feel you have a more creative pen and prefer marketing-like translations, let your project manager know your preferences.
- Do you love to write for websites? Well, think about search engine optimization. Would it be an idea to provide a short list of the key words that you feel should be used on a localized website?
- Perhaps you are a software localizer. Your project manager

will love you if you ask the queries in such a way that she can forward them directly to her customer, instead of having to clean them up from personal remarks like 'What the hell does this mean in this context?'
- If you are interested in the automation of translation, show that you are not afraid of using new technologies or editing machine translation output.

In the above scenarios, you will mainly be communicating with your project manager. Do make sure you do not forget about the decision-maker, the vendor manager. Just as a translation company does with its customers, pick your main customer, and ask for their vendor manager's feedback on the quality of your work, on your communication, and on your turnaround times.

Conclusion

Emphasizing to the translation company what you are good at, and showing it in practice distinguishes you from the crowd. In my opinion, this is the main diversifying element that translators need to become better at. Don't see it as adding even more tasks to the list. Try to see it as making sure that you concentrate on what you are truly good at, and that you communicate that to whoever should know. Your translation company will become loyal to you, as its customers will become loyal to the translation company, thanks to you. We could not wish for a better partner.

Interview with Judy Jenner

Judy A. Jenner is a seasoned Spanish and German business and legal translator, conference interpreter and court-certified Spanish interpreter in California and Nevada. She holds an MBA in marketing and runs her boutique translation and interpreting business, Twin Translations, with her twin sister. She was born in Austria and grew up in Mexico City. She co-writes the award-

winning translation blog, Translation Times, *pens the 'Entrepreneurial Linguist' column for* The ATA Chronicle, *and is a frequent speaker at conferences around the world. Judy co-authored* The Entrepreneurial Linguist: The Business-School Approach to Freelance Translation, *which has sold more than 3,000 copies. In addition, Judy teaches in the online certificate for English/Spanish interpreting and translation at the University of California, San Diego Extension.*

1) Judy, you make no secret of the fact that you work exclusively with direct clients. At what point in your translation career did you decide to target only direct clients? What were the reasons?
When my twin Dagy and I decided to start a translation business in Austria in late 2002, we didn't really know translation agencies existed. I am not joking here! This story doesn't make us look particularly smart or entrepreneurial, but this was in the early days of the online world, and we were in much more of an isolated bubble than we are now. In 2013, translators are very connected, worldwide. In 2002, we were not.

I had just finished an MBA, so we asked ourselves: how do we get clients? My MBA answer was: we find clients who have a need for our services and pitch to them. And that's what we did. We ended up doing a very basic marketing campaign, but it worked, and hilariously enough, all the market research we did was pretty much wrong. We predicted that we'd probably be the ideal provider for small to medium sized businesses, as large companies would have in-house translation departments, but we were quite wrong about that: our first client was Sony.

After we landed that first direct client, we heard about translation agencies through colleagues, who told us that agencies pay significantly less than we were charging, so we thought: why rely on a broker if we can find our own clients? And we've never looked back. Don't get me wrong: I am not inherently opposed to agencies, quite the contrary. I think it's a business model that works very well for freelancers who don't want to look for their own clients, and it's a win-win situation for many people. It's just not the business model we've chosen to pursue.

2) What impact has this decision had on your translation business?
We don't have to work as much because we charge our direct clients higher rates than agencies would pay. We work less, earn more and have time to donate to the profession, which is something we love to do. We are also in the lucky position that we are able to pick and choose our clients.

3) What would you say to freelance translators who are sceptical about the developments in the language industry and the increasing level of diversification we are experiencing?
I would say that all entrepreneurs must adapt to change to be successful in the long run.

4) Where do you see freelance translators in five years' time in terms of diversification?
I think that many fellow freelancers see the value of working for direct clients, but they also realize that it's a lot of work to find them. In terms of keeping them happy, direct clients are no more work than agencies, but finding them is a challenge that requires a significant investment in terms of time and energy. There are fundamentally two ways to acquire clients – online and offline – and you have to do both, including going to awkward networking events. I've found that many freelancers want direct clients, but shy away from the amount of work that's involved in the client acquisition process. However, I think as downward pressure on rates continues from agencies, more and more colleagues might begin to look for direct clients. I really don't get downward pressure on rates from my clients – they just want the job done, and they want it done well. We deliver that, so they are happy. Once a year or so, I get an email from a client who thinks that we are so valuable that they want to pay more. I am not kidding.

Passive diversification
INCOME THROUGH PRODUCTIZATION

A RISK ALL FREELANCERS face is what happens if we get injured, go on an extended holiday or are otherwise unable to work? The moment we stop working, our income stops – unless we have a couple of passive income streams lined up!

The keyword here is productization, that is, turning your service or expertise into a product clients can buy without consuming your time. As freelancers we typically only earn money while we are putting in the hours. Given that we only have 24 hours a day, our resources from a time point of view are limited and we simply cannot make ourselves more available. This means there is a limit to what we can earn unless we raise our rates astronomically and/or work day and night. One solution to this is to create products we can sell time and time again without needing to sit at our desks and actually perform any work after the initial product creation stage. In this way, we stop trading time for money and being the product. All too often we wrongly assume that everyone else knows what we know and don't realize that our personal combination of experiences, trials, encounters, skills and ideas are valuable, and that clients are willing to pay for them. The key is to productize this knowledge to create a passive income stream.

The traditional approach to creating a passive income stream is to develop publications such as books or e-books, which can be sold even while you are out of the office. The advantage of offering publications is that you only need to invest the time and resources to create them once and can sell them over and over again. It must be said that the market for freelance translator publications is becoming increasingly saturated, but there will always be a need for high-quality products that contain useful information for your target audience. You may also want to consider offering publications for your clients, for example, on selecting the right translator or on the translation process in general.

This chapter also investigates the option of setting up a business offering continuing professional development (CPD) for translators and online training in general. As with publications, this option would allow you to continue to sell recordings of online training events without any additional time investment on your part. If you have an entrepreneurial streak and are keen to share your expertise with fellow freelancers, this may be an option worth exploring. You could, of course, consider setting up your own learning platform, or you could become a trainer through one of the excellent existing online learning platforms for translators, two of which we'll hear about in this chapter (eCPD Webinars and Wordsmith University).

Another very interesting option that is becoming increasingly popular in this context is that of automated online training environments. Today, a number of companies offer online course environments that let you create your own customized courses, including webinars, videos and audio presentations. Although many trainers prefer interactive courses, it is also possible to design entirely self-directed courses for students to go through at their own pace. The automated platforms that are available for coaches today – usually at very little cost – make this possible. It's entirely conceivable for you to create an online course, video or webinar once, and then resell it (or recordings of it) time and time again in the future – a typical example of productized expertise.

Companies such as eCPD Webinars and Wordsmith University, online teaching platforms specifically for freelance translators, not only offer live webinars but also have extensive video libraries where freelance translators or other customers can purchase video recordings of past events. In this chapter, online teacher Désirée Staude writes about her take on diversification, while Lucy Brooks from eCPD Webinars shares her experiences with selling CPD. As a bonus, Lucy has also included mini-interviews with Marta Stelmaszak, Jost Zetzsche, Suzanne Deliscar and Tuomas Kostiainen.

PUBLICATIONS

Joy Mo *is a freelance translator and certified Mandarin/English court interpreter based in Vancouver, BC, Canada. She is the author of* Say Goodbye to Feast or Famine, *an e-book for translators on how to attract clients and create multiple income streams. Joy is also the owner and founder of www.translators-biz-secret.com, a website/blog that promotes practical and effective marketing strategies for language professionals. With no formal business training, Joy obtained marketing and business skills through her own experience of trial and error. From barely making ends meet to running a successful business while taking care of two very young children at home, she understands the challenges and problems freelancers face these days and how to deal with them. Joy publishes a free bi-weekly e-zine,* Translate Your Way to Success, *helping freelancers build a profitable business with their language expertise.*

A FEW YEARS BACK I HAD A very heated debate online with a fellow translator. I was talking about how important it is for translators not to rely on the traditional translation service model alone. I was also urging language professionals to start developing multiple sources of income. This gentleman became upset with me. He said, 'The translation industry has been around forever, it's not right for you to change the way things are done in this profession.

If it ain't broke, why fix it? Translation is what we do, we are translators, not marketers or entrepreneurs. Translation is what we do. And we are not in this profession for money.'

I bet this gentleman is not alone; many translators feel the same way. Why do you have to be business savvy when all you want to do is translation? Isn't that counter-productive? Isn't that being untrue to yourself? These are exactly the same questions I asked myself many years ago before I had a clue about running a profitable business. The truth is, no matter what you do, marketing is always more important than mastery of the skills.

One thing I would say is that as long as human beings use different languages in different regions and countries, and as long as we try to communicate with each other as we do, there will always be a huge demand for skilled translators. However, times are changing. It has become increasingly difficult these days for translators to make a decent living simply by offering one-on-one translation service alone. Many translators I know have either quit the profession entirely or keep translation as a secondary income while working other jobs – often because there isn't enough money and work for their translation business. Yet many translators feel uncomfortable talking about money. Some even believe that money talk would damage their professional image!

Here's the fact of the matter – the moment you choose to be a freelancer, you are responsible for your own success, and that includes your professional development and your financial wellbeing. You have worked hard to get to where you are now, but in reality people often don't get what they deserve. Many extremely talented and smart translators entered this profession not because they wanted to make lots of money, but rather to follow their passion. We all want to do what we love; at least, that's what we've been told to do. However, the longer a person keeps doing something without any rewards – whether financial or personal satisfaction, or both – the less likely they will be motivated to continue doing it. Sadly, this is what is happening to many professional translators.

As language professionals, we are faced with multiple challenges in a world where global communication continues to expand: rapid changes in modern technology and development of translation software; increased access to international markets for clients; the lack of legal protection in the translation profession (anyone who knows a second language can claim to be a translator, while very few would dare to give legal advice without a licence); increased pressure to provide more service for the same or less pay.

When something has been done the same way over a long period of time, it is often a sign that some change is needed. One thing you can do differently is to leverage your time and expertise. Publishing your own e-book or book is a great way to start.

Why publications?

When I say publications, I mostly refer to e-books, books and other reading materials that you offer to your clients, either free or for payment. For translators, selling your own publication is a great way to create your first passive income stream. It's easy to implement, your initial product can always be updated, and the upfront cost is minimum.

The benefits of selling a publication of your own are:

1. the ability to serve more clients in a bigger market
2. more credibility and visibility
3. increased expert status
4. the opportunity to attract loyal followers
5. leads for your higher priced services or products
6. the ability to create once and sell again and again
7. possible business partnership opportunity.

My story

I had been a professional translator and a certified court interpreter in British Columbia, Canada for over 10 years. Looking back, I had a fair number of clients to keep my schedule relatively full, but financially I was struggling to make ends meet and felt that my sense of job satisfaction was extremely fleeting. I thought about quitting the profession, but I simply couldn't find it in my heart to leave this business behind me. Finally I made a promise to myself that either I would make it work in a year or I would find a new job and forget about the translation thing altogether.

I will always remember those days when I spent hours and hours reading all the business books I could get my hands on and taking all the marketing and sales lessons that I could afford. Not long after implementing some of these strategies, I started to see results: a little job here and there and then some ongoing monthly and weekly jobs. Then our first baby arrived, followed by our second. I realized that I would have to create a business that had some flexibility and did not rely solely on my immediate availability. It simply was not possible to commit as much time as I had before my children arrived.

There was a period of time when I was receiving many requests to write English speeches for foreign politicians and officials who were visiting North America. After a few assignments, I realized there were some similarities in these speeches, so I created a template and started selling that to my contacts in China. It went very well, so I began to create other templates on different subjects. The client response was great and the income, although not big, freed me from always trying to meet multiple deadlines. I was able to keep the income going while taking care of my children. That was my first taste of passive income and I saw the potential of selling a publication from that point on.

In 2012, I published an e-book called *Say Goodbye to Feast or Famine* on my own website. From on my own experiences in the translation industry, I compiled the many tips and strategies I've used to attract clients and create multiple sources of income. The message I want to convey to fellow translators is that marketing doesn't have to be complicated and uncomfortable. It's not about pushing something onto others. It's about effectively communicating to your potential clients who you are and how you can help them (or their business) become better. It's about creating a product that you can sell over and over again.

The additional income of the book sales on top of my existing services and programmes is nice, but to me, the best outcome of this e-book is the buzz it creates. From comments by fellow translators and business professionals who have purchased it, I hear how it established my credibility in the industry. It showcases my expertise and spreads the word out there, and I'm now considered something of an expert. This is an advantage money cannot buy.

Since publishing my e-book, I've received more calls from clients and more requests to partner in webinars and online training sessions than anytime before. I have also been offered opportunities to be a paid guest speaker and a conference presenter. Needless to say, it has helped my business in a big way. Now who doesn't like that?

Some frequently asked questions and answers

Some people say to me, 'Joy, it sounds like a good idea to publish my own e-book. I'm going to do it when I have more experience under my belt.' Or 'I will get another degree before I start my book project.' Or 'I'm not good enough to take on a project like that yet.' I understand the fear that a project such as writing a book involves. You want to make sure that everything is perfect before you take any step. If this is you, don't let perfectionism hold you back. It's more important to get going than to be perfect. You can always improve and adjust along the way.

Many bestselling e-books are written by people who were previously unknown. I came from nowhere myself. I'm not a professor, nor do I have a PhD. I don't use big words or complicated sentences in my writing. I don't even have any formal business training. It doesn't matter – many of my clients have written to me saying that they bought from me because they liked the message I sent and they felt they could relate to me, that we shared similar experiences starting out. Being real, being authentic and offering value is all that matters to my clients. It will matter to your clients as well.

Don't get me wrong – I'm extremely honoured to be included in this book together with many very accomplished scholars and senior expert translators. I have tremendous respect for them. They'll give you their wonderful ideas and views on how to be a successful translator. I'm here to share my own experience with you in my unique way. So don't wait for someone else to validate you before you start your project. Just get going.

Once you are committed to the book project, the next step is to make sure you have a winning idea that will attract people to you. Here's an email I received from John, a fellow translator: 'Hi Joy, I would like to write an English-Spanish dictionary because I simply can't seem to find such a dictionary with good quality out there. Can you recommend any good resources to me?'

My first reaction to that was that this plan was huge and with limited possibilities. Why? Have you ever seen a dictionary? Noticed the long list of professors and scholars who participated in its publication? Can you imagine the amount of time each took to contribute to it? How can any one individual compete with a group of highly qualified people with lots of institutional support? You can't. That doesn't mean you should just give up the idea entirely. Instead of trying to write a big dictionary, you could come up with something more targeted: 'Your Spanish secretary in Cancun – a booklet filled with commonly used phrases or expression that may come in handy for tourists'. Or perhaps your own speciality or interest would be more to your liking: 'How to write a successful university application letter'. There are so many possibilities. Narrowing the subject area often helps remove the barrier of having insufficient credentials. If it's your first publication, don't make it too long. The sooner you complete it, proofread it and publish it, the more confidence you will have for the next project. Remember, you can always add more content when you edit.

A few things I've learned

To make sure your publication brings the impact and results you want, here are some key elements:

1. **Create something that people really want and need.** To achieve this, you first need to know who you are going to write to. That's your target readers. For most people, it would be your clients or potential clients. It can be your colleagues or potential business partners as well. After you have that clear in mind, start collecting feedback from these people, both online or offline. That's what I did before coming up with the content for my e-book. Often when you get the WHO, your content is more targeted and focused. That's a critical step in making sure what you create is indeed wanted and needed.

2. **Establish your credibility.** It's important to let your readers understand why and how you came to the conclusion you did. In other words, you need to show your readers that you know what you are talking about. I find telling my own story helps me connect with my clients. They feel they can relate to me and that my ideas and advice are credible as they come from my own experience and have been proven effective.

3. **Choose an interesting topic.** Writing a book is quite different from writing your thesis. A book titled 'How to use the past tense properly' is not as sexy as '7 deadly mistakes to avoid when creating a bilingual website.'

4. **Write as if you are talking to a friend.** It's interesting that many

people write to show off their language skills. Seldom do they feel that the primary reason for writing is to communicate with others. Instead of trying to impress clients or readers with big words or long sentences, think about your message and how to economize your ideas into simple, clear language. Unless you are writing a novel, I suggest you use easy-to-understand sentence structures. Not everyone reads at the same level, especially not your clients. Keeping it simple and to the point is the way to go.

5. **Go easy on yourself.** I've come to a conclusion that the power of one is the rule of thumb for anyone who is ready to write a book. Try to focus on one main subject in a publication. Too much information often overwhelms your readers and as a result, they will be less likely to give you the kind of response you want. Make sure you read, re-read and have someone else read your work before publishing.

6. **Have a marketing strategy in place.** Writing a book is a huge task, but marketing it requires even more work. Here are a few effective tools to market and promote your publication:

- your own website
- your own e-zine
- free chapters
- listings on major websites
- networking groups your clients are members of.

You can find more information in my e-book *Say Goodbye to Feast or Famine*. If you don't have an e-zine set up yet, let me tell you this: I've been publishing my e-zine for the past three years and it has been my number 1 marketing tool. I share free tips and strategies every two weeks with my readers who are translators and other language professionals. I also respond to my subscribers and try to answer their questions and requests. As a result, my subscribers have come to view me as a credible, trusted source of information. Each issue of my e-zine results in more sales for my services and my e book.

Because of my e-book, I've been able to expand my horizons to include translation, consulting, coaching and online training. I'm also in the process of launching more digital programmes. My business is me, and I love every minute of it. It is great to be able to help people with my bilingual skills, but it feels amazing to transform people's businesses and in some instances improve their lives because of what I do. And interestingly, it all started with the small, humble idea of self-publication.

Interview with Luke Spear

Luke Spear is a freelance translator (French and Swedish to English) of some 10+ years, based in the East Midlands, UK, who runs a small agency with a core of loyal clients, freelances with a healthy balance of direct and agency clients, and spends time working on his pet project, linguaquote.com. He likes to employ technology for its intended use – to make working life easier – in order to free up time for actually living life. In this search for ever better working tools he has borrowed and built upon the collective and current best practices of similar professions, as well as borrowing from the world of online commerce and startups. These practical strategies are then focused into making the most of their technological, yet ever human, methods to streamline and grow a translation business. His website, work and writing can be found at lukespear.co.uk.

1) Luke, you are a successful French/English translator, a fervent blogger for the translation industry and also the author of two books aimed at freelance translators who wish to build and grow their translation businesses. What motivated you to start offering publications for freelance translation professionals, and what are your experiences with this activity?
Given that it took just shy of a month to produce the *Translation Sales Handbook*, I was taking a bit of a risk. Yet time was my only outlay, with digital publishing not requiring a minimum-quantity cost barrier to get started. I had an idea of

how to get the online 'shop' together, and had a few years' worth of relatively new online/offline sales and marketing techniques behind me, so I thought it might be a professionally rewarding way to spend a week. Or four, as turned out to be the case, some 45,000 words later.

With my first book, *Build Your Business as a Translator*, aimed at pre-professional translators, now offered for free through the site, I spent much less time. It was just a case of collating the basics for making a start in translation. It may well be in need of an update at this point, but the idea there was to really make some connections in translation and share what little I could with colleagues. It was the book I would have wanted as I was starting out.

Both books were satisfying, professionally and personally, the second more so because of its potential for wider impact among colleagues. The idea of digitally publishing with the ability to send out updates and follow-up downloads to existing customers was something I was quite excited about on publication, and I plan to release some additional notes later this year. There are a fair few 'business of translation' books on the market (although not an abundance, it must be said) and so I wanted to be sure I had something new and unique to add. My computing/IT viewpoint for leveraging tech was the most obvious angle from the start.

Finally, when it comes to blogging, I only scribble the odd post to share a view or two on the industry. I'm certainly not as prolific as some of the more dedicated bloggers out there, but I like to take a small part in the discussion if I can.

Over time I've tried to become more helpful in my content, and it certainly is a nice way to raise the profile of a website in the search engines and have my voice heard on the trivia that interests me, for what it's worth!

2) What impact has publishing your books had on your translation business, and does the income you generate from these publications reflect the time and effort invested?

The first book had little or no impact (especially given its target audience) on the business, save a few mentions by clients who appreciated the attempt and perhaps saw me in a new light once I had created a new resource for the industry, no matter how small the contribution was. Since the publication of my latest book, there has been a modest increase in interest in my work. However, I have been working on a few fronts other than freelancing these last few years that might somehow confuse the picture. These are principally a small translation agency, in which I try to apply best practices as I see them, and a side project that I hope to finally release for general use this year, called Linguaquote.

With the latest book I was aiming to earn in sales enough to cover the month it took to write. I did take on freelance and agency projects throughout this period, but not as many as I might have, so a month's pay was owed to me by the book, essentially. I did manage to reach this target, with modest marketing efforts, and hope to raise awareness of the updated version later this year alongside the release of the aforementioned side project.

If the *Translation Sales Handbook* was to sell as I hoped, I knew the book had to be practical, actionable and fluff-free to justify its existence. I certainly felt the pressure to 'be useful' while writing it. It had to offer enough methods for readers to earn back the expense one or many times over. I hope to have achieved this, and to bolster its content as time goes on. Kind compliments offered by translation associations and high-profile bloggers have offered some reassurance since its release.

3) You are also the creator of Linguaquote, an online portal that allows agencies and end clients to obtain quotes from freelance translators and contact them directly. Can you tell us more about this platform and how it came about? How does it compare to the 'traditional' translation-related platforms such as ProZ.com or Translatorscafe?

At the moment (mid-2013) there is a complete rebuild of the site in the wings, soon ready to be launched. I'm slightly hesitant to direct folks there just now, but people can certainly visit to get an idea of what is to come. The site intends to put freelancers and agencies on a level playing field when it comes to making sales to direct clients. It will also allow both groups, as well as buyers, to securely and efficiently manage multilingual projects, avoiding the long email discussions and file version chains that accumulate in our inboxes. The use of encryption across files, passwords and messages will allay concerns about data security at all levels, with tight permissions keeping files accessible on an 'eyes only' basis.

In terms of matching expertise and speciality subjects to specific translation projects, Linguaquote does a great job, with extensive use of taxonomies and categorisation to give buyers an easy way to compare language service providers from freelancers to agencies. Quality is a major concern of the site, with extensive (human) vetting of accounts conducted before profile publication. This way I can create a user-friendly resource that even the disparate translation associations struggle to produce, offering as much value as possible to translation buyers.

With all of these factors at play, then, direct comparison with existing platforms is hard to do. It takes all the best modern practices for selling, marketing, project management and security and packages them into a usable, uncluttered site that 'gets things done' for its users.

4) Do you enjoy this type of diversification from the translation career you originally embarked on, or do you find it challenging?
Yes! I certainly do. With Linguaquote I get to spend time spinning up high-powered servers, administrating and securing these systems, designing, programming and learning as I go; all the things I wanted to do as an ambitious 11-year-old with a QBASIC 'operating system' in the works. The same goes for writing, where a finished product can emerge from nowhere in a matter of weeks. With any luck, these products and projects will be useful to their audiences and I can say that I have contributed at least something along the way.

As with freelance translation, I have tried to create my own little jobs and fill them with as much responsibility as I wanted at the time. There are indeed risks and challenges, but these are calculated, with the odds tilting in your favour the more (or better) you produce. That's how I see it, at least!

5) Are you planning to continue translating as your main business activity, or is your long-term goal to make a living from passive income?
Translation is my 'bread and butter', as the saying goes, and I hope for it to be so (technological breakthroughs notwithstanding) until I'm too old to work.

If I can supplement that income with a body of work that covers my later years then I'll gladly put in the time and effort to do that now. I've always been quite optimistic and excited by progress, so in that respect I could predict a few more projects and creations over the decades to come, but I'd be a fool to ignore my main source of income, itself the result of time and effort expended in years gone by.

6) Where do you see freelance translators in five years' time in terms of diversification?
I won't pretend for a minute that I can reliably predict anything, but trends that are quite plain to see are already in place. Businesses worldwide are striving for the supposed panacea of automated, machine translation for voice and text applications. Few people in the world recognize the interpreter/translator distinction anyway, nor their respective value, with prices being squashed year on year for professional translators, despite, or perhaps due to, the rapidly expanding market.

I don't know if the supply of translators is exceeding demand, or if the market is commoditising the profession as time goes by, but it's clear that the role of the translator is changing and will be vastly different by 2018. If I have to make a prediction, bearing in mind the above disclaimer, I'd say that the smart translators who move with the market will end up consulting on all things multilingual (particularly software and business services) while the slower-to-react translators will face tougher times in the face of ever more 'passable' machine translation reducing the quantity and quality of projects being commissioned.

Clients who appreciate quality and expertise will still turn to the best linguists, leaving those providers relatively safe. But then perhaps a boom in multilingual e-book publishing could fuel the resurgence of the literary translator, or the EU might legislate for or against mass translation, doubling or halving the industry in one fell swoop; it's all unknowable, really, but all completely possible at the same time. All I know is that, wherever possible, I'd like to be part of the progressive crowd who are, of course, not averse to a little tangential diversification.

CONTINUING PROFESSIONAL DEVELOPMENT

Lucy Brooks *has been in business for over 30 years, and for the past 22 has operated a successful commercial and industrial translation business. For some of those years she ran a mini translation agency serving, in particular, public relations specialists working in industrial fields. She is a fellow of the Chartered Institute of Linguists (CIOL), a Qualified Member (MITI) of the Institute of Translation and Interpreting, and in 2008 she was one of the first to attain the newly created professional chartered status for linguists. While serving on the Translating Division Committee for the CIOL in 2009, Lucy instituted a series of webinars for the institute and drove forward a dynamic programme of professional development. She went on to found eCPD Webinars in 2010, pioneering online education and training for translators and interpreters. Since that time eCPD Webinars has become a byword for high-quality professional development for language professionals. The eCPD catalogue now contains subjects to cover virtually every training need a translator, whether new to the profession or a long-standing practitioner, may have. Yet the team still develops new and interesting courses. They work in partnership with a number of like-minded enterprises.*

WHEN NICOLE ADAMS ASKED ME to contribute a chapter to her book in which I would discuss how translators might offer additional income-boosting services, she asked me to concentrate on continuing professional development (CPD) as a way to develop a career. It is a massive subject. As a translator, just about every job you ever do contributes to the overall learning process.

While learning new skills and fields might not be lucrative immediately in terms of earning power, in my view it is absolutely essential if one is to maintain earning power and adapt to change. In this chapter I interview four prominent translators who have diversified by developing portfolio careers for themselves.

Anyone born before the 1980s has witnessed massive technological advances in their lifetime. Technology continues to advance at a hectic pace. Many people are working past the standard retirement age these days – by necessity or by choice – so there is even more need to adapt to the times and to new situations.

This chapter will explore the options for translators to become providers of CPD to their peers, and will show how making a contribution to the profession – even where not actually financially beneficial – can aid career advancement. I have talked to prominent translators who have, while continuing their core profession, branched out into the provision of services to translators. I asked each one what prompted them to diversify their activities, whether the effort they put in has been financially lucrative, and whether they enjoy this diversification and consider it part of their own CPD. I also asked myself the same questions.

What is CPD?

Let me begin by defining CPD. It stands for continuing professional development. In the US it is known as continuing education and in Australia as professional development. Essentially it simply means 'keeping up' with developments in your professional environment. Lawyers, accountants and medical practitioners, to name only a few professions, must undergo CPD in order to practise, and so should translators. As translators we can keep up in many ways: we can attend formal training courses and lectures, we can do informal background reading, and, of course, we can carry out unstructured CPD by watching television, or visiting our source (or target as appropriate) countries, and simply talking and listening.

Most qualified translators log their CPD in some way or another. Certified members of the American Translators Association are required to, as are Chartered Linguists in the UK, for example. Members of most professional organizations are encouraged to keep CPD records and if they are to follow their codes of conduct, are obliged to. Having established successful careers themselves, some translators feel that they would like to put something back into the profession by speaking to students, mentoring, or giving seminars in their specialist subject. These activities also count as CPD. It is this last area of providing training and information to other translators into which I have diversified, and which I intend to write about here.

About myself

I trained for a trilingual secretarial and translating career in the 1960s. I spent a few years working in travel and tourism before becoming an early user of word processing systems. My career morphed into one where I found that I had become the local expert on personal computers. As local businesses and individuals purchased their brand new Amstrad PCW and found that the most they could do with it by themselves was take it out of the box, I was in hot demand as a freelance trainer.

During that time I taught myself simple programming. I recall that for one local business I devised a program to cut out metal parts as economically as possible from a square sheet of metal. I also devised a booking system for a small coach tour business, but mostly I was called upon to set up accounts systems and databases for a wide variety of businesses.

I then spent 13 years in local government and also became very involved with an industrial PR company. In the 1990s, while still working in local government, I decided to come back to what I had trained for all those years ago – translation. With the support, advice and help of my husband, I refreshed my language skills and started to advertise for freelance translation work. I look back on my first translation jobs with a certain amount of horror and amusement now. I made mistakes, but learned from them. In 1991, there was little support for new translators and I made my way by myself. You could say that I devised my own continuous learning programme. I also quickly realized that all my previous work had been part of one long CPD programme, assisting me to become a better translator with knowledge of many specialist subjects. It had also helped me understand how to run a business, how to submit VAT returns, and how to produce an invoice, so the business side of becoming a translator was not hard for me.

By the mid-1990s my professional institute (the Institute of Linguists, as it was then) had started TransNet, a peer support group, and I joined it at an early stage. Although I did not know it at the time, it was from that point that diversification from a straightforward translation career began.

Putting something back – and gaining at the same time

You probably realize that I do not stand still for long. A decade is about as long as I have ever done the same thing on a constant basis. Now that I am old enough to draw a pension, the mortgage is paid off and my son is earning more than I do, I no longer have to worry about where the next penny is coming from and can spend more time doing what I want.

My contribution to the profession started when the aforementioned TransNet became electronic. I became its volunteer coordinator and promoted the e-group to translator members of the Institute of Linguists. Anyone with a question relating to translation and the business of translation could post it on the forum and receive almost instant advice. It was a godsend for many members and the work I did was appreciated. If I had something to contribute I did so, but I gained as much from the forum as I put in. TransNet was the first of its kind and I am proud that the network continues, now moderated by fellow members of the institute.

Voluntary work of this nature generates no income. What it does, however, is raise one's profile among colleagues and peers. Whenever I attended a function or a conference I found I was among friends, even if we had to peer at each other's nametags first! Having said that, networking, whether in person or electronically, can sometimes generate work. Members of TransNet often post jobs that they cannot handle themselves, or seek colleagues to collaborate with.

Organizing functions was the next step in my diversification path. Having set up the electronic version of TransNet, it was a logical step for me to stand for election to the Translating Division Committee at the Institute of Linguists (by now the Chartered Institute of Linguists). This committee works hard to provide training for translators.

During my time on the committee, events were held three or four times a year in London. Many people found it difficult to get to London (though it's surprising how far some would travel to these events – I met people who had travelled from the Isle of Skye and Spain to be there), so in 2009, I started to investigate a new medium of providing training that had recently appeared on the scene – webinars.

Online learning – the way to go

After a season of running several webinars for the Chartered Institute of Linguists on a voluntary basis, I decided to dedicate more time to the venture by setting up a commercial company.

In the summer of 2010, eCPD Webinars was born. It has now grown and developed to the point where the company offers training courses and a very wide range of single webinar topics for translators and interpreters.

I had to learn new skills – new softwares and how to use social media being just two – and the learning curve was steep. Initially I found that finding speakers was a problem. Not only did I have to convince people of our integrity and professionalism, but I was also faced with the need to train speakers who had never presented online and were, understandably, nervous. We were beset by tragedy, too. One of my original partners in the venture died soon after we opened for business, and with the changed dynamics the second felt unable to continue.

After a period of working with my wonderful co-director in Australia, Sarah Dillon, things changed again when Sarah decided to concentrate on her family. For the past year the business has been run with two directors. My 'other half', Maia Figueroa, is a translator of fiction into Spanish. She intends to maintain her translation workload, so has to juggle her deadlines with eCPD commitments. I have eased off on the amount of translation work I do – partly because I stopped working for agencies a couple of years ago when I opted to take my pensions, so I am able to dedicate a lot more time to the myriad tasks involved in keeping a lively and constantly evolving company going.

Public speaking

Heading eCPD meant that people in our industry became aware of my name and I found that I was being asked to speak at conferences and to MA students about my experiences as a translator. While fees for such events are, typically, fairly low (and sometimes non-existent) for the amount of work involved for one presentation, it is often possible to re-use presentations – with a few tweaks – for a different audience. Presenting is a very rewarding experience and a good way to get your name known outside your own small circle. In my role at eCPD Webinars, I spend a lot of time seeking out potential speakers, many of whom had not considered such a venture, but find that in fact they quite enjoy it. Some even go on to develop a very active public speaking career.

More ways of contributing to the profession as a method of development

This year I have started to mentor a new translator. I was pretty nervous about this, since my own qualifications are fairly ad hoc and random, but I have found the experience very rewarding. It has been illuminating to discuss the fine points of a tricky text with someone who looks at it from a different point of view. So, although mentoring is not technically you learning, in effect it is. A moderate fee is usually paid to the mentor for this service.

Blogging

Part of my work for eCPD is to find interesting articles and resources for our newsletter and our blog. I keep an eye on tweets and blogs from industry leaders and pass on tips and hints, as well as industry information while, of course, absorbing the information myself.

Speaking outside the industry

I believe strongly that as translators we have to broaden our outlook and talk to our potential end customers. It is a sad fact that most people outside our industry have little idea of what we do. Nataly Kelly and Jost Zetzsche rectified this recently with their bestselling book *Found in Translation* which attempts to tell the outside world just what a myriad of functions we linguists undertake.

Some years ago I wrote an article about choosing a translator. I had no idea where to publish it, so put it on my website. The article follows the lines of the excellent booklet published by the American Translators Association on buying translations.

I would urge all translators to approach their local chambers of commerce and business networking clubs and ask to give a talk about translation in general and their services in particular. Giving such a talk free of charge could well lead to some excellent contacts and potential work. Another way is to give a career talk to students of modern languages at a local school.

The case studies

I shall start by answering the four questions I asked of four prominent translators myself:

> *What spurred you to start training for translators?*
> eCPD Webinars came about because I could see from my work with the Translating Committee at the Chartered Institute of Linguists that there was a need to provide online training for people who, for various reasons, were unable to travel to city centres for training.

> *Would you say that the income you generate from this activity reflects the effort you put it?*
> eCPD Webinars makes a profit, but I am sure I put in more hours than are truly reflected in the income I earn from the venture.

> *Do you enjoy this diversification from the career you originally trained for?*
> I love it. I get to see all the presentations, which is great, and I also meet and get to know the movers and shakers of our industry, which has been an exciting development for me. I am beginning to be invited to present at face-to-face events, too.

> *Do you consider this activity to be part of your own personal CPD programme?*
> I consider a great deal of my work in this area as contributing to my own career development as a translator, but I don't log everything I do on my personal record. It would fill up too quickly!

Marta Stelmaszak *of WantWords is a professional translator and interpreter from Polish. She has made a name for herself as a public speaker and trainer in marketing skills and business for translators.*

(See also her own contribution to this book in the sub-chapter entitled Coaching and business training)

There are three key issues that made me diversify into providing business training to colleagues. First, when I was starting out I met a handful of wonderful people across all industries whose willingness to share their knowledge and expertise helped me enormously in getting established. I have always felt that I owed it to them.

Second, I think that knowledge is much more purposeful when shared. If I know something, only I know it. But if I share a marketing tip with 10 people, who pass it to another 10 people, it already makes a crowd.

The third issue is the whole profession. I agree that the stronger and more aware the whole profession is, the better situation we are in as individuals.

I am satisfied with the income from public speaking, writing articles, and my blog. It certainly covers the time I spend on preparation and actual delivery, and at the moment it is a steady source of income for me. But looking at the bigger picture, it is not only about the money. Public speaking and other profession-oriented activities strengthen my bond with the profession, make me feel fulfilled, and satisfy my abandoned teaching ambition. In this sense, the income is much higher.

My original career in translation was never a stand-alone. I have been participating in business and marketing training since I decided to become established as a translator. I even won a marketing competition a while back. One of the key things I have learned about doing business is the need to diversify and maintain a variety of sources of income. Diversification has been my plan from the very beginning! My current career mix contains just about everything I enjoy doing.

The skills I acquire and develop when engaging in training are certainly on my CPD list. Over the years, I have managed to work on my public speaking, online marketing, copywriting and interpersonal skills. You would be surprised how helpful business skills are in working as a freelance translator!

Jost Zetzsche *is an English to German translator, a localization and translation consultant, and a widely published author of books and articles on technical aspects of translation. A native of Hamburg, Germany, he earned a PhD in the field of Chinese translation history and linguistics, and began working in localization and technical translation in 1997. In 1999, he co-founded International Writers' Group on the Oregon coast. His computer guide for translators,* A Translator's Tool Box for the 21st Century, *was published in 2003. With Nataly Kelly, he is co-author of the hugely successful book* Found in Translation.

I felt that I was in the same boat as the majority of freelance translators: I loved language but I really was not well equipped to work with the computer. What differentiated me from many was that I was inquisitive enough to learn more about the computer and make it into a useful tool for my translation work. This seemed like a good place to start talking about my experiences and views, since I could speak the language of the technical novice explaining how he succeeded in making technology work for him.

I earn some money from it, but it's much less than what I would earn through translation working the same amount of hours. It benefits me in other areas, though. I am, for instance, often invited to give keynote speeches at conferences, and it also feels good to see the appreciation that many of my colleagues have for my writing. Another reason I started the work on my e-book and my newsletter was that I have MS and I am sometimes not able to work the long hours that are often required of a translator. The book and newsletter give me a little more flexibility for at least one part of my working life.

Even though my master's and doctorate theses in Chinese studies were on translation (history), I did not go through a typical translation programme. My current combination of actual translation combined with research about it seems like a perfect combination for me that in many ways reflects what I was trained to do, and I am very thankful that I was able to carve that niche for myself.

Suzanne Deliscar is a Canadian lawyer-linguist who translates in the French-English and Spanish-English language pairs. She focuses on legal and official document translation, as well as contract abstraction and e-discovery in Spanish and French. She is also the developer and presenter of numerous webinar programmes for translators and interpreters, focusing on legal translation, official document translation, and marketing.

I was spurred to help my fellow linguists/language service professionals learn about the industry initially when I saw how many found marketing their businesses to agencies and direct clients challenging.

In 2010, I taught my first training webinar, entitled 'Be Special: Standing Out in the Language Services Industry', when I shared the tools that I had used in marketing my lawyer-linguist services. The webinar was well received and I enjoyed incorporating a training aspect into my business.

Since that time, I have developed and presented many training programmes focused on legal translation, official document translation and marketing. I have plans to deliver even more webinar programmes in 2013.

It is important to distinguish between times when you speak as a contribution to your professional community, and times when the information you are offering should be exchanged for payment. I have spoken to the broader translator and interpreter community on numerous occasions for free, and find that work just as rewarding and a way to give back to my profession. If a particular training event is not profitable, I believe that all involved should consider the factors at play, for example, poor marketing, high cost, vague marketing copy, and rectify them.

I very much enjoy this addition to my career. In the legal profession, there is an expectation that a lawyer will be able to make a presentation in an articulate, successful fashion. However, I have found that although many linguists have superb expertise that they could share with others, they often seem hesitant to do so. I believe this to be true judging by the high demand for the courses that I and other linguists offer.

I find that by preparing to teach others I further refine my own skills, as I have to think through how to best present the material. I believe that most certifying bodies in the translation and interpreting industry acknowledge that teaching is one way to keep a certification current.

Tuomas Kostiainen *is a freelance translator from English to Finnish, residing in Northern California. A member of the American Translators Association, he is also an SDL-approved Trados trainer and now provides Trados and MultiTerm training, consultation and troubleshooting for translators and translation companies on-site and online.*

It all started because I wanted to learn Trados really well for my own translation work. Little by little I started helping my colleagues and realized that there was a big need for the knowledge among translators. I did not really consider it as a professional service or a source of income at that point, but rather a way to do something enjoyable and share my knowledge.

I do not see my training activities as being part of my own continuing education (CE) programme but certainly my own learning about Trados and other tools (for myself and for training purposes) is part of that.

Now that I have been doing it for about 10 years, the income reflects the amount of effort I put in, but it certainly did not during the first few years.

I enjoy teaching and it is a nice counterbalance for solitary translation work. It is also a good way to diversify my working day and business in general. This diversification also helps to even out occasional slow periods in translation work and supports my own translation business in many ways (knowledge of the tools, client contacts, recognition).

Being a provider of CPD – is it worth it financially?

From the case studies above it is clear that the main gain from developing a portfolio career and helping other translators is intense satisfaction, getting to know other industry leaders, and a feeling of self-worth. For some, the income generated from such activities is substantial, and with the increased exposure that such activities generate, there is also a greater likelihood of gaining new translation clients. The case studies show that translators already working in a specialized field feel passionately about passing their expertise on to others by presenting training courses and lectures.

Undertaking CPD – is it worth it financially?

As a translator, I think the single most lucrative step – and the one with the fastest returns – that I took with regard to learning new technologies was to encompass the movement towards computer-aided translation. I believe that without it, my earning power as a translator would have dropped drastically. With it, my accuracy and consistency increased and possibly my output increased. More output = more income.

Attending CPD lectures or webinars can be an entry into a new field of translation or income stream. Knowledge of a new field can mean new opportunities for translation and localization work. Learning to specialize in a particular subject can take many forms. In my case, it was mainly by doing, rather than by formal courses. I am a great believer in self-education. It is great to have a string of degrees but these days education is so expensive you have to be really sure that the course you enrol for will pay off with increased earning power in the future.

Meanwhile, a secretarial job with a firm of solicitors, or in a high-tech production company, pays the bills and provides good background for legal or technical translation later on. If working in the sector is not possible, the next best thing is to immerse yourself by reading about it in specialist trade press reports, journals and blogs. This can be a spare time activity that eventually pays off in more work opportunities.

To sum up, although providing CPD to fellow translators is a revenue stream, the main things gained are satisfaction, peer appreciation, personal development and a thorough knowledge of the industry.

The future

I am already thinking hard about a career for my seventies, as I begin to lay down some of my current work tools and activities and wind down towards retirement. But that is a still few years off!

ONLINE TRAINING COURSES

Désirée Staude lives in Frankfurt am Main. She has worked for over 21 years as a certified bilingual secretary for various corporations, including ANZ Bank, the legal firm Oppenhoff & Rädler and KPMG; she has also served as a project assistant for both AT&T and Lufthansa Systems. She started working part-time as a freelance translator in 2008 when a friend of hers, already a freelancing translator, suggested this to her and helped her with useful tips on how to begin. In 2011, Désirée founded her own company in order to work full-time as a freelancer and enjoy an ever more diversified working life. With this full-time business she continued to learn a lot more about freelancing and also improved her skills in improving productivity and time management. In 2012, she had the opportunity to hold an online training session at Wordsmith University, in which she passed on her combined knowledge about the change of role from employee to freelancer. From then on she made up her mind to diversify into the training sector as she finds it very satisfying to help and motivate others on their unique and individual path.

AS THE TRANSLATION INDUSTRY IS growing very fast and we all have to face the negative influences of low-price agencies and low-price performers, life is becoming pretty hard and uncertain. Given that, living by only offering translation services might not be possible much longer, unless you are so good at marketing that customers are queuing at your doorstep. If you don't have to worry about your translation business decreasing because you are so well known, or you work in such rare language pairs that you have nothing to fear from strong competition or low-price offers, you might be in a minority of freelancing translators who are doing well. The rest of us will have to think again.

Nowadays, a translator has to diversify in order to ensure his or her income. There are many ways of doing this. One person might be able to offer interpreting services, another transcription. If you are very good with graphics, you might choose desktop publishing (DTP) services. Enhancing your portfolio is all about gaining and using new skills. As all skills can be learnt, one cannot say, 'I don't know how to do it', 'I don't know how I should do the marketing', or 'I don't know if there will be a market'. The Internet contains a vast amount of information about everything and anything. You can learn new skills by reading blogs by successful people working in that field or business area. You can take courses (online, face-to-face or distance) and read lots of books about the new subject. You can ask fellow colleagues for help and tips. You will find that much information is freely available or, at least, doesn't cost much. Enhancing one's knowledge has never been as easy as it is these days. You just have to take advantage!

If you are not sure what kind of diversification you should try, think about what you like doing most apart from translation. What is it that makes you happy? What is it that you are interested (and possibly already well read) in? What kind of talents do you have? Define what it is you could do besides offering translation services.

My way

I attended so many online courses and learnt so much in 2011 and the beginning of 2012 that I thought about offering my (so far) accumulated knowledge in online training. I also felt that I wanted to help and motivate others as some of the teachers and authors had helped me so much by passing on their knowledge. So I began to compile all the information and tips I had learnt so far into a presentation. I contacted one of the teachers and told him about this idea, as I had always enjoyed his courses and had good conversations with him before. It turned out that he, also a translator and an agency owner, had already started to set up an online university called Wordsmith University, in which freelancers could attend online courses and learn about the industry and languages themselves. He was looking for teachers, and suddenly I was part of this university, doing exactly what I wanted to do: passing on knowledge to other freelance translators in order to help them.

I diversified in this way because I wanted to help others, as I was very grateful to have had the chance to learn from other fellow translators myself, and also to earn some extra money as my translation business was decreasing. I was vehemently refusing to accept low-price projects because I did not want to bring down the rates for my fellow translator colleagues and make it an even worse living for all of us. Then I realized how much I loved what I was doing. Of course, I was a beginner and had to learn how to give presentations. I not only needed to rehearse over and over again and felt weird at the live webinar session, but I also needed to learn techniques to make it really good. I listened to the recordings and made notes of where my weaknesses were, and continually tried to improve the following session until I was satisfied with the result and so were the attendees.

Benefits and successes (so far)

The biggest benefits and successes have been meeting a lot of interesting people who attend my training, and receiving positive feedback after the sessions and via the platform that keeps me going when I have a bad day and doubt my skills. Seeing some attendees register for other training sessions I offer gives me an additional boost and reassures me that I am doing the right thing and am good at it. I want to continue to improve and be worthy of their trust in me.

There has been another great side effect: as I had to re-read and re-watch a lot of materials to prepare and back up my training sessions, I absorbed the subject through continuous repetition. Theory became something I can rely on, something I feel I can actually touch; theory has turned into a well-loved practice. Now I offer webinars on a regular basis at Wordsmith University and have the opportunity to give training sessions at one of the leading translation platforms as well. My diversification has really taken off and I want to become established in the highly competitive training and speaking industry.

I have learnt that I do not have to limit myself to a single business and I enjoy the different kind of work immensely. My self-confidence about my abilities in every aspect of life has grown due to this experience and I hunger to go further.

Get started

To prepare myself when I was starting off as a trainer, I actively searched for people in the training and speaking business in Germany. I checked their websites, watched their promotional videos (when they had one), and even contacted one or two via social media networks. Guess what: most do not think of you as a competitor but as a possible future colleague who might pass on projects to people you know and like when you yourself cannot take them over.

Please consider that starting a diversified business means that you will have to spend much more time in front of your computer and that you will have even less spare time. As for offering training, the preparation for training sessions does take quite a while, as you have to find a subject that will be interesting and helpful to the potential audience, do lots of research, define the content of the presentation, set up the presentation, prepare what you will say alongside each slide, and decide if you want to include quotes or statistics (this should be really well researched). When all this has been taken care of, you'll find yourself presenting this training to yourself over and over again in order to sound professional when you finally hold the presentation, otherwise people will not continue to grant you their time (and money) to attend it.

Whatever you plan to do with regard to diversification, dare to ask people who are already successful in that area if they might be able to help you and give you tips on how they made it. I met interesting people doing so and they can be assured that I will pass customers on to them if I cannot handle a project for whatever reason. Get as much background information as you can about the new business area. Read whatever you can lay your hands on, check out youtube.com for additional information (a great source of knowledge from different perspectives), and then give it a go! You are only limited by yourself. But you do not have to limit yourself; dare to dream and whatever you put your mind to you can achieve – no matter how difficult the obstacles and odds of life!

Determination

It is possible to make things work when you like doing something and are determined to be as good at it as you are at translating. With regard to diversifying, there are some things you should know. One is never born a master, and on your way to mastery you may make a number of mistakes, have to face setbacks, feel completely lost or lose faith in your own abilities. These things will happen from time to time (more often at the beginning), but you can take the opportunity to accept the (partial) failure and learn from it.

The more you practise the better you get. The more you learn and ask questions, the better and more self-confident you will become. Share your thoughts with others – translators or colleagues in the new field of business. Join forums and be active. All you have to do is to be determined and commit yourself to never ever giving up. When you stumble, get back on your feet and carry on! Look back in order to learn, but look forward in order to see where you are heading. Commit yourself to reaching the top 20 in this new field. The more well known you become, the more your translation business will be also recognized. Diversification should be seen as a win-win situation – a tough one at the beginning, but always win-win.

External diversification
SPECIALIZED SERVICES FOR LANGUAGE SERVICE PROVIDERS
AND FELLOW TRANSLATION PROFESSIONALS

IN RECENT YEARS, A NEW TYPE OF diversification has started to emerge. An increasing number of freelance translators have started to offer services targeted specifically at their peers and colleagues. Many freelance translation professionals are excellent linguists but lack skills in other areas, such as business, CAT tools or desktop publishing. A new generation of 'diversifiers' in the language industry has identified exactly these gaps in expertise.

Today, freelance translators have access to an impressive range of choices when it comes to business and marketing training specifically geared towards them. They can attend CAT tool training sessions, or have their websites designed by a team of experts who specialize in websites for translators. In this chapter, we'll hear from business coaches, public speakers, web designers and desktop publishing specialists, all of whom are targeting freelance translators or LSPs and have become well established in their new niches.

COACHING AND BUSINESS TRAINING

Marta Stelmaszak BA (Hons) NRPCI MCIL DipTrans IoLET is a Polish–English translator and interpreter working in law, IT, marketing and business. She is a member of the Management Committee of the Interpreting Division at the Chartered Institute of Linguists and a Co-head of the UK Chapter of the International Association of Professional Translators and Interpreters. She is also an Associate of the Institute of Translation and Interpreting, a qualified business mentor, a member of the Institute of Enterprise and Entrepreneurship and the Chartered Institute of Marketing. She is working towards a master's degree in management, information systems and innovation at the London School of Economics and Political Science. In 2013, she was awarded a Higher Education Social Entrepreneurship Award. Marta runs the Business School for Translators, where she shares her experience and business knowledge with other translators and interpreters. Marta gives regular talks and webinars, writes articles for The Linguist *and* ITI Bulletin, *and speaks at conferences.*

TRANSLATION HAS ALWAYS BEEN the centre of my professional life, with my daily routine evolving around different time zones, holidays adapted to quieter and busier seasons, and deadlines being more important than regular working hours. I have been translating for some six years now, working mainly in IT, business, and marketing, and completing a healthy number of interpreting assignments here and there. Translation has shaped my working environment, creating the need to have at least two panoramic screens and drink more coffee than is clinically advised. Looking at it, one might say I had it all; I matched the definition of a successful freelance translator. But I wanted more.

Discovering the business angle

The more came from this other part of me, the part that has always been up for a challenge, up for a new deal, up for organizing a meeting, a conference or a charity ball. The other part insisted on taking business and marketing courses and, to be fair, turned me into quite a good translator. However, for a fair bit of time I never took the other part of me quite seriously. Startups, coaching, mentoring… it all sounded like a meaningful and productive hobby. To me, I was primarily a translator, and if I wanted diversification, I could say I was an interpreter.

Freeing the business person inside

It all started to change when the profession was buzzing about diversification. I understood the concept and agreed with it: offering more services does provide more stability and reliable sources of income. However, I decided to diversify not because I was concerned about a lack of assignments, but because I realized I could put into practice more of my skills and passions. My first try at diversification was to become more formal about my interpreting, and it worked fine for me at the time. I also decided to offer transcreation and some desktop publishing (DTP) services.

As a long-term diversification plan, I decided to polish my French and resurrect my Norwegian. At that point, I also decided I wanted to try my hand at translation project management, so I joined a small company on a part-time basis. Gradually I began to realize that the business skills and know-how that I took for granted were in fact precious and sought-after qualities. I decided to free the business part of me and acknowledge its existence. We had a long and honest meeting, like the one you have with a potential business partner, and we discussed the options. I agreed to treat the translator and the businesswoman in me equally.

Using the business you to help your translation business

The real challenge was to combine the two in a fair and non-conflicting manner. The first and obvious step was to use the business skills I had just rediscovered to revamp my own language business. I had another look at my business model, pricing, strategies, marketing and branding. In a way, I hired myself as my own business coach and I wasn't scared to criticize my previous choices or decisions, made by a translator but not a skilled business thinker. All the changes that I have introduced in my translation business have brought interesting results. In the end, by being more of a businessperson, I became a much happier translator.

After freeing the businessperson in me and rediscovering my skills, I decided to take it further. In an extremely productive meeting, where I told her about the hurdles and problems translators have with marketing and business skills, Meg from Websites for Translators came up with the idea of offering websites and a range of marketing services to freelancers. Not a translator herself, she immediately fitted in and found a way to make the entrepreneurial side of her clients shine. In many cases I witnessed these transformations myself. Seeing people enjoying being entrepreneurial and taking charge of their businesses has been a deeply inspiring experience.

I know people who left the overworked and underpaid freelancer's lifestyle behind them and transformed themselves into independent and appreciated experts with some encouragement and a few pieces of advice from a business mentor.

Setting up the Business School for Translators

In a conversation with a colleague about two years ago, I mentioned that my biggest dream would be to set up a business school for freelance translators, to share our experience and skills in running a successful translation business. I started by writing a business-oriented blog for translators, covering issues as simple as what to put on a business card or how to network with clients. I published a guide on CV writing and then became fascinated with social media. I gave my first presentation and first webinar, then a published article, then a guest post, and the ball started rolling. I realized that the demand for sound and practical business advice was there, and the feedback I was getting from my colleagues encouraged me to work even harder. In this first stage, the Business School for Translators was a blog and a few presentations I gave. However, even at this point, it was already bringing return on investment high enough to make the time I spent on it profitable.

Now the Business School for Translators is not only a blog, but I have launched regular online training sessions hosted by eCPD Webinars with help from Lucy Brooks, and I have developed my portfolio of publications. The idea behind the school is to encourage a more practical or business-minded approach to the art of translation. When students are at school doing their degrees in languages or translation, they learn a lot about translation theories, interpreting modes, or how to find the best equivalent, but they are not usually told how to actually work as a freelance translator or interpreter and earn money from it. My school equips students with a set of practical tools to help them survive or even flourish on the market.

Apart from the training and the blog, I run a thriving Facebook page and a Twitter account. I'm also working on starting in-person training sessions on everything that's practical about translation and interpreting with Valeria Aliperta of Rainy London Translations. Our idea is to run smaller workshops, rather than seminars or presentations, where colleagues can work on the various aspects of their business with some help and coaching from us. I have to admit that it was Valeria who came up with the name, The Freelance Box , explaining that every freelance translator should have a symbolical (and why not tangible?) box with tools needed to run a successful business.

Combining the two

At this point, I can say that I am a fully-fledged provider of business skills training for translators and interpreters. Each month I spend about eight hours writing blog posts (or 'lessons'), plus about 30 hours delivering online training, and about four hours on one-to-one or in-person sessions. It comes to about 42 hours a month, so just over a day of work a week. As a result, I can't translate five days a week, but about four. I have also hired a part-time assistant to help me with the administrative side of running the school.

However, finding a different source of income encouraged me to fire the lowest paying clients. It is not the only benefit I have experienced after diversifying into providing business skills training. I feel more confident because I have a range of sources of income and I am not solely dependent on translation or interpreting work. I have more stability and I can predict my income more easily, eliminating the issue of the feast and famine. I can expect a certain level of income from the training and it helps me to cover basic expenses. Speaking and presenting is financially satisfying, but most of all it is extremely rewarding.

Because I have a steady source of income, I don't feel tempted to accept less profitable offers. Moreover, I feel more satisfied and fulfilled in terms of creativity. By promoting my business skills training and the Business School for Translators, I've learned a whole lot of tips and strategies for successful marketing. Needless to say, I've used them in my own marketing, enhancing my profile and developing a client base. Meeting clients at marketing and business-related events is a perk as well.

I can certainly say that translation and providing training fit together quite well. I meet plenty of people every week, and I am always happy to offer business advice to colleagues. In return, they recommend my translation services to their clients. Believe it or not, I actually found a couple of clients who read my 'How to write a translator's CV' guide and decided to work with me, appreciating the business angle of my services.

Overcoming challenges

The biggest challenge I experienced when diversifying into providing business skills training for translators was the issue of my own confidence. I am largely a self-made person, and as I mentioned, for a long period of time I used to ignore the business part of me. As a result, in the beginning I lacked the confidence to share my skills and knowledge. Being a translator doesn't help either, as the majority of us tend to be more introverted. By providing such services, I was also risking being perceived as a ninja entrepreneur rather than a reliable professional. However, I met a number of wonderful people whose encouragement and support made me feel more and more confident that what I was doing was right and needed. The results speak for themselves, too.

At the moment, I am still trying to find the best way to manage being a translator and a business trainer at the same time. One can quite easily dominate the other, and I have to be very careful not to end up drained after a long project, with no energy to spread the entrepreneurial spirit around. Providing business skills training requires plenty of preparation, as well as a certain level of enthusiasm and creativity. I find that I have to be in the right mindset, or even put my businessperson hat on to be up to the task. On the other hand, translation requires a more meticulous and scrupulous approach. Switching between the two extremes can be quite challenging. In order to manage the workflow, I had to invest in another computer, a tablet, two whiteboards and a flipchart. I try to keep the two separate, and while I still have just one office, I have different desks for different tasks. Sometimes I even find myself being in a different mood, depending on the part of my business I'm devoted to at a given moment.

Diversification as the way forward

Diversification into providing business skills training required me to change my lifestyle and way of thinking. Some people are a bit confused when I can't answer straightforwardly when asked what I do for a living. In general, we're used to the fact that people have one vocation or profession; it helps us assess and understand the world around us. We all know someone who is a doctor, a lawyer, a gardener or a hairdresser. Simple answers signpost our professional lives. That is why diversification may seem alien, or unnatural, in the beginning. But one of the reasons why I am an independent professional is that I have a few ideas about my career, and I find it hard to imagine a single occupation or workplace that would allow me to combine them all. When asked what I do, I can't say I'm a translator, because I'm also heavily involved with business and marketing. On the other hand, having this skill set has already attracted a few clients who were interested in intercultural marketing services. Yet another venture to diversify into?

Appreciating both the translator and the businessperson in me has brought a range of benefits. I feel more satisfied as a professional, because I can do more things that I like. I have managed to establish diverse sources of income and this has provided me with financial stability, so important in a freelancer's lifestyle. Most certainly, one aspect of my business drives the other at the moment. And seeing other colleagues flourish makes me feel very optimistic about the future of the whole profession. If you have more than one passion, do not be afraid – diversify.

TEACHING AND PUBLIC SPEAKING

Konstantin Kisin is a trainer, speaker, business coach and freelance translator who gives workshops and webinars on topics like negotiation and communication skills, productivity and work/life balance. With over 10 years in the language service industry and an extensive knowledge of the psychology of communication and human behaviour, Konstantin offers practical solutions based on his hands-on experience of running a successful freelance business. A dynamic and engaging trainer, Konstantin shares his attitude to doing business with his customary passion and enthusiasm and is known throughout the industry for his out-of-the-box thinking and counterintuitive ideas.

IT IS A GENUINE PLEASURE TO have been asked to contribute a chapter to this book. I will focus on a specific type of diversification with which I have some personal experience: training and continuing professional development but first, by way of disclaimer: The discussion of what many people call the 'need for diversification' in the language service industry has become louder and more prominent since I became a translator over 10 years ago.

It is not uncommon now to hear people talk of diversification, particularly offering training and mentoring, as the 'only way to achieve a good income' in our industry.

My position on this could not be clearer: people who don't know how to make money in this industry have no business teaching or mentoring others, in the same way that you would not go to a yoga class taught by someone whose personal mantra was: 'Yoga is impossible!'

Early on in my career as a trainer and speaker, I read a wonderful book called *The Way of the Peaceful Warrior* by Dan Millman. The book is a treasure trove of beautiful stories and metaphors, one of which had a particularly strong impact on me as a budding trainer, the story of 'Gandhi and the Boy Who Ate Sugar':

> One day, a distressed mother took her son to see Gandhi. They waited in the queue for many hours and when her turn came, the mother stepped

forward and asked Gandhi to tell her son to stop eating sugar because it was bad for his health.

Gandhi looked at her, then at the boy. He considered them for a short while and eventually said that he would not be able to help at this time and asked them to come back in two weeks.

Frustrated, confused and discouraged, the woman took her son home but decided to return two weeks later. When she did, Gandhi looked at the boy and said 'Stop eating sugar!' Amazed and confused further still, the boy's mother pleaded with Gandhi to explain the reason for his strange behaviour: 'Why couldn't you have told him this two weeks ago?' she asked.

'Because two weeks ago, I was still eating sugar,' he replied.

Anyone can offer training that will be of value to others. The trick, for want of a better word, is to identify something you do or know extremely well. And when I say 'extremely well' I am talking about being one of the best in the world at what you do. This could be anything from Norse mythology to working with a specific CAT tool to accounting to negotiating with clients. We all have different skills, life stories and experiences that give us a unique perspective on life, business and just about anything else. All of these different perspectives can be of value to the right audience.

If you are reading this book, you are probably an expert in some aspect of what you do. Maybe you have never thought about how much of an expert you are in these areas because, as an expert, you take your expertise for granted: you know what you know and see nothing special in knowing it. If you are thinking about offering training to others, these are the fields you'll want to focus on.

It is often said that one of the hardest things in life is to practise what you preach. The solution, however, is simple: only preach what you practise. Providing language services continues to be my main occupation and the source of most of my income – I wouldn't feel comfortable teaching people something I wasn't doing myself on a daily basis. Being a trainer and showing colleagues how to do more and do better is a wonderful privilege that comes with many responsibilities, including the responsibility to continue to do more and do better yourself, a topic to which we will return.

If you have reached the point in your life where you feel that your expertise is worth sharing with others, the modern world is brimming with opportunities. There are hundreds of conferences and workshops happening every year all around the world, webinars are quickly becoming a powerful and easy way to reach your audience and CPD is increasingly recognized as an essential part of a freelancer's career. With online venues such as ProZ.com actively embracing the concept of in-person and online training, you have the opportunity to share your knowledge and reach people who would benefit from it easily, quickly and with little to no expenditure.

There are a few boxes that have to be ticked before you can embark on your journey as a trainer and speaker:

- You have to know what you know and what you don't know.
- You have to know which skills you'll need and which of them you don't currently have.
- You have to identify and understand your audience.

What you know and what you don't know

From the outset of your career as a trainer, you have to make a commitment to authenticity. Not because this is 'morally right' and 'proper' but because it is the only way to long-term success.

You have to be clear about what you are an expert in and what you are not. For example, I never run webinars on CAT tools because it's not something I know well enough. With enough research, I could probably present a decent workshop on this topic but I am not interested in running 'decent' workshops – I only want to show people things I know inside out. If someone woke you up in the middle of the night, put a knife to your throat and demanded that you tell them about some part of your work that you know like the back of your hand, what would you talk about? The answer to this question is usually a good indication of what you really know!

Skills you need and don't yet have

It is an obvious fact that there is a massive gap between knowing something and being able to teach it to other people. No amount of expertise can make up for poor communication skills or a lack of flexibility in adapting your message to the audience. Training is an act of persuasion: the trainer's job is not simply the delivery of information. Like a farmer planting crops, you have to locate and prepare fertile ground for the seeds you wish to plant. Telling people what you think is not enough – you have to captivate, entertain, challenge, inspire and lead.

Most of us are not born with these skills. I certainly wasn't. In fact, for most of my life the thought of standing up (let alone speaking) in public filled me with a sense of foreboding and dread. I also lacked the mental and linguistic flexibility to be able to communicate my message in a way that could reach people who had different personalities and ways of thinking. The good news is that all these abilities are learnable. They are skills, just like riding a bicycle, and all it takes is the desire to learn and the right teachers.

The most important part of my career as a trainer and presenter happened before I came anywhere near a microphone. I spent several years and a lot of money learning about different branches of practical psychology and public speaking, and even dabbled in hypnosis and guided meditation, learning from many incredible teachers and mentors. And I continue to do so.

There is an obvious and stark contradiction in the training industry where many people talk about the importance of training in order to promote their workshops and webinars while they themselves no longer undergo any training themselves. The best trainers, coaches and workshop leaders I have met are people who continue to learn from others and have no attachment to their status as a teacher. Deciding to become a trainer is a commitment to lifelong learning.

Your audience

There is an audience for every subject. To reach your audience you have to understand who you're talking to and what they want that you can offer. You can do this by thinking about things from the perspective of the other person, asking people directly and observing online discussions. If you're offering training in CAT tools, what do people want to know? What is it that they need to know but probably don't? What are the most commonly asked questions on CAT tool forums and at conferences? If your webinars are going to be about business skills, which skills are both necessary and lacking in the translation industry? What do people want to learn about? How can you connect your expertise and what you can talk about authentically with the needs and wishes of others?

The biggest mistake you can make as a trainer is thinking that everyone is your audience. If you speak regularly at large conferences and other industry events, one of the things that becomes apparent very quickly is that not everyone who attends your presentation actually came to hear what you have to say.

A typical conference audience of 100 people usually contains 60-65 people who hold that intention. Of the rest, a handful came to ask a question. That is their only objective and they will ask a question regardless of what you say. You will learn to recognize these people because they go from presentation to presentation looking for an opportunity to demonstrate their knowledge and expertise.

As you are giving your presentation, their eyes will typically have a glazed look and, while they may pay attention every now and again, most of their focus is internal: they are rehearsing their question or replaying the response to the question they asked at the previous presentation in their mind.

A few others came because there was nothing better to do. The other presentations on offer were of even less interest to them and in coming to your presentation they may be open to the idea that you have something of value to offer or they may not. And some people simply walked into the wrong room and are too embarrassed to walk out halfway through. As a speaker, you have to learn not to take this personally. Any presenter who enters a conference room expecting to reach and convince everyone is in for a disappointment.

Not everyone who walks into a shop buys something, not every person who contacts you for a translation ends up being your client. That's business. It is therefore important to think about the type of people you want to reach and speak to them, both in your webinars, workshops and presentations and in your promotional materials. What do they want and what makes them want that?

For example, if you want to teach people about negotiation skills your audience will be people who:

- already have clients
- believe that their work is or could be worth more than they are currently being paid
- feel that their negotiation skills are insufficient to achieve their objectives
- are open and interested in learning.

What do they want?

- more money
- better rates
- more confidence and skill in challenging negotiation scenarios
- an enjoyable learning experience.

Once you identify your audience and understand what they want, you can begin to explain how what you are offering will meet those needs. A lot of the time practical reasons are driven by underlying psychological factors. If asked, people who want to be better negotiators will tell you they want to make more money and charge better rates, but on careful observation you'll usually find that, more than anything, they want to feel comfortable and in control when they're negotiating with clients.

Your ability to reach your audience in promotional materials depends, first and foremost, on communicating your understanding of people's needs and explaining how what you are offering meets them. What's more, the process of doing this actually gives you, the trainer, a much better understanding of what kind of course would best serve the needs of your audience.

For me, the decision to become a trainer came primarily from a desire to contribute to the conversation about how the translation world is and ought to be and to share useful practical techniques with colleagues. A successful trainer's focus is always on the audience. If you aim to make sure that the people who spend their time and money on attending your training events get what they need, the personal rewards will follow.

CAT TOOL CONSULTING

Nicole Keller finished her translation studies (English and Spanish) at the University of Heidelberg in 2000. After a short period of time she went back to university and started her dissertation on web-based terminology databases, which she published in 2006. During her dissertation Nicole also started to work as a freelance trainer and translator. Today, she is a university lecturer at the Institute for Translation and Interpreting of Heidelberg University and specializes in medical translation from English into German as well as translation memory tools and terminology databases. She also works as a freelance trainer and consultant for different translation memory systems and terminology databases. She still works as a freelance translator and specializes in medicine and IT from English into German. She is a member of the German terminology association (DTT) and the German professional association for technical communication (tekom). She is also very active in the German translators' and interpreters' association (BDÜ) giving training and writing articles on different technologies for freelance translators.

AT THE BEGINNING OF MY UNIVERSITY studies, none of our lecturers talked or even knew about CAT tools as a supporting device for translators, and the Internet was still in the early stages of development. I remember that I had to complete a full semester course to receive my first email address. In the course, we learned how to do commands in DOS and the email program Pegasus Mail for DOS. It is a blessing that we do not have to use this platform anymore.

By the end of the 1990s, the situation regarding the use of computer-based tools and information research on the Internet was changing very rapidly. At the end of my studies we had actually heard of the computer-aided translation tool Trados Workbench, and we knew that translators used those tools to optimize their daily work, but there were no courses for such tools at university.

Reality struck when I started out on my first job as a project manager in a small translation agency. We had to use several CAT tools for different customers, and I had to get up on them to cope with my everyday work. The typical learning-by-doing process started. My colleagues supported me as best they could, but most of the time I had to consult the user guide to improve my knowledge and solve my individual problems, so my relevant experience and knowledge was increasing every day.

After a short period of time, I decided to go back to university and embark on a dissertation on terminology systems and the advantages of their web-based interfaces, which were at this stage mainly offered by the bigger CAT tool providers. During my work I came into contact with all the leading CAT tool producers and as I familiarized myself with their terminology systems I also got to know their complete solutions – the translation memory systems. At one translators' conference, I met one of the leading members of the German translators' and interpreters' association (BDÜ) and we decided to start the first seminar series comparing different translation memory systems with a view to supporting freelance translators in opting for the right tool. The seminar series was, and still is, very successful. That means that freelancers are keen to use those tools in their daily working lives.

In the course of time, more and more companies not only introduced translation memory systems but also combined them with additional products or modules like workflow modules, machine translation systems or supporting interfaces for technical documentation. Buying those systems and using them in-house made the companies more independent and more flexible in choosing their language service provider. In recent years, there has been an increasing trend for companies to revert to direct contact with freelance translators rather than giving the whole translation package to one translation agency. The agencies usually work together with a big pool of freelancers who are unknown to the actual customer. This transition and the fact that the computer has now turned into a main work tool for a translator means that freelancers have to extend their knowledge to encompass computer-based problems and challenges if they want to satisfy the technical requirements made of them by their direct customers. This is one of the main reasons why a lot of translators today have to work with several different translation memory tools and why CAT training has become more and more popular and important.

In the complex setting of translation memory tools and the processes they imply, translators only cover one part of the sometimes long chain of different tasks. Quality management or European standards like EN 15038 (Translation services – Service requirements) make it necessary to integrate more people than used to be the case. See Figure 6.1 for the departments/people potentially involved in translation processes.

Figure 6.1: Departments/people potentially involved in the translation process

I am in an advantageous position. On the one hand, I teach at university, offering workshops and seminars on different CAT tools and terminology systems. This means that I automatically stay up to date. After all, we cover a broad variety of different tools so that the students get a good insight into their functions and features before they enter the language market. On the other hand, I still work as a translator using translation memory systems for my translation jobs. This combination is an ideal precondition for someone supplying training courses on translation memory systems, as I can compare different systems and I know all about the problems that can occur from my everyday experience at the coalface.

In my opinion, it is absolutely essential to acquire the relevant technical knowledge as early as possible because in today's market-place it is important, not to say crucial, to work with at least one translation memory tool if you want to stay competitive as a freelance translator.

Training options

At the beginning of my trainer career, I only offered workshops for freelance translators. That means all attendees used their own installations on their personal notebooks, followed my explanations and tried to repeat the steps on their computers. We divided the workshops into two different groups: beginners and advanced users. The advantage of this is that the participants can really work with the system and solve actual problems from the word go. The disadvantage is that, especially with the beginners, there can be a lot of time-consuming problems that have to be solved, so the topics covered in one day are very limited.

Accordingly, I also tried out presentations instead of workshops, since here the groups were relatively big (up to 12 attendees). I set up PowerPoint presentations with matching handouts so that the attendees could take notes during the seminar and follow the practical examples without trying to replicate them on their notebooks. The theoretical parts contained enough screenshots and explanations so that they could use the written material as a basis for their work at home.

The advantage of this method is that the attendees are not distracted by trying to repeat the single steps on their system. On the other hand, they have no opportunity for encountering practical problems at the outset and solving them with the help of the trainer. Today, I use a combination of both methods, so the attendees get some practical experience with the system and also a good overview of the main modules and functions.

With the increasing speed of the Internet, webinars also became attractive as a training medium. The advantages are clear: they are cheaper, you can reach more people anywhere in the world and you can serve a larger group of attendees. Another advantage is that webinars can be recorded and people can watch them twice or more. Usually, they are not planned for a whole day but split up into two-hour sessions focusing on one main topic. This means that you learn the different topics step by step and not all of them in one day. Before the next webinar session you can practise handling the features you've learned about and are likely to have a better understanding of them at the next session. The disadvantage is that they are not as interactive as classroom training formats, where attendees can ask questions and make comments.

In my experience, companies in particular prefer a mixture of classroom training sessions and webinars. They use webinars as a follow-up after basic classroom training. Webinars enable participants to deepen their knowledge at a later stage, while in the classroom context they can ask any questions they may have about specific issues.

The situation today

Today, CAT tools are used by the majority of freelance translators. In fact, they are very often forced by their customers to work with a certain, sometimes company-specific, tool. The unfortunate side of this is that they have to invest a great amount of time in getting to know the different software products and solving the specific problems involved instead of actually doing their translation jobs.

Another very critical problem often discussed in translators' forums and at conferences is that companies tend to look for translators who can work with a certain tool instead of asking after their professional competence, for example, what they specialize in. The result is that the stipulated tool is used at the expense of translation quality.

Recent discussions at translators' conferences have shown that translators are not very happy with a situation that forces them to work with several different tools instead of focusing on the real translation process again. As long as standard exchange formats are not offered and supported by the tool producers, there is probably no choice. But in recent years there has been an observable trend towards standards like XLIFF, TMX and TBX that make it easier – at least for freelancers – to work with a (possibly) different tool of their own, while maintaining compatibility with other tools.

One important point I want to refer to in this context is that in my view this great diversity of tools is mainly a problem in Europe, especially Central and Eastern Europe. In the rest of the world, freelance translators are not confronted with these problems to the same extent. This is because in other countries CAT tools are not used as often and the diversity of tools is limited to two or three different products. Not all the translation memory tools known and used in Germany are available in the rest of the world as well.

If you think of globalization and the way it has opened up the worldwide market, translators do not only have the advantage of offering their portfolio to companies all over the world, they are also confronted with new pricing situations and new software used in different countries. For many translators this is a good opportunity to earn more money than in their own country. But you also have to keep in mind that you might have to invest in new software products – an investment that calls not only for money but also intellectual effort.

Where will translators be in five years' time?

The whole software industry is going through a big change at the moment. You can observe an unstoppable trend towards cloud applications (see Figure 6.2). Just look at the new Windows 8 or the new options in Microsoft Office 2013. This trend will not stop short of translation memory tools and terminology database systems. Traditional tools already offer web-based interfaces for their local installations, but the new tools on the market work with pure cloud applications requiring no installation at all.

These solutions present new opportunities both for companies and for freelance translators. One advantage is that these installations are much cheaper, since licences mostly have to be offered by the customer. Since a cloud-based application does not require any installation, technical problems are reduced dramatically.

Translators are also much more flexible as far as choice is concerned. It does not matter anymore if you work with a Windows- or Macintosh-based computer, or any other operating system.

This diversification is probably something that will not vanish but this is a phenomenon that can be seen with almost every (software) product. You will always have several competitors on the market. I am convinced that the cloud application will also offer small groups of freelance translators the opportunity to position themselves better on the market in order to offer a greater variety of languages and services without investing in expensive offices and software.

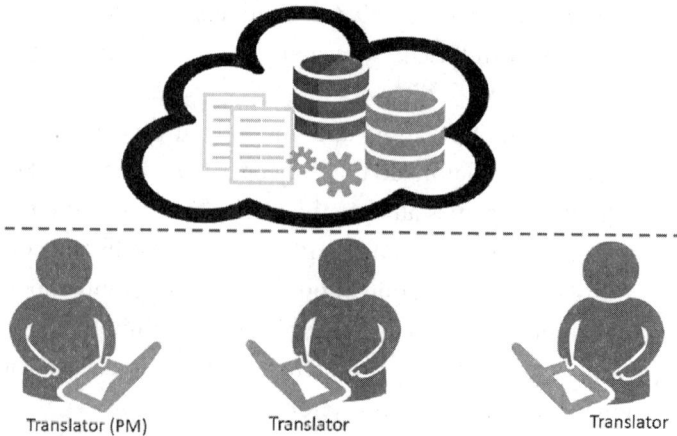

Figure 6.2: Cloud-based work as a translator

Conclusion

The market offers great opportunities for translators, but to be competitive, it is essential that freelancers acquire very good technical knowledge of the system(s) they use. The better their knowledge, the more independent they are and the better the quality they can offer to their potential customers.

In my opinion, CAT tool training sessions will remain an important element in a translator's life and it is fortunate that with the help of translators' associations they can be provided at affordable prices. My experience has shown that the more knowledge you have in one tool, the easier it is to learn how to work with a new tool, since the underlying principles and central features are most often comparable.

The training sessions have helped me a lot and even improved my daily life as a translator. I still do translations, though not full-time, and hardly ever have any problems using different tools. I do not want to suggest that everyone should now start coaching other people on how to use CAT tools. But the days are over when freelance translators should close their minds to new technology. Hardly any translation is done without a computer. The more familiar you are with yours, the more exclusively you can concentrate on the translation itself.

WEBSITES AND WEB-RELATED SERVICES

Magdalena 'Meg' Dziatkiewicz is the owner and managing/creative director of Websites for Translators, a Twisted Marketing Ltd project born in the heart of London with the help of an interesting blend of creative, entrepreneurial minds. Meg decided to work on Websites for Translators because of her intense love for languages, IT and marketing. Apart from her native language (Polish), Meg speaks English, Finnish and French. Although she was tempted to become a translator (it runs in the family!), her creative energy went into a different direction, making her an ambitious web developer and an aspiring marketing mind. Meg's background in advertising and marketing helps to create a balance between the translation industry and the latest marketing trends. Websites for Translators shares the business-minded approach amongst translators and freelancers, whilst emphasizing the values of entrepreneurship, professionalism and self-employment. Through our web design, marketing, and management services the project aims to help translators grow their own businesses worldwide.

BELIEVE IT OR NOT, WEBSITES FOR TRANSLATORS was an idea that came to us one day, not after a long, exhausting brainstorming session (although we love those!), not after poring over a huge piece of paper weighing up the pros and cons of every idea we had; it wasn't forced out. The whole concept of having a web design company had been with us for some time, as we had the skills and the people (we have translators, programmers and marketers on our team), but since there are a whole lot of other design companies and web designers out there, we really wanted to create something more focused and exciting.

Our group's skills are varied, but mostly come from two fields – IT and languages. We've been doing language-related projects for a while, as many of our friends and relatives are in the industry. Spending some time on the research within the translation industry sector was a valuable exercise, as we learned a great deal about its needs and requirements. Right after finishing our first translation industry website, we realized that we'd like to help the whole industry to establish a strong presence in the online world, so that it would be easier for potential clients to find a reliable translator to take care of their text. We see the website creation process as an art and so we thought that a tailored and customized service with a personal approach would be an interesting blend.

A tip for freelancers: Always think of your best skill set and try to identify your main strengths – then see if the skills you think you score the highest in can be combined in some way. Don't forget that the things you enjoy doing the most and are good at give you a massive advantage in the business world! And it doesn't have to be anything that anyone's ever done before!

What is Websites for Translators?

Sometimes the idea of what we do is confusing for many people, and they ask all kinds of questions about us. What exactly do you do? Do you list translation jobs on your website? Do you translate websites? Are you an agency? When I start explaining, they realize that we actually design websites as an online advertising opportunity for individual translators, freelancers, agencies or translation associations.

So what we actually do is a pure IT stuff – no language-to-language creative work – and yet somehow we feel connected to the translation industry. There are many similarities, such as the possibility of working from anywhere in the world. Flexibility and creativity also characterize both professions, and, of course, the extreme focus while working! In the same way as one word may quickly become another with a click of a button, a line of code may result in a completely different layout (or mess up your whole page!) if you forget as little as a bracket sign or a quotation mark. So we do understand the translation business. Although visually different, the translation and IT share a similar level of involvement.

When we say we only focus on the translation industry, some like to discredit us by saying 'How can you limit the provision of such services to a one industry sector? You're missing out on so many clients from other industries!' In today's environment, focus seems to be the main attribute. Just as translators choose their specialties, we choose ours. Focus gives you much more insight into the industry you're aiming to work in. The longer we do this, the more knowledge we gather about what structure of website is the most popular, what keywords to include in the text, what the clients are looking for, or how to maximize their chances of being contacted to do the job. Then there's the technical side of it – the development of plug-ins and apps, non-invasive design, and the creation of an overall positive experience for the visitors.

Occasionally, we create a cake shop or a rock band website, because we have the skills, but the research, the resources and the knowledge about the industry are focused and streamlined to one market only. Being niche is no longer a problem when you can trade worldwide – and that also applies to languages.

A tip for freelancers: Don't pay attention to people who have no previous experience in doing business, or are totally unrelated to your area of trade. Believe me, if they knew what they were talking about, their business would be already the most famous. Look for successful mentors in your industry who will offer you advice worth thousands of pounds – and it might just be a few email conversations!

How do we help translators?

I started out by putting together some websites for my dad, but later on set up translators' websites for my family and relatives. It was fun; doing research helped me tremendously, but also allowed me to discover some shortcomings in the worldwide web of translation. I thought, why not offer such services to other professionals and see if they would like it? As it turned out, they like it very much. Imagine a business card you give someone after a business meeting. How many people do you think will see it? I'd say one to three. Imagine an online business card. How many people do you think will see that? Definitely more than three.

But simply having a website is not enough. If I go outside and start giving my business cards to some strangers on the nearest street, I can guarantee you nobody will come and get a website from me, because this was not the target market I was aiming for. An informative and engaging website helps to present your skills to the widest audience possible. The key is to think about your end customer group and shape your online presence 'for them' or 'with them' not 'to them'. The most important aspect is to think of the way private clients or agencies will assess your compatibility with their expectations based on your specializations.

And of course, there is the marketing side of it! Having a website is just one of the marketing tools used to promote your services. There you can highlight your USP – unique selling proposition – focus on your specializations, engage potential customers in a dialogue or build your own brand.

Word of mouth is one of the most powerful communication tools. By having a well-thought-out online presence you increase the chance of being mentioned and recommended – even if people who have seen your website have never bought anything from you!

A tip for freelancers: So here's another area for development. Marketing is the key. No, wait. Marketing communications is the key. Think of your skill set. Is there a marketer inside you? Do you enjoy research, planning and linking creative ideas together? You could help many other translators by developing online marketing plans for them!

What else can you do for your colleagues?

The translation industry is a very versatile business. You may sometimes think that it's 'just' about the message re-creation from one language to another. But it can be so much more fun! We all want to do what we *like* doing; people get bored and frustrated doing things they *have* to do. The *have* to part is often required during the education process, and that's fine – you *have* to explore many options and get to know the industry and that's what courses and assignments are for. But your ultimate goal should be feeling so comfortable with your job that you will love what you're doing.

At this point in my career I have managed to get to know the industry better, and the people I've met are all doing amazing things! Some of them focus on aspects of accurate translations, technicalities of the process, language structure and best practice. Others show their entrepreneurial spirit by launching translation agencies, engaging in industry associations and helping to make the industry grow and set standards. Then again, there are marketers who recognize the need for promotion and differentiation of services nowadays. This is an emerging trend in the industry to which Websites for Translators vaguely belongs, but it mostly concerns the entrepreneurial translators. They embrace the social media hype, customer relationship management, branding and other elements of the marketing mix, making them relevant to the industry.

Such a creative approach opens up another mine of jobs to take or create. If you've been in the industry long enough, you can think of consultancy services for young graduates who are planning a career in translation. You can become a personal translation career coach, and you could speed up their careers. Or maybe copywriting is your thing? Offering marketing, or SEO-optimized texts for websites and marketing materials can be a creative thing to do, I can assure you of that! Since you know the language so well already, why not consider it as a form of diversification? Only you know what's best for you and what you like doing. I'd say, if you're pretty good at it, you have a huge chance of success.

A tip for freelancers: The bad news – or the good news depending on how you look at it – is that you need a plan. I find mind maps and timelines very helpful in setting goals and visualizing the milestones I need to achieve before reaching the ultimate goal. I start with an idea, and then figure out how to get there. Then the most important part – I do it!

How do I figure out the best way to diversify and love my job?

Ways to diversify? There you go!

- Career coaching – Are you an experienced translator? Do you know the industry inside out? Help other translators to establish their freelance businesses, too! Be their mentor, advisor and planner.
- Marketing – It's a growing area. Have you previously worked in marketing? Teach people how to market themselves and what tools to use, and work closely with them to establish the best way to promote their services.
- IT – Do you have programming skills? It's not only the web design industry that needs you! There are plenty of CAT tools that could be improved; and applications, dictionaries, online databases and directories to be programmed. Think of an interesting idea, ask other translators what would they need or expect from such a project and go ahead!

- Teaching – that is a pretty self-explanatory one, but there are different ways you can approach it. Yes, you can become a lecturer, but you could also go freelance and hold courses, workshops and seminars on every aspect of a translator's life, depending on your experience. People love to learn from others – why not share your knowledge?
- Admin – freelance translators face the reality of having to manage their own invoicing or set up financial schemes. Do you have a financial or accountancy background? Do you know how to handle the numbers in the most productive way? Please share the knowledge!
- Art/design – web design, promo materials, business cards, banners, posters, merchandise, illustrations, you name it, translators and translation companies need all of them, so there shouldn't be a problem with finding your customer base!
- Copywriting – Do you enjoy translation, but would like to produce texts, too? This is a great way to diversify if you're working closely with languages. Be creative and become a copywriter in your areas of specialization since you already have all the words in your head.

There are so many ways to make your job lovable. Good luck in developing your diversification strategy!

MULTILINGUAL DESKTOP PUBLISHING AND OPTICAL CHARACTER RECOGNITION SERVICES

Jaber Maycid earned a Bachelor of Information Technology from Carleton University in Ottawa, Canada, and majored in Interactive Multimedia and Design. Since 2005, Jaber has had the pleasure of working with language service providers across Canada and around the world. Over the years he has provided multilingual desktop publishing (DTP) services in over 60 languages for materials including brochures, pamphlets, posters, labels, logos, stationery and websites. His ability to read and write Arabic gives him a great advantage when working with right-to-left languages. A graphic designer by education and trade, Jaber possesses the skills needed to work with various desktop publishing and optical character recognition (OCR) software. He is committed to working closely with clients to deliver his services with professionalism and expertise and allow him to create work of the highest standard.

WITH SO MUCH UNCERTAINTY IN today's economy, now is the time to look at what you can do to keep your freelance income stream flowing. In this chapter, I will discuss my views on diversification in the language industry as well as my experience providing multilingual desktop publishing (DTP) and optical character recognition (OCR) services.

Background and experience

I'll begin by giving a little background information as to how I got started in this industry and went from a graphic designer to a foreign language typesetter. Several years ago, I was asked by a cousin of mine, who knew I was a graphic designer, if I could assist him in pasting some Japanese translations into a corporate brochure for a company he was working for. He explained to me that he had a corporate brochure designed and laid out in Adobe InDesign and all he needed me to do was copy and paste the Japanese translations from a Microsoft Word document into the brochure in place of all the English text.

This sounded easy enough to me, as I was very familiar with both software applications. What I didn't expect was the Japanese translations to be much shorter than the English, leaving a lot of empty space. That was when I realized that there's more to multilingual desktop publishing than just copying and pasting. After adjusting the font size and line spacing, I successfully typeset my first DTP project. More and more projects came my way, with different languages each time. I learned something new every time.

Since then, I have had the pleasure of working with translators and language service providers all over Canada and around the world. Over the years, I've gained experience in working with over 60 languages as a foreign language typesetter. My ability to read and write Arabic gives me a great advantage when working with right-to-left languages. I am able to properly mirror layouts, reading directions, and paragraph structures based on these languages.

Being very familiar with Adobe Acrobat, I began to also offer OCR services. This is a technology that converts text from a scanned document or image to be searchable and editable. In the language industry, this is a very handy tool. For example, a client needs a lengthy legal document translated, but they only have a physical copy. One can use a flatbed scanner to scan the document, and then use OCR to convert the document so that all the text can be copied and inputted into machine-assisted translation software such as SDL Trados.

After gaining more experience in the DTP/OCR field, I decided to put a name to my typesetting services: Lingo Bravo. It was a carefully selected name that breaks down as 'lingo' (a foreign language or dialect), and 'bravo' (brilliant and showy technical skill – derived from the Italian word 'bravura'). Together I interpret these two words to sum up what I do: excel with great technical skill in foreign languages.

Over the years, I'd say about 10% of the projects I get are handed to me as incomplete projects in which a translator has tried their hand at typesetting. The result is always the same: the translator did not know what to do when faced with the many obstacles of foreign language typesetting. Although I'm always appreciative of the extra work that comes my way, I'm sure it's a blemish on the résumé of the translator who tried and failed at typesetting.

What exactly do the duties of a multilingual desktop publisher consist of? Let us take a common example of when I put my services to work. If a business has a corporate brochure, there may come a time when it would need to translate its material for the purpose of marketing to a broader, more diverse and international audience. The number of languages into which they would like to translate depends on their needs, and it could range from one or two languages to as many as 30 or more. The business would approach a translation firm and provide the text to be translated. Once the text is translated into however many languages, the next step is to insert the translations into the brochure. This is where I come in.

Multilingual DTP (also known as foreign language typesetting) refers to the practice of formatting translated content to fit the foreign layout of the original text, while simultaneously taking into account typographical variations between the native and foreign languages. To have a translated text that is precisely the same length as the original is rare. An example of this is a bilingual (English-French) lid labelled:

See side of pack for use by date
Voir sur le côté de l'emballage pour la date limite d'utilisation optimale

Typically, non-English languages take up 30% more space than English text. It is therefore worth planning to leave enough white space to account for the word growth that is common when the text is translated out of English into non-English languages. A conservative but safe assumption is to add 50% for length when designing a layout for a document that will be translated into multiple languages. If not enough space is available, paragraphs, line breaks and page breaks have to be adjusted accordingly, along with any graphics or charts that surround the text. Alternatively, the typesetter may have to reduce the font size or alter the amount of space between lines of text within the document.

Typesetting in a foreign language is to examine the macro typography of the original text in order to correctly input the document to the end language. When typesetting, the typographical customs of the respective language have to be considered so that the final document changes from the original as little as possible. It is important to identify and adapt your text to fit the different reading style in your target country. Nothing from font size, font style, line spacing, and reading direction (left-to-right or right-to-left) should be overlooked.

This profession can be very tricky when different writing methods are used in a single text. For instance, a French business would like to have its booklet translated into Chinese. In many situations, the name of the business would still be written using the Latin alphabet. This would result in selecting a Chinese font that matches the Latin characters. The typesetter must possess a wealth of fonts for dozens of languages, which will ensure that the overall design of the foreign layout remains as consistent as possible with the original.

Many typesetters struggle with languages that are read from right to left (Arabic, Farsi, Hebrew, etc.). If you need multilingual typesetting for a right-to-left language, the layout needs flipping. In right-to-left typesetting, bullets, flowcharts, and tables all need reversing, which can incur extra cost and time. A meticulous and methodical process must be followed in which all elements are mirrored to better suit these respective languages. The ability to read and write one of these languages (in my case, Arabic) provides a key advantage when working with right-to-left script. A professional foreign language typesetter is able to produce a final document that flawlessly complements all types of languages, creating a geographically-tailored text. He/she must format and typeset localized text to match the original layout of the publication and comply with foreign language typographic standards.

Multilingual DTP can be very tedious and tiresome. A translator with no design background will overlook many key details such as font style, weight, colour and size. This is when a background in graphic design is a great advantage. It provides the skills needed to work with desktop publishing software such as Adobe InDesign and QuarkXpress. On most occasions when graphics are involved, other software from the Adobe Creative Suite, including Photoshop and Illustrator, is also put to use.

Like multilingual DTP, OCR can get complicated at times. The conversion of scanned documents into digital, searchable text can be done relatively easily with today's technology, but it doesn't always work well. If the document you are scanning is wrinkled, has stains or is damaged in any other way, many words in the document may be misread during the conversion process. This can happen even if the physical document has no wear on it at all. Therefore, it is imperative to always proofread the converted document to ensure the content has not changed.

Diversification in the language industry

Now, let's take a look at whether or not to diversify your services. As an expert in the design field, I can only give advice on whether or not to add DTP/OCR services to someone's résumé; I cannot speak for other potentially viable services one may add to their CV. One must be very cautious if considering offering DTP/OCR services. As I mentioned earlier, there have been several times in which I've taken over projects from translators who attempted to dabble in DTP. It involves a lot of creativity at times and a translator with no design background may find it extremely difficult to tackle. On the other hand, if he/she does have a creative side to them, then it would definitely make their overall services more valuable.

Probably the most challenging part of freelancing is finding work. The burden is on you, the freelancer, to draw business through nonstop advertising and self-promotion. When work is slow, it becomes tempting to accept any work that comes your way, regardless of whether it's part of your specialization or not.

Specializing in only translation services can make you too dependent on one source of income. If you're relying on your one specialization to keep yourself progressively busy, there's always the likelihood that, for whatever reason, that market might slow down and be done with your translation services. What will you do then? Fortunately, a great number of successful translators are capable of branching out beyond just translation.

The wise course of action, in my opinion, is to diversify your services. To do so in any industry is a prudent move and has the potential to grow a business. Take, for example, a country rich in oil wealth. It does not just rely on the flow of oil to keep its economy going. In fact, the day will come when the oil wells run out. So the country also invests heavily in other industries such as tourism and real estate. The same thinking can be applied to a translator's career. With computer-assisted and machine translation advancing at an exponential rate, there's no telling what the future holds for the translation industry. My view is that if a translator can offer other services besides just translation, then their future will certainly be brighter.

This is undoubtedly true in a troubled and fragile economy. By diversifying your services, you will not be tied economically to the translation industry. If ever that market is struggling, then so too will your business. Once you find the right balance between the need for specialization with the need for diversity, your target market will grow, leading to more opportunities for sales and revenue. This can also lead to selling your primary translation services to new clients. Another benefit is that you'll have much less down time as your customer base increases. Your diverse services will deliver stability for your business while allowing you to stay focused on the translation industry.

As a business owner, I receive dozens of résumés every week from people offering translation services. When filtering through these résumés, I always place in a special category the ones who offer services aside from just translation. These other services vary from typesetting to interpreting, from graphic design to marketing. However, as much I'd prefer to hire someone who has more than one skill in the language industry, I tend to stray away from those who offer too many services and spread themselves too thinly. The key is always quality before quantity.

My recommendations for any translator looking to begin offering desktop publishing services is to have some sort of degree, diploma or certificate in graphic design or a closely related field, or at least five years of professional experience as a graphic designer with an emphasis on printed publications. If looking to offer OCR services, I'd suggest learning one of the many OCR software applications available today. Typesetters would already have Adobe Creative Suite, which includes Acrobat. Acrobat has an OCR tool that works well and can be learned easily by any tech-savvy person. If looking to add multilingual desktop publishing or optical character recognition to your list of services, be sure to have several years of experience in the graphic design world.

In conclusion, my thoughts on diversification in the language industry are that it provides you with numerous streams of income. In this case, for example, if you're experiencing down time with your translation services, you would still have your other skill set to fall back on. Having another stream of income that balances your main service will fill the void when a project is finished. Diversifying your translation services can help you maintain stability in your workload and finances. Lastly, your portfolio will quickly expand, since you'll find it easier to find work with your newly diversified client base.

7

Distinctive diversification
CREATING A UNIQUE NICHE

A SMALL NUMBER OF KEY PLAYERS in the industry provide a one-of-a-kind, innovative service that every freelance translation professional has heard of or actively uses. These 'distinctive diversifiers' have created distinct products or services that did not previously exist in the language industry but are household names among freelance translators today. Their ideas may have started small or seemed bold initially, but have proved hugely successful for their entrepreneurial creators, as illustrated in this final chapter.

What this shows us is that if you have a unique idea or a special skill from which you feel others could benefit, have the courage to pursue your idea and make it a reality, no matter how outside the square it is. Even if you start small, you never know where it may lead!

CASE STUDY 1: MOX'S BLOG

Alejandro Moreno-Ramos is a full-time English and French into Spanish translator and cartoonist. Since 1999 he has translated 3,494,568 words and 520 technical manuals, but, had he known that one can earn money drawing stick figures, maybe he would not have bothered earning a MSc in electromechanical engineering, or he would not have bothered to begin translating at age 19. His translation-related cartoons published online enjoy huge popularity among translators and interpreters and bring some fresh air into the industry. Alejandro is also a conference speaker and contributes regularly to several translation magazines.

Thomas was making decent money as a freelance translator. His strategy of specializing in finance proved useful and, after several years in the industry, he charged high rates, had several reliable good paying clients, and there was plenty of work. One of his clients in particular offered him regular jobs, interesting texts to translate and paid in two weeks. This client alone provided 40% of his income. On a typical week, Thomas received too many proposals and had to decline several offers. His wife complained that he worked too much, but, as Thomas always replied, 'Is there any freelancer who doesn't work long hours?' At €4600 net per month he supported on his own his wife and two children. It was far from being a life of luxury, but they managed to pay the mortgage and save a little for college. Life was reasonably easy and they were happy.

But one fatidic Sunday, during a skiing vacation, Thomas fell badly and fractured his right hand, suffering a severe tear of the ulnar collateral ligament of the metacarpophalangeal joint of the thumb, a common injury in skiing. Fortunately, the insurance took care of all related charges, and he only spent some hours in the hospital and was sent back home. However, he was told that he would be unable to use his right hand for eight months and had to follow very time-consuming rehabilitation or risk losing the use of his hand permanently.

After taking a couple of days off to recover from his bruises, Thomas tried to get back to his translation work. He had to type with only one hand. Work was slow and he had no choice but to accept very reduced amounts of work. He also began to train a voice recognition software. His clients were truly nice people and were understanding at first. 'Thomas, take it easy, do not force it. You may extend the deadline two days if you need.' But soon, they started calling other translators and his main customer, who up until then had provided him with 40% of his work, stopped sending him texts altogether.

In three months, Thomas had lost all but one of his regular clients, and his monthly turnover decreased by 80%. Despite being prudent and having good reserves in the bank, he started to worry. How long could they go on like this? To make matters worse, his left hand began to hurt, probably as a consequence of overuse. Also, the voice recognition software he was using was not providing the expected results, in part due to his regional accent, but mainly because of the very specific terminology used in the finance field, which forced him to spell so many words that the process was excruciatingly slow.

He applied for social welfare, but since last year he had earned a well above-average wage, he didn't qualify for any help. He even made some attempts to get an in-house job in the financial industry, which he knew so well and where he had some contacts, but he discovered that at the age of 36, which he considered to be fairly young, it was not so easy to be recruited. His habit of being frank and honest, acquired through long years of freelancing, didn't help in interviews.

Thomas wished he hadn't put all his eggs in one basket, specializing so much and depending on one source of income.

Introduction

Do you know Mox? Even if he doesn't exist in real life, he's probably one of the most famous translators among freelance translators. Mox is the name of a comic strip centered on the life of Mox, 'a young but well educated translator with two PhDs and six languages who hardly earns the minimum wage.'

Origin of Mox – using a hobby to promote your career

Mox was created in 2009. At the time, I had recently switched from a very promising career in engineering to full-time freelance translation and, though things were going well, I had not enough work yet to fill all my time. Tired of sending out CVs, I spent some time thinking about creative solutions to find customers. Although my drawing skills are almost non-existent, I had always liked to draw stick figures and funny doodles, so I decided to create a comic strip blog about freelance translation in order to gain visibility on the Internet.

Initial success – ego boost

I drew some comics, posted them on a blog and sent the link to some colleagues and friends. The results were immediate and beyond my expectations. The comic strip soon gained huge popularity, links multiplied in the very first weeks, and visitors came in waves of thousands. Feedback was abundant and 100% positive. There are some translators who don't like Mox, but who will waste his time expressing his dislike of a comic strip? Only translators who enjoyed Mox bothered to contact me. Needless to say, I enjoyed all this attention.

The reason behind Mox's success

In my opinion, my comic strip is only funny-ish. The key of its success is that the situations described are – or could be – true. This might seem trivial but it's well appreciated by its target audience.

Imagine this typical scenario: a freelance translator receives an email from a new customer asking for a quote. The customer knows nothing about translation, so he does not even attach the document to be translated and doesn't specify the target language. The translator feels frustrated, and would like to complain to her colleagues about the clumsiness of this new client, but she has no colleagues nearby. She tries to talk about it to her spouse, but he won't listen anymore when she talks about work. She discusses it with her cat, pretending it is listening. Then she finds a Mox cartoon with the same situation and thinks: *Exactly! That's what happens in real life! I'm not alone.*

It is clear to me that most freelance translators are happy with their work, but at the same time they can't help but miss human contact. In this line, I like to think of Mox as my friend, and I guess that as a result he is a nice guy and other freelance translators see him as a friend, too.

Not the expected results – where is my money?

Yes. Mox was popular and the blog was receiving lots of visits. Unfortunately, this did not translate into any significant increase in translation work, which was the original objective. That is, the success of Mox was not what I expected: Mox was becoming very popular, but I wasn't. To be fair, I did find some clients thanks to Mox, and the position of my professional website in Google increased dramatically, but the benefit was not worth the time I dedicated drawing the cartoons and keeping the blog.

After realizing that advertisers were not willing to pay decent money for advertisement space in the blog, I considered abandoning it. It is true that I was having fun, and the idea of making other people laugh was very satisfying, but I didn't like the idea of working for free.

Last try – getting physical

Experts in marketing usually say that it's easier to sell products than services. This proved to be true with Mox. In 2011, I tried a last effort to monetize the blog, and wrote and published a comic strip book[1] with the help of 13 well-known translators and interpreters. The book sold well, and I soon began working on a second volume,[2] which also sold well. My business model is now based on the books, and their sales fully justify the time I spent working (having fun) with Mox. Even if in the future

---

1 Moreno-Ramos, A., et al. *Mox. Illustrated Guide to Freelance Translation.* Vita Brevis, 2011.
2 Moreno-Ramos, A., et al. *Mox II. What They Don't Tell You about Translation.* Vita Brevis, 2012.

I abandon Mox, it would continue to be a source of passive income, as translators would presumably continue to buy the books.

Why I see Mox as a gold mine – flexibility

Currently, Mox represents about 18% of my income. This doesn't look impressive, but from my point of view it is a gold mine. The biggest advantage of Mox as a revenue source is that I can work on it whenever I want. This flexibility is a huge perk that allows me to fill the gaps between translations and avoid the feast-or-famine trap.

Additionally, my translation business received a boost, since I became more selective when accepting jobs and can focus on more interesting or better paid projects. After all, we translators sell our time, and it is only natural to try at all costs to minimize workless periods. This tendency can be damaging to our career, since we may be inclined, for example, to accept lower rates in exchange for regular work and the associated stability.

Advantages of micro-niche markets – becoming a guru

My niche market (comic strips for freelance translators and interpreters) is so small that I know everything and everyone in my niche. Curiously enough, even if the market is tiny, there are some competitors, translators who also draw translation-related cartoons, but they offer no risk to my business. This is not because I'm better than them; it is simply because the market is big enough for all.

Have you ever struggled to convince anyone that freelance translation is a real job? I have. When I say that I am a freelance translator and that I work at home (in my pyjamas), I often get questions like: 'But, how do you make a living?' or 'I learnt some Spanish in high school; can I be a translator, too?' Those awkward moments are nothing compared to those when I explain to people that I publish comic strip books about freelance translation. The ineffable expression of my interlocutors (probably thinking 'Is he joking or not? How can one earn money with that?') makes me feel privileged. Yes, I do what I like and (partially) make a living from it.

Lessons learned from Mox

- If any of your writing/activity gets lots of attention, that may well mean that you have a potential source of business.
- If you convert a hobby into a business, try to define clearly your business model, i.e. how you will make money out of it. I often have to remind myself that in order to go on with Mox on the long term, I have to sell books. This can certainly kill some of the fun, but otherwise you'll run the risk of feeling frustrated.
- Freelance translators are in a great position to start a business. Among many other virtues, by definition they speak several languages fluently and, equally importantly, are familiar with two or more cultures, too. That fact alone multiplies their ability to reach their market for any entrepreneurial initiative. Also, they are also efficient in closing operations via the Internet.
- Curiously, for the same reasons stated in the previous point, translators also make a good target market.
- If your diversification attempts do not work as you expect, see if you can take advantage of the results in a different way.

How not to diversify – do the numbers

Life is a bowl of cherries and every translator should find alternative sources of income. Despite being invited to participate in this book because of Mox, I also have some less positive experience of diversification, which

I will share, hoping it might be useful to the reader. Some years ago, besides looking for alternative sources of income, I was also longing to leave the office (home) and socialize. As a natural service expansion, I began giving Spanish lessons in German companies. It was fairly easy to find clients, and I soon found that I could be a good teacher because the sad truth is that many language teachers are not professional teachers, just native speakers who don't know what else to do. Probably this is the reason why it is so badly paid. Thus, even if it was nice to leave the computer and talk with real people, the money was not worth my time. It was a nice experience and, above all, it's an excellent back-up job in case for some reason I must stop translating in the future, but I should have done the numbers before.

What I did	What I should have done
90 minutes of teaching @ €25/hour + 60 minutes of commuting	60 minutes of translating @ €40/hour + 90 minutes of true socializing (grabbing a beer with a friend)
= €37.50 + 90 minutes of moderate socializing	= €40 + 90 minutes of quality socializing

Conclusion – have fun

If you decide to diversify your income, take advantage of the freedom of being a freelance translator and try doing something you really like.

CASE STUDY 2: TRANSLATOR PAY

Paul Sulzberger *was born in New Zealand and studied second language teaching methodology at Moscow State University in the late 1960s. He completed his MA (Hons) degrees in modern languages and political science at Victoria University, Wellington. Later in life he completed his PhD in applied linguistics. During the 1970s Paul taught Russian at New Zealand's Otago University and then worked as a translator for the New Zealand government in the early to mid 1980s. In 1986, in collaboration with several other colleagues, he established his own translation company, New Zealand Translation Centre Ltd, which grew into the largest professional document translation provider in Australasia. Dr Sulzberger has had wide experience in virtually all aspects of the translation industry from working as a professional translator, and as an IT specialist dealing with computing in foreign languages, to managing a translation company with a full-time complement of approximately 50 staff. Paul is an enthusiastic grandfather, and blogs on translation issues at* The translation business.

WHY WOULD A TRANSLATOR want to diversify into money transfer? Well, I'm certainly no finance guru. But I've been a professional translator for well over 30 years, and have seen that as the industry has evolved from a purely 'local' business into a global one, the question of getting paid across currency zones has assumed greater and greater importance to translators.

When I set up my own translation company in New Zealand in 1986, access to translators in foreign countries was simply not an option. At that time, I certainly had no access to the nascent Internet and I had never heard of email. The translation business was a very local affair – local customers and local suppliers. With the arrival of the Internet, the transition to a globalized business was very swift, but paying foreign translators (and getting paid by foreign customers) was always awkward – and very expensive.

The need to diversify into areas outside the purely linguistic side of the business has been constant over the years. When Britain joined the

European community in 1973, New Zealand was faced with losing its primary export market. Suddenly our exporters had to look for markets outside the English-speaking area for the first time. Translators were faced with questions such as how to label products in Arabic or Chinese. Diversification into areas such as foreign language typesetting and graphic design became problems that needed urgent resolution. The advent of the computer age and the Internet raised fresh questions that required many translators to master knowledge that previously had been well outside their normal range of interests – programming, handling databases or developing and managing local area networks. Such matters were once obstacles which needed urgent innovation. Today we take all these things pretty much in our stride.

Despite the fact that the translation industry continues to grow in global scope, the nature of the international banking system remains a major obstacle in the way of translators fully participating in the global marketplace. It is simply a system that was built for much bigger players than us. For really large transactions between suppliers of goods in one country and buyers in another there are many financial instruments available – such as letters of credit and insurance arrangements – that ensure the seller gets paid.

But what about small businesses and individual professionals like translators? They also need to trade globally and to get paid across national borders. But freelance translators typically get paid in relatively small amount, like $US 50, $US 500 or $US 1,000. There are no safety nets for small players like these who want to take on new (and often unknown) foreign customers. To get the work, they typically have to carry the full risk of not getting paid. And when they do get paid, it's often at a high cost.

For multinational companies, the cost of transferring millions of dollars across national boundaries via the international banking system is tiny in comparison with the huge amounts being transferred. But relative to the small sums earned by individual translators, the cost of transferring money between currency zones can be huge.

There are many options for transferring money across national borders and currency zones – and the cost of different methods can differ wildly.

Foreign exchange and money transfer companies can provide currency exchange rates that beat the banks. But you typically have to be sending more than $US 2,000 across currency zones to find a foreign exchange company that will not charge you a hefty transfer fee. The average small translation company that pays out lots of relatively small amounts to their freelancers is probably losing money every time it sends money abroad because of poor exchange rates and high fees. More often than not, however, it's the solo professional translator at home who ends up paying for it all.

Was there a way to solve this problem?

I often wondered whether there was something that could be done. Would the day come when individuals could do global business from home as easily and inexpensively as doing business locally?

So, I went looking for someone who might be sympathetic and who might be able to help. In 2011, I found Neil Hamlin, a chartered accountant who lives in Auckland, New Zealand.[1] I discovered that over the past 20 years he had set up and run a successful international software development company – one of his projects included developing the tax revenue infrastructure for numerous South Pacific governments. His experience in these small island nation states alerted him to the plight that many local people have in transferring money abroad – the banking costs are simply horrendous. Given that a large number of Pacific Islanders work abroad and remit money home, the banks were making a killing. Neil decided to do something about it and built an international money transfer business that would empower individuals to send money home without incurring the huge fees demanded by the banks.

I told him about the problems translators have with the high cost of international payments and asked him whether anything could be done to make it easier for individual translators and small translation agencies to do business globally. Translator Pay was the result.

Translator Pay's offer was startling to many. It offered free international

---

1   Neil is the founder and CEO of Money Move IT. MoneyMoveIT is the money transfer machine behind Translator Pay.

money transfers to translators, that is, a system where no fees are charged to either the freelancers or the translation agencies. Was this idea just too good to be true? Many were sceptical and feared that it might be some sort of a money laundering scam. When something is offered for free, many people will inevitably ask, 'What's the catch?'

It's true that there's not much in life for free, but there is actually no catch here. We designed the system as a win-win-win business. Agencies win because they are not charged any fees to pay their foreign translators and so they reduce their overheads. Translators win because they get paid more – not only because no fees or bank charges are deducted from their payments, but because when payments have been negotiated in the agency's currency, the amount they receive in their pocket is likely to be significantly more. This is because the exchange rates Translator Pay can offer are generally more favourable than they are able to get from their local bank, and most other providers.[1]

There's a third 'win' too… Like any business, Translator Pay expects to make a sustainable profit to continue offering the service. But here is the intriguing part – offering a 'free' service and making a profit at the same time just doesn't make sense to many people. What then is the mechanism that allows Translator Pay to make a profit but allows it to offer a valuable service to translators at no direct cost to them?

How does it work?

There's no magic in how Translator Pay can provide a better service to translators than the banks and still make a profit. While Translator Pay charges no fees to either translation agencies or their freelance translators, it can still make money on the difference between what it can buy foreign currency for and the price it sells it.

The crucial difference, in comparison with the banks, is the size of that margin. Translator Pay's margin is tiny in comparison with the banks and other payment providers. Translator Pay is able to buy foreign currency on favourable terms on the wholesale market, better than you can get from

---

[1] If the payment has been agreed in the translator's currency, then of course, the agency will get the benefit of Translator Pay's more favourable rates—it will cost them less to ensure that the translator gets the agreed amount in his or her local currency.

pretty much any other provider. Unlike the big banks, it has low running costs. The small margin however, is large enough to cover its costs and to make a reasonable profit, and translators still get an exchange rate better than they can usually get from their bank. In this way Translator Pay can pass the savings on to the translators who earned the money in the first place.

It takes two to tango

For translators to get the benefit of better foreign exchange rates and receive their payments free of any fees, deductions or bank fees, the translation companies need an incentive to pay them using the Translator Pay system. So we looked at the problems language service providers (LSPs) have to deal with when paying their freelancers, and how we might solve them. We found that it's a fairly messy and time-consuming business: each freelancer's banking details have to be stored (and kept up to date when they change); and different freelancers often want to be paid in different ways – some want payments via bank transfer 'wires' and some want to be paid by PayPal or some other money transfer system. Keeping track of all this information and making many individual payments using different systems can be an administrative nightmare.

Translator Pay simplified this process for LSPs in a variety of ways. The easiest is where the LSP simply uploads a data file for Translator Pay to process all the payments for all their translators each month. From the LSP's point of view, it means just making one single payment to cover all the payments and letting Translator Pay do all the work of getting the right amount in the right currency into the bank account of each translator – at no cost to the LSP!

So why would a translator like me want to diversify into international money exchange? The answer is simple really. To me, the money transfer problem was just another of the many obstacles that needed a good solution.

CASE STUDY 3: TRANSLATORS WITHOUT BORDERS

Interview with Lori Thicke

Lori Thicke *is the founder of the machine translation services firm LexWorks, an innovator in translation technology and a leader in machine translation. LexWorks is a subsidiary of Lexcelera, which has been providing translation services since it was founded in Paris, France, in 1986. Lexcelera was the first translation company in France to receive ISO 9001:2000 quality certification. Lori is also the founder of Translators without Borders, the world's largest community of humanitarian translators. As a US-based non-profit, Translators without Borders supports global aid organizations by donating millions of words of professional translations each year. With the founding of its translator training centre in Nairobi, Kenya, Translators without Borders is actively taking down language barriers to knowledge for some of the world's most disadvantaged people. Lori, who holds an MFA from the University of British Columbia, is a frequent speaker and blogger.*

1) Lori, as the founder of Translators without Borders, can you share with us how the idea to start a language-centred non-profit organization came about?

Since my university days, I'd wanted to do volunteer work. But I never had the time. I almost worked on a crisis line, almost read books for the blind, almost helped out in a soup kitchen... In other words, I spent my time 'almost giving'.

I certainly never dreamed that translation could be the humanitarian work I was looking for. But one day in 1993, Medecins sans Frontières (Doctors without Borders) knocked on the door of Lexcelera, my translation company in Paris. They asked for a quote on a translation project. They are a great organization, so I asked them, 'If we do this work for you pro bono, can you use the funds you save to do more work in the field?' They said yes, and since then we have donated around $3 million worth of translation services to Medecins sans Frontières and other non-profits such as Oxfam, Action Against Hunger, Partners in Health and many others.

I'm proud of this contribution. The non-profits tell us they can use the funds we save them to send more doctors and nurses into the field, vaccinate more children, build more schools and so on. Not only this, but our translations help them raise money. For example, last year a website we translated into Spanish and French for a non-profit supporting Haiti generated $600,000 for building homes for people. So many families have been able to move out of shelters into their own homes because of the work done by our translation volunteers.

In 2010, we added a second activity to Translators without Borders. During the Haiti crisis I noticed that non-profits were trying to communicate with the population affected by the earthquake in English and in French. But the people most affected didn't speak those languages! Then I noticed the same phenomenon later on in the year, on a trip to Africa: health information was being delivered to people in European languages!

I was astounded by this. I'm Canadian, and it would be very strange if someone came into our schools with information in Russian. So I started looking at the translation problem in non-mainstream languages. And I found that every day, all over the world, aid information is being delivered in the wrong language. So this has become our second mission: to raise awareness that not everyone speaks a European language, and also to train translators in local languages like Swahili, so they can help translate critical information for their communities.

2) What impact has your involvement with Translators without Borders had on your actual translation business, and do your achievements with Translators without Borders reflect the time and effort invested?
I have to admit that the humanitarian work with Translators without Borders takes a considerable amount of time away from my translation business. But I have a great team running Lexcelera, so it works out fine.

3) Could you briefly outline the role machine translation and crowdsourcing play for Translators without Borders?
Translators without Borders is based on crowdsourcing. But it's crowdsourcing with a gateway in the sense that the translators are all professionals who have

undergone our test, or else have been certified by a professional organization such as the ATA. We work via an automated platform that was donated by Proz.com. Having an automated platform to distribute projects to our volunteers is critical because it helps us scale. When we first started out in 1993, Lexcelera donated the project management. But we didn't have an unlimited number of project managers, so that put a limit on how many non-profits we could serve. Today with an automated platform we can better scale to meet the need.

Machine translation isn't currently in our workflow for European languages, but we are working to build machine translation systems for local languages to increase access to knowledge. What's happening now is that the Internet is becoming increasingly available to people via their smart phones. Even simple phones will soon be able to access Wikipedia, which means that they will have all of human knowledge in the palms of their hands. But language is a barrier, and we need to solve that. For some local languages like Swahili we are training machine translation technology to take down those barriers to knowledge.

4) Do you enjoy this diversification from the translation career you originally embarked on, or do you find it challenging?
The translation industry isn't just about translation per se. We need to see our industry in a wider context. We are about taking down the language barriers that stand between people and the information they need.

5) What would you say to translators who are sceptical about the developments in the language industry, such as machine translation, crowdsourcing and increasing diversification?
Translation is both an art form and a utility. Throughout history it has moved between those two poles. When I first entered the industry, translators typed their manuscripts, so the quality wasn't unimpeachable. They had one chance at it, and if it wasn't perfect, they didn't necessarily want to type their pages over again. But they resisted the computerization of translation because it meant someone could correct their work. But no one is perfect in their first draft, and quality did improve.

There was also quite a lot of resistance to translation memory technology. I wouldn't say that translation memory improved quality, but I'd say it maintained the quality of the original translation.

When we regard translation not as an end in itself but as a means to opening up information, the quality requirements change. Taken from this point of view, the quality and accuracy of the information is what is important.

Machine translation can be improved to quite a high level of quality, but even raw it serves a vital purpose. With so much content available in English, we may not realize how much the world depends on machine translation – if it exists in their language – to take down the barriers to knowledge. And that's what it's all about.

CASE STUDY 4: RAINY LONDON BRANDING

Interview with Valeria Aliperta

Valeria Aliperta (Associate of the ITI, MCIL, member of ASETRAD and IAPTI Head of External Relations) is a conference interpreter and translator. She works from English, Spanish and French into her native Italian for IT and web, fashion, design, marketing, legal and advertising. Valeria has a soft spot for blogging and social media (she organized the Tweet-Up at the 2010 and 2013 ITI conferences). She was included in the Language Lovers 2012 and 2013 contest, gives talks and webinars, and has been a speaker at recent conferences (ITI Conference 2013 and ProZ.com International Conference). A writer of articles on branding and identity, she is regularly featured in the ITI Bulletin. She also offers branding consultancy under Rainy London Branding *and is co-founder of* The Freelance Box, *offering seminars and hands-on courses for freelancers.*

1) Valeria, you are an Italian, French and Spanish freelance translator and interpreter, better known as Rainy London Translations, who has recently launched Rainy London Branding, an identity and branding consultancy specifically geared towards freelance translators and interpreters. What motivated you to add branding consultancy to your service portfolio, and do you enjoy this diversification from the translation career you originally embarked on?

Well, that's an easy one! My partner is a web designer so I am back to back with that inspiration all the time. Having seen so many examples of good and bad logos, identities and websites – and being in the process of revamping mine – I thought why not share what I know that directly applies to my field? I have not studied design or marketing per se, even though the branding side of it is fascinating and who knows, I may do that soon. I've gained my little know-how just out of curiosity. Books, guides, articles, events, even translations, can teach you lots about another field. I've always liked drawing and admiring stylish things around me (art, nature, fashion, objects, people, shapes, architecture... anything!) so I guess I can say that what I know is self-taught. There is lots of good reading material nowadays that can really help expand your views on so many topics! It's still early stages and of course it is a secondary business, but I think it can definitely work and will help many find their voice and identity. I mainly talk about my case study – I present what I did and hopefully inspire others to start their branding – at conferences and events, which I enjoy very much. I love talking and helping out because sometimes all people need is a little shake, a push in the right direction.

Plus, I do get translations in the field and when you know your Pantone from your CMYK colours, that's an added bonus!

2) What impact has your branding consultancy business had on your core translation/interpreting business, and does the income you generate from this service reflect the time and effort invested?
As I said, my core business is still interpreting and translation but it has evolved, integrating more and more creative work. I love voice-over, because as an interpreter I get to learn how to make the most of my voice skills, and transcreation because it involves inventing and adapting – it's like a stepped-up localization that also needs the hype and kick typical of brand-new, created-from-scratch marketing copy. As for design and branding, not being a designer myself, I work in collaboration with Fabio from Artscode/Cocorino who carries out the practical graphic part after I've consulted with prospects sharing what I think is best for their business. The effort is worth it and it keeps me stimulated, but as I said, I have just launched the services so I will keep you posted. The main reward is from seminars, webinars and events – the feedback is so refreshing. Sometimes the examples I give are self-centred, but I think they have to be, as I'm showing what worked for me and hoping to inspire others to find something similar for themselves. In the near future, I want to expand and go into the branding process in more detail, to make sure everyone has a full picture of what it involved, not only for Rainy London but for others, too.

3) Something that caught my eye on your website was the statement that 'diversification and differentiation are the key to the success of your

business'. **So what would you say to freelance translators who are sceptical about the developments in the language industry and the increasing level of diversification we are experiencing?**
I need to remain inspired and bring variety into my life; that's why I want to keep changing and trying new things. Don't get me wrong – I like my traditions, I'm Italian! But I am a great supporter of 'new' and 'innovation' when it really helps and works for you, making your life easier. That's why differentiation for me means keeping abreast with new things and this has brought about new topics I could translate – design, fashion, etc. For me it also means combining your passion with work. Cliché, I know, but it's true. I have (I swear) met people who really love electrical manuals. They love them, and that's probably because they spent their childhood disassembling gearboxes and the likes and now they relive that passion in those texts.

Diversification is just another way to talk about being specialized in a skill, being an expert in one subject. In my case, I used to do lots of renewable energy work but then it eventually died down and other topics came in. Never underestimate the power of hobbies; a friend who is into fitness ended up with copy on that very subject and she's becoming an expert. Because of her passion she is happy to work on copy related to that.

In my experience, it's always better to have a plan B (and C, and D), as work has ups and downs and translation subjects go in waves, too. So, to translators who are sceptical about developments I say: find what works for you – sometimes it's very easy, right under your nose – and don't feel bad if you're not as 'diverse' in your offering as others.

Freelancers are personal brands, offering personal services, and each of us has different backgrounds. Just because one person does something in a certain way does not mean it will work for all of us. Plus, there is always going to be an edge to your business that you will be able to offer clients: find that something that makes you different and don't be afraid of offering it as your 'strength'.

Of course, don't do things you're not comfortable with and make sure your service is compatible with the profile you have (don't pair dog grooming with translation; set up a different website or profile if you want to work in that field!)

Try to find that space outside the oh-so-overrated comfort zone, that space where the 'magic' happens.

4) Where do you see freelance translators in five years' time in terms of diversification?

I think wherever they want to allow themselves to go. It all goes hand in hand with technology, in my humble opinion. While it now seems so normal, just the other day I was thinking about how I got my first computer at the tender age of 21. Yes, 21. And nobody I knew even had broadband Internet at home. Five or so years ago, would you have believed that we would be able to open PDFs on the go, share videos and audio files and have tablets from which we can technically make others believe we are in the office? Joking apart, I am very much looking forward to the moment – I hope it comes – when CAT tools are compatible with mobile devices. I also hope that translators will start seeing themselves as entrepreneurs (I hate that word, but that's what we are) and not mere human tools for carrying the meaning from a source to a target language. That's where diversification, variety and creativity come in.

Of course, you should not be a 'Jack of all trades' but if it makes you happy and you're good at it, why not? It can only balance the (in)famous periods of famine that freelancers complain about in cycles and keep life interesting. Of course, it all depends on your profile: if you only translate from/into one language and are not keen on teaching or interpreting or any other side activity, then don't. But maybe you're good at gardening and that's your diversification. That can make you stand out so that a client will pick you and not another competitor. So, five years could mean the world – provided you make them count.

Conclusion
FREELANCE TRANSLATOR – QUO VADIS?

I N THIS FINAL CHAPTER, I WILL sum up the reasons for diversifying based on the experiences shared by the contributors, investigate the best possible diversification strategy and outline the situation for freelance translators today and in the future. If one thing is evident, it is that all contributors have different viewpoints on different services, products or business strategies. What they all have in common, however, is that they embrace diversification and take an entrepreneurial approach to the freelance translation industry. They all exemplify 'success beyond translation'.

Reasons for diversification

The selection of personal experiences shared by the contributors to this book has shown that diversification typically happens for one or more of the following reasons:

- **Opportunity knocks on the door:** often, diversification is not

a planned strategy but simply happens because a freelancer comes across an unexpected opportunity and decides to seize it.
- **Responding to client and/or market demand:** in many cases, a freelancer's client may expect or request the practitioner to offer a certain service in addition to pure translation, or the changing market conditions may make it necessary to add to one's portfolio in order to remain competitive.
- **Desire for variety:** many freelancers make a comfortable living from, or at least get by with, translation. However, they dislike the monotony of 'just' translating day in and day out or feel like they want to get out and meet people. Hence they expand into different areas.
- **Tapping into existing skills to boost business:** some freelancers identify certain skill sets they are not yet maximizing and decide to tap into this unused potential to become more well-rounded professionals and thus boost their business.

Formula for success

At the moment, 56% of freelance translators surveyed believe that in order to succeed, it is more important to become a better translator and grow their existing translation business than expand their businesses beyond translation services (38.8%, see Figure 8.1).

As translation is our core business activity, I agree that it is important to grow this side of our businesses on an ongoing basis. I don't, however, see this as excluding diversification; rather, the two should complement one another. Concentrating on becoming a better translator does not mean neglecting alternatives or additional services altogether. In fact, offering other products or services may increase your credibility or your status as an expert, or lead to word-of-mouth recommendations, resulting in a boost to your translation business. Achieving a good balance is the key; and doing something else doesn't mean you have to stop translating; quite the contrary.

What all the contributors to this book have in common is that they have diversified into an area for which they already had the necessary skills. Diversification does not mean dabbling in areas you know little about, but rather exploiting your existing knowledge and expertise, and putting your talents to good use.

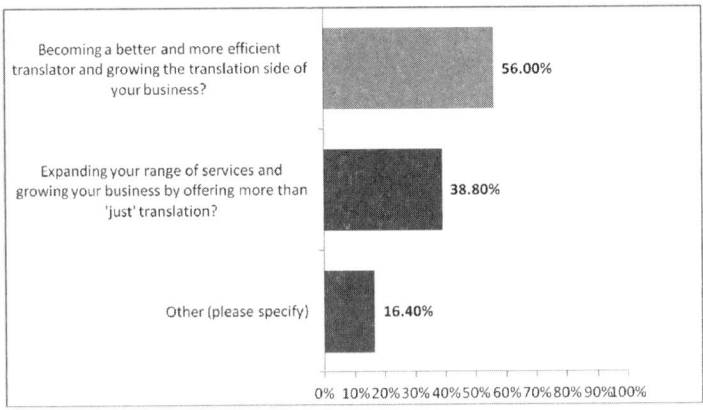

Figure 8.1: What would you say is more important in order to succeed as a freelancer in the translation industry over the next 3-5 years?

Take stock and ascertain what you are good at and which skills you are not maximizing at the moment. Check if you are already doing something that you have never thought of as a way of diversifying (e.g. terminology services or proofreading). Diversification is not about spreading yourself too thinly, but about tapping into your areas of expertise in addition to being a good translator.

Diversification strategy

Most contributors also agree that it is important to have a solid translation business first before expanding into new, additional areas of business. We are professional translators after all. Before tackling diversification, freelance translators need to be sure they have a strong core translation business, which forms the basis of all their activities. It is advisable to diversify from the inside out, or from bottom to top in the Diversification Pyramid (see Figure 8.2) as a freelancer becomes more established and experienced in the industry.

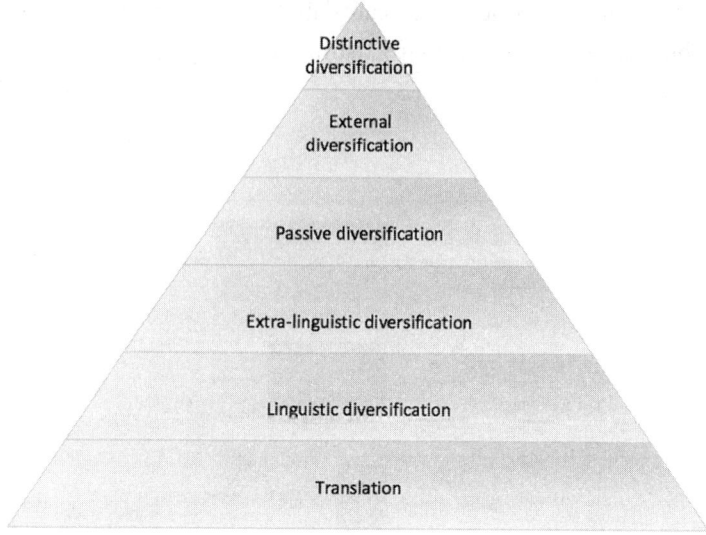

Figure 8.2: The Diversification Pyramid

I have spoken to another freelancer, Lisa Carter, who is successfully diversifying and has established a second line of business alongside translation.

Interview with Lisa Carter

Lisa Carter is an acclaimed Spanish to English translator with seven major titles and several short stories to her credit. Her work has won the Alicia Gordon Award for Word Artistry in Translation and been nominated for the International IMPAC Dublin Literary Award. Through her company, Intralingo Inc., Lisa offers translation, writing and editing services, including online classes.

1) Lisa, you are a Spanish to English freelance translator who also provides online courses for literary translators. What motivated you to add online courses to your service portfolio, and do you enjoy this diversification

from the translation career you originally embarked on, or do you find it challenging?
There wasn't just one thing that motivated me to begin offering online classes in literary translation, but several. There was a financial component, sure; I believe it's good for any small business owner to have a diverse portfolio. When one area of the market wanes, another area might boom, and though we might love what we do, we're also doing it to earn a living.

More importantly in my case, though, I felt the need for these types of courses in particular. Having written a blog on literary translation for a long time, I was receiving a few emails a week with questions about everything from how to break into the industry to what to charge for a book project. There were no courses of this type anywhere to be found, so I felt I was filling a need.

Related to this, I remembered all too well what it was like starting out in literary translation, when information was very hard to come by. The wall of silence, the barrier to entry seemed very artificial and unnecessary. In my own small way, I wanted to break through that and share all I had learned so far.

There's no doubt that diversification can be challenging, though. As many small business owners will tell you, you've got to be everything from CEO to janitor. Adding other components to a business means wearing even more hats, and that can be draining.

I like diversity, though. The range of tasks on my plate each day keeps things interesting. And interacting with my students, seeing them make real strides in a career they're passionate about (a career I'm passionate about!) – gives more energy than it takes.

2) What impact has diversifying into online teaching had on your core translation business, and does the income you generate from this service reflect the time and effort invested?
My online classes haven't had a direct impact on my core translation business. The number and type of clients I have as a translator are a result of my publications and professional reputation. Many may not even be aware that I teach literary translation.

Financially, my courses are viable, but I do acknowledge that because it's in my nature to give and give some more, my per hour earnings may not be that significant. Still, I think some payment is to be found in the satisfaction I feel when a student says she has found the confidence to pursue this career, or had a positive response from an author, or had a first story published. A happy student is likely to recommend the class to others, which allows me to keep offering classes each session.

3) Which path would you advise freelance translators to take in order to prepare their business for the future: focus fully on their translation skills and become a better translator to grow their core business, or diversify and add additional services or products to their portfolio as a systematic business strategy to grow their business beyond 'mere' translation?
There's no one simple answer that will suit everyone, in my view. If you're just starting out in a freelance business, then I would suggest you dedicate yourself to that and become the absolute best translator you can be. Once you have established your business and your reputation, then leverage those to branch out. However, if an opportunity that interests you, feels right and is feasible presents itself along the way, then by all means pursue it.

What anyone else does may not be right for you, so follow not only your head but your heart. Whenever I'm faced with a new type of client or am considering a slightly new direction for my business, I always step back and think about how it will enrich me personally, not financially, in order to decide if it's worth pursuing.

4) Where do you see freelance translators in five years' time in terms of diversification?
Overall, I think we'll be in a similar situation, with a wide range of options to suit each of us and our individual reality. There will always be those who stick to their core business because it's what they love and are good at and they have found a way to make it financially viable. Others will find themselves in a position where larger market factors change and they have to branch out, albeit unwillingly at first.

And there will be those who want to pursue different tracks in order to feel more secure in their business or simply because they want to follow their interests. The beauty of running a small business is that more than one of these might be your reality over time.

Present and outlook

I strongly believe that the future for freelance translators is positive if you are open-minded and embrace change. This includes exploring options to diversify your business in order to have secure income streams in any situation. While diversification is not a 'must', it makes good business sense to have alternatives at the ready in order to account for unforeseen circumstances (whether that's a broken wrist, market changes or technological advances).

It is encouraging that 30.8% of freelance translators surveyed see themselves as successful freelance translators making a living from selling translation services *and* other services (see Figure 8.3), that is, diversifying successfully, and 43.6% state they expect to do this in five years' time (see Figure 8.4).

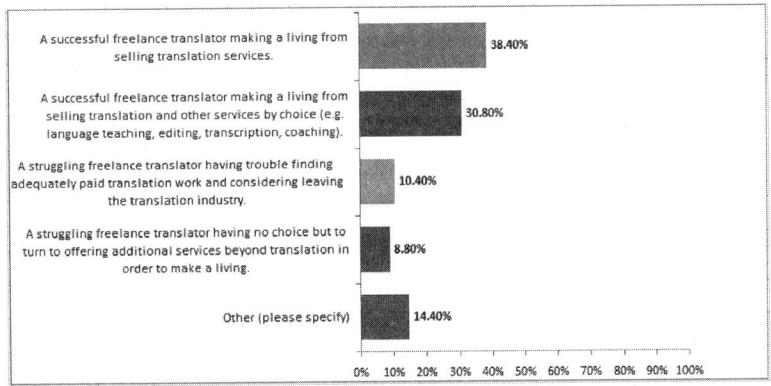

Figure 8.3: How would you define yourself today?

What's even more positive is that while a total of 19.2% of respondents consider themselves 'struggling freelancers' today, only a total of 4.4%

expect to be struggling five years down the track, with 6.4% seeing themselves working in-house or in another industry. The general mood in the translation industry is positive, and I am convinced that the increased level of diversification we are experiencing is contributing to this positive outlook.

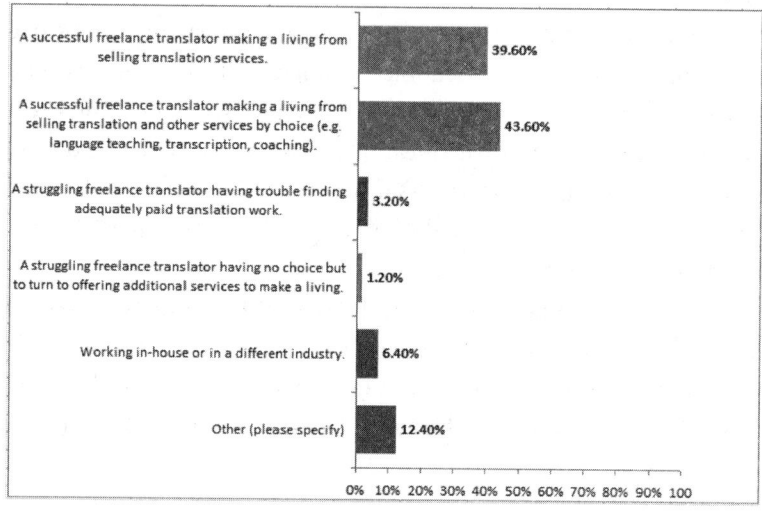

Figure 8.4: Where do you see yourself in five years' time?

In my experience, those colleagues who are the most positive about our industry and its future are those who have established themselves as successful freelancers and have also embraced the concept of diversification. Colleagues sceptical of diversification and change, on the other hand, tend to display a more negative outlook and are more likely to consider themselves to be struggling.

Conclusion

Diversification is not a race, and it is not a competition. Just because someone else is doing something doesn't mean you need to follow suit. You need to choose what is right for you and your business. You may want to translate 95% of the time and offer another service 5% of the time. You may want to work on establishing your core translation business and then explore additional options a year or two down the track. You may need a change of scenery and choose to translate only 60% of the time, developing another line of business for the rest of your time. The choice is yours, and the opportunities are endless.

It is clear that the translation profession has changed considerably in the past decade and will continue to do so due to technological advances and changing customer requirements, in some cases leading to increased pressure on translation prices. Today, just being an excellent translator is hardly enough anymore. Each freelancer will need to identify their own additional skills and talents and find a way to distinguish themselves from the competition in order to stand out in the market. Moreover, customers today often expect us to offer services beyond mere translation, and if we refuse to consider diversifying into additional areas, we risk getting left behind pretty quickly.

It is your business and your future. What is not optional is being aware of the myriad options out there and having a risk management strategy in place. As freelancers in an ever-changing industry, we cannot afford to wear blinkers and hope for the best. Being proactive is a must-have trait for any freelancer today. I hope this book has given you some valuable ideas and suggestions for expanding your business, now or in the future. Whether covering *linguistic diversification, extra-linguistic diversification, passive diversification, external diversification* or *distinctive diversification*, the stories featured in this book clearly show that the language industry can be your oyster.

List of contributors

Aliperta, Valeria
Arakelyan, Olga
Arnall, Annamaria (Foreword)
Balemans, Percy
Ball, Laura
Berner, Sam
Bhattacharyya, Pritam
Boonen, Inge
Brändle, Diana
Brooks, Lucy
Carter, Lisa
Christaki, Catherine
Clark, Jeana M.
Colliander Lind, Anne-Marie
Diamantidis, Anne
Dietterich, Tea C.
Dziatkiewicz, Magdalena
Ferreira, Alberto
Freeman, Jane
Gallagher, Clare
Heine-Kilic, Martina
Hussain, Eva
Jenner, Judy
Kastenhuber, Karolina
Keller, Nicole

Kelly, Nataly
Kisin, Konstantin
Lange, Meike
Martelli, Alessandra
Maycid, Jaber
McKay, Corinne
McMahon, Melissa
Mo, Joy
Moreno-Ramos, Alejandro
Mueller, Felicity
Nissen, Vanda
Piróth, Attila
Rudavin, Oleg
Spear, Luke
Staude, Désirée
Stelmaszak, Marta
Sulzberger, Paul
Thicke, Lori
Tomarenko, Valerij
Torres, Nora
Van Beukering, Tineke
Walker, Fernando D.
Wilson, Sheila

Index

AALC Inc., 132
ABIE France, 132
ACBC, 132
Action Against Hunger, 303
administrative work, 168, 171, 282
Adobe Acrobat, 284
Adobe Creative Suite, 286
Adobe InDesign, 283, 286
Adobe Soundbooth, 94
advertising, 43, 118–24, 188, 205–6, 278–9, 287, 307
AEC/AIEX, 132
agencies, 34n.3, 50, 168–72, 215–220
 vs. direct clients, 46–8, 167, 200, 220–21, 235–6, 271
 money transfer, 300–01
 project management, 166, 169, 172
 and specialization, 54–6, 167
 as a threat, 80, 138
 transcreation assignments, 124
 voice-over assignments, 90–95
 see also translation companies
Aliperta, Valeria, 260, 307–10
American Translators Association, 27, 80–1, 90, 92, 181, 187, 196, 239, 243, 248, 305
 annual conference, Denver 2010, 189
 ATA Chronicle, The, 81n.1, 221
Amnesty International, 119
Anderson, Adele, 12
ANZ Bank, 251
APCS, 159
Arabic, 134, 283, 284, 286, 299
Arabic Communication Experts, 175–80
Arakelyan, Olga, 198–202

Arancho Doc, 215
Arnall, Annamaria, 12
art, 282, 307, 118, 123, 206
Artesis University College, 101
ATA *see* American Translators Association
AT&T, 27, 251
Audi Akademie GmbH, 110
AUSIT *see* Australian Institute of Interpreters and Translators
Australasian Association of Language Companies, 132
Australian Business in Europe, 132
Australian China Business Council, 132
Australian Export Council, 132
Australian Institute of Interpreters and Translators (AUSIT), 12, 37, 96, 101n.11, 132, 159, 175, 178
Australian National University, 37, 96
Australian-Polish Community Services, 159
automated word count, 177
Avira Operations GmbH, 172

Balemans, Percy, 118–24
Ball, Laura, 153–8
Barry, Bridie, 133
Bausch, Pina, 99
BDÜ, 31, 117, 203, 270, 271
Beninatto, Renato, 46
Berner, Sam, 175–80
Bhattacharyya, Pritam, 60–65
blogging, 65, 187–97, 243, 260, 291–97, 315
blogs
 Adventures in Freelance Translation, 187
 Anmerkungen des Übersetzers, 203

Business School for Translators, 259
Freelancer's Freelancer, 60
Mox's Blog, 291-97
Rainy London Translations, 307
The translation business, 298
Thoughts on Translation, 196
Translation Times, 221
Translators Biz Secret, 199, 226, 232n.1
Your professional translator, 198
Blue Ocean strategy, 207, 211
books, 197, 295-6
  publishing, 63, 194, 196, 224, 228, 233-4, 246
  reading for self-development, 92, 94, 120, 156, 177, 228, 252,
  translating, 40, 103, 194, 196
  see also publications
Boonen, Inge, 215-20
branding, 188, 258, 281, 307-8
Brändle, Diana, 110-117
Brandt, Willy, 132, 133
British Chevening Scholar, 60
Brooks, Lucy, 225, 238-50, 259
Build Your Business as a Translator, 234
burnout, 70, 107, 161, 176, 180
business
  development, 60, 63, 169
  model, 14, 21, 20, 33, 167, 221, 258, 294, 296
  partners, 169, 185, 214, 231
  skills, 127, 177, 226, 246, 257-62, 267
  strategies, 19, 105, 165-222
  training, 85, 245, 257-262
Business Class programme, 133
Business School for Translators, 257-262

CALL, 150
Cancer Council of Victoria, 162
Carter, Lisa, 314-17
CAT, 44, 49, 78, 80
CAT tools, 44, 45, 94, 270-76
CAT tool consulting, 270-76
CAT tool training, 95, 256, 264, 267
CCDA, 161
CELTA, 157
Centre of Cultural Diversity in Ageing, 161
Certificate IV in Aged Care and Patient Services, 163

Certificate in Teaching English to Speakers of Other Languages, 157
certification see also NAATI accreditation, 27, 68, 146, 181, 197, 248, 303
challenges, 63, 83, 125, 130, 184, 227, 261
chambers of commerce, 133, 140, 159, 243
Chartered Institute of Linguists (CIOL), 154, 187, 238, 242, 244, 257
Chinese, 163, 229, 246, 286, 299
Christaki, Catherine, 187-195
CIOL see Chartered Institute of Linguists
Clark, Jeana M., 78-85
clients, 66-7, 132, 180, 204, 228, 230, 231
  client base, 34, 79, 90, 126, 155, 167, 180, 215-20, 220-2, 261
  direct, 46-7, 128, 141, 167, 189, 193, 200, 207, 221-22, 235, 247
  interpreting, 160-2
  low-paying, 260
  potential, 133-4, 184, 187-8, 192, 193, 195, 231, 279, 288
  and specialization, 44, 124, 126, 208-10, 213-14
cloud, 26, 45, 49, 79, 84, 216, 218, 275-6
coaching, 110, 224, 257-62, 263, 268, 281
cognitive debriefing, 139, 142-5
collaboration, 26, 177, 183, 219, 308
Colliander Lind, Anne-Marie, 22-6
Colorado Translators Association, 196
Common Sense Advisory, 54, 121
competitors, 23, 67, 88, 115, 162, 207, 209, 275, 295, 319
computer assisted translation see CAT
computer guide, 246
conferences
  American Translators Association, 92, 189
  AUSIT, December 2012, 101n.11
  ITI, 307
  ProZ.com, 307
  Media for All, London 2011, 100n.7
  UTIC, May 2013, 46
consultancy see consulting
consultants, 27, 31, 125, 129, 246, 270
consulting, 233, 237, 270-76, 281, 307
  cross-cultural, 132-6, 136-8, 162
Consumexpo, 205
content optimization technologies, 172

continuing education *see* continuing professional development
continuing professional development, 12, 26, 81, 82, 125, 129, 224, 227, 238–50, 264–269
copy-editing, 85
copywriting, 14, 31, 119, 120, 123–31, 172, 189, 207, 245, 281, 282
CPD *see* continuing professional development
creative writing, 122, 213
courses *see* online courses
cross-cultural training *see* cross-cultural consulting
crowdsourcing, 57, 100, 304–5
crowd translation, 146
CSA, 54
cultural awareness, 134, 163
cultural competence, 29, 162
cultural diversity, 161, 162
currency, 298–302
customer base *see* client base
customer orientation, 208–09
customization, 210
CV writing, 259

DAAD, 157
DAF, 157
Danish, 100, 148
dbterm terminologieservice, 110
Deliscar, Suzanne, 225, 247
Der Lernladen, 154
design, 123, 126, 287, 308–9
desktop publishing, 31, 32, 55, 104, 132, 172, 179, 206, 251, 256, 258
  multilingual, 283–9
Deutsch als Fremdsprache, 157
Deutsche Akademische Austauschdienst, 157
Deutscher Terminologietag, 117
Diamantidis, Anne, 31–7
dictionary, 23, 114, 211, 230
Dictionary of Americanisms, 211
Dietterich, Tea C., 132–6
differentiation (strategy), 25, 127–31, 209, 280, 308–9
digital publishing, 233
Dillon, Sara, 242
disintermediation, 22, 24–5
DIT e.V., 110

diversification, 62–3, 90, 102, 252
  categories of, 19
  challenges, 76, 315
  of client base, 215–20, 220–2
  definition of, 17–19
  distinctive, 19, 290–310
  as a door opener, 105, 106
  external, 19, 20, 257–89
  extra-linguistic, 19, 20, 165–222
  health measure, 11, 106–7
  linguistic, 19, 20, 66–164
  passive, 19, 20, 223–255
  Pyramid, 313, 314
  reasons for, 201, 249, 258, 262, 288–89, 311–12, 317
  reasons against, 20, 165, 198
  as specialization, 78–9, 126–7, 158, 166–7, 203–11, 211–14, 309
  strategy, 63, 90, 258, 313–14
  tips, 64–5
DTP *see* desktop publishing
DTT, 270
Durban, Chris, 184
Dutch, 73, 118
Dutch Translation Services, 73
Dziatkiewicz, Magdalena, 277–82

EasyEnglish, 154
e-books, 194, 224, 228, 230
eCPD Webinars, 224–5, 238, 242–4, 259
ECQA Certified Terminology Manager, 110, 116
editing, 14, 20, 46, 66, 100, 107–9, 141, 207, 213, 314
  of non-native texts, 78–85, 85–9
editors, 27, 37, 78, 83–9, 96, 100, 105, 118, 206
Einstein, 181
EFL, 85, 87, 154–8, 198
e-learning, 93
ELIA, 132, 195n
Entrepreneurial Linguist, The, 221
ERP/CRM system, 172
ethical business practices, 181
EU, 42
European Language Industry Association, 132, 194

European Union, 42
exporting, 133–4
e-zines, 63, 226, 232–3

Facebook, 36, 188, 190–3, 200, 202, 260
FairTradeNet, 139, 141–2
Fanboys, 100
Fansubs, 100
Farsi, 286
fashion, 118, 120, 123, 307, 309
Faust, 100
Ferreira, Alberto, 172–4
Fichte, 203
Figueroa, Maia, 242
film, 97 102, 103 4, 203
Finnish, 248, 277
foreign exchange, 300, 302
foreign language typesetting, 132, 284–5, 299
Found in Translation, 26, 30, 243,246
Freelance Box, The, 260
freelance translators, 14, 296
  in five years' time, 39, 76, 88, 104, 138, 158, 174, 185, 197, 214, 222, 237, 275, 310, 316
  survey of, 14–15, 17–21, 166, 312, 313, 317, 318
Freeman, Jane, 53–9
French, 31, 85, 103, 114, 187, 196, 233, 247, 258, 277, 285, 286, 291, 304, 307

GALA, 132
Gallagher, Clare, 136–8
Gandhi and the Boy Who Ate Sugar, 263
Gaultier, Jean Paul, 120
generalist, 78, 91, 166, 167, 212
German, 31, 37, 38, 79, 82–3, 90, 93, 95, 96–9, 105, 118, 125, 136, 153–4, 187, 198, 203–10, 220, 246, 270–1
German Institute for Terminology, 110
German professional association for technical communication *see* also tekom, 203, 270
German terminology association, 270
Gile, Daniel, 96
Global English, 83
globalization, 22, 23, 42, 105, 165, 275
Globalization and Localization Association, 132
Globish, 83, 84
glossaries, 44, 47, 71, 111, 114, 140, 197

Goethe, 100
Google+, 200
Google Translate *see* machine translation
Gotschall, Jonathan, 209
graphic design, 286, 288, 299
graphic designers, 283, 288
Greek, 163, 187, 194
GxP Language Services, 31, 36

Hamlin, Neil, 300
health of translators, 106–7, 175
Hebrew, 113, 286
Hegel, 203
Heine-Kilic, Martina, 90–95
Hobbes, Thomas, 62n
hobbies, 52, 258, 293, 296, 309
Hobsons Bay City Council, 162
How to Succeed as a Freelance Translator, 196
Hungarian, 181
Hurst, Dan, 93
Hussain, Eva, 159–64

IAPTI *see* International Association of Professional Translators and Interpreters
IBM, 118
income, 33, 64, 75, 77, 87, 138, 156, 186, 223, 234, 244, 245, 248, 249, 251, 258, 264, 287, 317
  additional, 32, 45, 51, 129, 135, 139, 149, 175, 188, 238
  multiple sources, 38, 168, 226, 229, 260, 262, 288–9, 296–7
  passive, 19, 223–4, 228, 229, 236, 295
  residual, 63
  secondary, 227
in-country investigator, 139, 144
InDesign, 283, 286
information architecture, 174
in-house translation work, 13, 40, 49, 54–5, 118, 139, 169, 172, 221, 318
Inkrea.se Consulting AB, 22
in-person training sessions, 40, 260
Institute of Linguists *see also* Chartered Institute of Linguists, 187, 240, 241
Institute of Translation and Interpreting (ITI), 257
Institute of Translation and Interpreting (IÜD),

270
International Association of Conference
   Interpreters, 37, 96
International Association of Professional
   Translators and Interpreters, 181, 203, 211,
   257, 307
International Baccalaureate, 148, 149
international markets, 135, 136, 227
International Network for Terminology, 116,
   117
International Writers' Group, Oregon, 246
Internet, 40-1, 101, 144, 165, 252, 270, 293,
   296, 298-9, 305
   access, 57, 99, 141
   for language teaching, 150-3, 155-8
   marketing, 35
   webinars, 273
*Internet Freelancing: Practical Guide for
   Translators*, 40
internships, 78, 172, 183
interpreters, 15, 27-30, 32, 42, 50, 53, 78, 98,
   114, 152, 159-64, 203, 257, 294
   community, 37
   conference, 37, 96, 132, 220, 307-8
   court, 27, 96, 220, 226, 228
   telephone, 27, 29, 151
   military, 40
   training, 37-8, 82, 238, 242, 247, 260
interpreting, 14, 32, 97-102, 152, 159-64, 251,
   258, 288
   on-site, 50
   remote, 50
   web-conference, 50
Intralingo, 314
Iowa Interpreters and Translators Association,
   78
Irish Gaelic, 29
isolation, 12, 154, 181, 185, 186
IT
   skills, 102, 158, 159,175, 277-8, 281, 298
   translation specialization, 90, 118, 187, 257,
   270, 307
Italian, 40, 120, 125, 130, 163, 307
ITI Bulletin, 307

Japanese, 283
Jenner, Dagmar (Dagy), 221

Jenner, Judy, 167, 220-22

Kastenhuber, Karolina, 105-9
Keller, Nicole, 270-76
Kelly, Nataly, 26-30, 121n, 243, 246
Kharkiv State University, 40
Kisin, Konstantin, 263-9
Knopp, Guido, 99
knowledge management, 110, 113, 175
Kostiainen, Tuomas, 225, 248-50
KPMG, 251
Kritikakis, Lefteris, 184
Kurz, Ingrid, 96

Lange, Meike, 168-72
Language Lovers competition, 187, 194, 307
language service providers, 46-7, 53-9, 107,
   114, 236, 256, 271, 284, 302
language teaching, 51
   online, 148-53, 154-8
Latin, 154
Leningrad Conservatory, 203
Lexcelera, 68, 303-5
LexWorks, 68, 303
Lingo Bravo, 284
Lingua Greca Translations, 187, 189
Linguaquote, 233-6
Linguist, The, 257
linguistic validation, 139-146
LinkedIn, 31, 191-3, 198, 200-2
literary translation, 100, 204, 314-15
literary translators, 40, 237
localization, 22, 51, 53-4, 111, 117, 172, 215,
   246, 308
   game, 106
   software, 32, 42, 132
   website, 50
localizer, 139, 198
Loctimize GmbH, 110, 117
London School of Economics and Political
   Science, 257
Lovatto, Luciana E., 212
LSP *see* language service providers
Lufthansa Systems, 251
lulu.com, 63

machine translation, 23, 25, 39, 43, 45, 49-50,

56-8, 67, 68-73, 73-7, 79, 88, 102, 124, 146, 165, 172-4, 177, 185, 237, 305-6
Google Translate, 80
Microsoft Translator, 80
LexWorks, 68, 303
Mandarin, 226
Mandela, Nelson, 136
Mann, Thomas, 100
marketing, 40, 124, 190, 196, 229, 259, 261-2, 280-1
Internet, 31, 35
online, 37, 166-7, 194, 198-202, 234, 280
skills, 102, 129, 136-7, 212, 220, 226, 228, 244, 245, 252, 256, 257, 277
strategy, 130-31, 176, 189, 200, 226, 232
teaching, 247, 280-1
translation specialization, 56, 85-6, 120, 121, 125, 128, 129, 203, 210, 219, 307
Marketing for freelance translators (LinkedIn community), 198, 201
Martelli, Alessandra, 125-31
Maycid, Jaber, 283-9
Mayfield Education, 161
McClure, Katalin, 181-2
McKay, Corinne, 196-7
McMahon, Melissa, 103-4
Medecins sans Frontières (Doctors without Borders), 303
mentoring, 78, 163, 178, 179, 181, 183, 243, 258, 263
mentors, 79-80, 106, 175, 257, 259, 279, 281
Metroplex Interpreters and Translators Association, 90
Microsoft Translator *see* machine translation
Millman, Dan, 263
MITA, 90
MLVs, 24, 41, 46, 47-8, 50, 53-8
Mo, Joy, 226-33
Money Move IT, 300n
money transfer, 298-302
Moreno-Ramos, Alejandro, 291-97
Mox's Blog, 291-97
MTM Translations, 130
Mueller, Felicity, 37-9, 96-102
multi-language vendor *see* MLVs
multilingual desktop publishing, 283-9

NAATI accreditation, 37, 96, 97, 132, 148, 159
NASA, 30
National Accreditation Authority for Translators and Interpreters *see also* NAATI accreditation, 97
National Association of Judiciary Interpreters and Translators, 27
National Council on Interpreting in Health Care, 27
negotiation skills, 268
networking, 12, 186, 191, 193, 194, 195, 198, 222, 232, 241, 243
social media, 62, 166, 176, 187-95, 196-7
New South Wales Department of Ageing, Disability and Home Care, 163
New Zealand Translation Centre Ltd, 298
Newcastle University, 154
niche, 19, 25, 37, 89, 93, 158, 167, 168, 185, 186, 211, 212, 247, 279, 291-310
Nissen, Vanda, 148-53
non-native texts, 78-85, 85-9
North American Academy of the Spanish Language, 211
Norwegian, 258

OCR, 177, 283-9
online courses *see* online training
online language teaching *see* language teaching
online learning platforms, 224
online marketing *see* marketing
online portal *see also* Linguaquote, 235
online presence, 35-7, 192-4, 279, 280
online training, 116, 224, 229, 233, 244, 251-5, 314
Open Translation Project, 101
Oppenhoff & Rädler, 251
optical character recognition, 177, 283-9
Organization for Security and Co-operation, 37, 96
output *see also* productivity, 176-7
Oxfam, 303

PACCI, 159
Partners in Health, 303
passive income, 223-4, 228-9, 236, 295
payment *see also* rates, 100, 247, 300-3

PayPal, 302
PEMT see also post-editing, 67, 158
Pentasect, 63
Petrov, Ljubica, 161
Phan, Sarina, 161
Philosophy of Mind, 203
Piróth, Attila, 180–6
Polaron Language Services, 159
Polish, 148, 159, 163, 244, 257, 277
Polish-Australian Chamber of Commerce and Industry, 159
portfolio careers, 238
post-editing, 25, 39, 50, 55–8, 67, 68–73, 73–7, 158, 185
pro bono work, 31, 32, 142, 303
Prodexpo, 205
productivity see also output, 41, 44, 56, 58, 69, 107, 173, 185, 251, 263
  enhancement by technology, 22–6
  tools, 177
productization, 19, 223
professional development see continuing professional development
project management, 53, 90–1, 95, 159, 166, 168–72, 172–4, 183, 215, 258
project managers, 91, 166, 169, 172–3, 218
Pro Tools, 94
proofreading, 14, 46, 51, 85–6, 106–8, 140, 141, 172, 185–6
Prosperous Translator, The, 184
ProZ.com 36, 63, 141, 148, 178, 188, 192, 201, 235, 265, 305
  conference, 307
public speaking, 242–5, 263–9
publications see also books, 196–7, 224, 226–33, 233–7, 259, 315

qualifications, 125, 137, 148, 157, 216
quality assessment, 185
QuarkXPress, 206, 286

RaDt, 117
Rainy London Branding, 307–10
Rainy London Translations, 260, 307
rates, 223
  agency, 217, 222
  bargaining, 47–8, 184

downward pressure on, 39, 55, 58, 77, 88, 100, 102, 125, 138, 222, 252, 295
  excellent, 88
  fair, 141, 268
  foreign exchange, 300–2
  increasing, 33, 158, 166
  structure, 50
Remael, Professor Aline, 101
renewable energy, 40, 211–13, 309
retirement, 238, 250
reviewing, 55
reviews, 194
revisers, 100, 181–6
revision, 87, 184, 185
right-to-left languages, 283, 284
risk management, 20, 319
Rudavin, Oleg, 40–52
Ruprecht Karl University of Heidelberg, 90
Russian, 37, 40, 96–7, 105, 148–9, 198, 199–201, 203–6, 298

Saarland University, 110
sales, 22, 53, 137, 170, 199, 215, 233–5, 288
Say Goodbye to Feast or Famine, 226, 229, 232
SBS see Special Broadcasting Service
School of Translation and Interpreting, Maastricht, 118
search engine optimization, 36, 43, 219
Senior, Jonathan, 200
SEO see search engine optimization
Serbo-Croatian, 97
service providers, 66, 111, 209–10 see also language service providers
Sharp End Training Russia, 198, 201
single-language vendors, 24, 58
skill set, 14, 55, 57, 67, 78, 80, 106–9, 126–7, 129, 186, 262, 278, 280, 289, 312
Sky News business channel, 133
Skype, 149–53, 154–8, 199
Slavonic languages, 37, 96
SLVs, 24, 58
Smartling, 26–7
Special Broadcasting Service, 37, 96–8, 103
social media, 26, 31, 57, 93n.3, 130, 133, 144, 176, 242, 259, 281, 307
  networking and marketing, 35, 166–7, 187–95, 196–7, 198–202, 254

software, 44, 50, 177, 184, 229, 237, 242, 274, 275
 applications, 150
 desktop publishing, 286
 developers, 169
 editing program, 94
 freeware, 149, 150
 localization, 32, 132, 219
 OCR, 283, 288
 open source, 94, 150
 subtitling, 100
 testing, 90, 95
 transcription, 108
Solidarités, 182–3
Sony, 221
Spanish, 27, 40, 105, 114, 125, 134, 136, 139, 146, 211–12, 220, 230, 242, 247, 270, 291, 307, 314
Spear, Luke, 233–7
specialization, 25, 39, 44, 50, 52, 54, 59, 88, 102, 118–19, 119–20, 124, 125–8, 287–8
 specialization as diversification, 19, 29, 79, 166–7, 203–11, 212–14
staff translator, 140
standardization, 210
Staude, Désirée, 225, 251–5
Stein, Peter, 100
Stelmaszak, Marta, 225, 244–6, 257–62
Stenhøj, Claus, 100
Stevenson, Vivian John, 185
Storytelling Animal, The, 209
strategic alliances, 167, 175–80, 181–2
Strathclyde Business School, 60
subject matter expertise see also specialization, 54–6
subtitling, 37–8, 96–102, 103–4, 132
Sulzberger, Paul, 298–302
sustainability see renewable energy
Swedish, 148, 233

teaching, 51, 63, 263–69, 282
 English, 87, 140, 157, 199
 interpreting, 38, 96
 translation, 37–8, 96–7
 university, 38
 see also online teaching
technical writing, 56, 174

technology, 22–5, 27–8, 44–6, 67, 77, 79–81, 105, 177, 220, 276, 310
 see also machine translation
 see also IT
TED, 101
tekom, 117, 203, 270
television, 97, 100–1, 103, 119, 122, 203
templates, 229
term extraction, 177
terminology, 71–2, 84, 219, 270
terminology courses
 Terminology Summer School of the International Network for Terminology, 116
 TermNet, 116, 117
terminology management, 110–17, 183
terminology management systems
 crossTerm, 116
 flashterm, 116
 MultiTerm, 116
 qTerm, 116
 TermStar, 116
terminology service providers
 across, 116
 Kilgray, 116
 SDL, 116, 248, 284
 Star, 116
 termsolutions, 116
TEFL see EFL
text-alignment tools, 177
Thicke, Lori, 68–73, 303–6
Thoughts on Translation, 196
Tkaczyk, Karen, 192
Tomarenko, Valerij, 203–11
Torres, Nora, 139–47
Torresi, Ira 120
touch-typing skills, 106, 108
trade fairs, 204–10
Trados, 79, 248, 270, 284
transcreation, 50, 51, 55, 118–24, 125, 128–9, 136, 258, 308
transcription, 66, 105–9, 213
trans-l'artisan, 139
translation
 agencies see agencies
 audiovisual translation, 96, 100n7, 101n11
 automation of, 23, 24, 215, 220

backward translation, 143, 146
companies *see* agencies
computer-aided *see* CAT
forward translation, 143
legal translation, 89, 119, 196, 220, 247
medical translation, 31, 119, 146, 270
memory, 56–7, 271–3
official document translation, 247
process, 49, 55, 272
quality, 25, 42–3, 58, 68–73, 74, 78, 81, 88
scientific translation, 181
volume of translation, 22–5, 57, 67, 81, 174
Translation Sales Handbook, 233, 235
Translator Pay, 298–302
translatorscafe.com, 141
Translator's Tool Box for the 21st Century, A, 246
Translators without Borders, 22, 68, 303–4
TREMEDICA, 146
Twin Translations, 220
Twisted Marketing, 277
Twitter, 36, 187–94, 200–2
2M Language Services, 132
typesetting, 288
 foreign language typesetting, 132, 283–9, 299

unique selling proposition, 207, 209, 280
United Nations, 42
University of Adelaide, 148, 149
University of Antwerp, 101
University of British Columbia, 68, 303
University of Buenos Aires, 139, 140
University of California, 221
University of Cambridge, 146
University of Graz, 105
University of Groningen, 73
University of Heidelberg, 90, 270
University of New South Wales, 97
University of Sydney, 37, 96, 97
University of Vienna, 37, 96
University of Western Sydney, 97
US Lincoln Library, 140
usability, 172

Van Beukering, Tineke, 73–7
vendor managers, 217–20
Venuti, Laurence, 99
Victorian Transcultural Psychiatry Unit, 161

Viki, 101
virtual classrooms, 148–52
Vivid Meaning, 136–7
Voice for Hire: Launch and Maintain a Lucrative Career in Voice-Overs, 92
voice-over, 90–5, 132, 308
Voiceovers: Techniques and Tactics for Success, 92
Voice-OverXTRA, 93
volunteering *see* pro bono work
Voronezh State University, 148

Walker, Fernando D., 211–4
Walsh, Caitilin, 80–1
Way of the Peaceful Warrior, The, 263
webinars
 attending, 116–7, 183
 presenting, 193, 224, 238–50, 253, 265, 267–8, 273–4
websites, 31, 86–7, 189, 232, 277–82
 website design, 256, 259
Websites for Translators, 259, 277–80
Wilson, Sheila, 85–9
word of mouth, 119, 128, 156, 179, 191, 194, 280, 312
Wordsmith Communication, 60
Wordsmith University, 60, 63, 224, 225, 251–3
World Summit on the Information Society, 139
WSIS, 139

YouTube, 116

ZAO Expocentre – International Exhibitions and Conventions, 205–6
Zetzsche, Jost, 225, 243, 246–7

About the author

NICOLE Y. ADAMS IS A certified commercial German/English translator and editor based in Brisbane, Australia. She has been practising since 2003 and specialises in marketing, corporate communications and public relations. Nicole holds a master's degree in Contemporary English Language and Linguistics from the University of Reading, UK, is an AUSIT Senior Practitioner and was awarded Chartered Linguist status for Translation in 2014. Awards won by Nicole include the 2013 Australian Excellence Award and the 2012 Australian Business Quality Award.